QUESTIONS & ANSWERS:
Secured Transactions

Multiple Choice and Short Answer
Questions and Answers

By

BRUCE A. MARKELL
Doris S. and Theodore B. Lee Professor of Law
William S. Boyd School of Law
University of Nevada, Las Vegas

TIMOTHY R. ZINNECKER
Professor of Law
South Texas College of Law

LexisNexis™

ISBN#: 0820556661

Editorial Offices
744 Broad Street, Newark, NJ 07102 (973) 820-2000
201 Mission St., San Francisco, CA 94105-1831 (415) 908-3200
701 East Water Street, Charlottesville, VA 22902-7587 (804) 972-7600
www.lexis.com

(Pub.3180)

DEDICATIONS

To Douglass G. Boshkoff, a better mentor and friend there never was.
B.A.M.

To my beloved wife, Lisa, truly a "Proverbs 31" woman.
T.R.Z.

ABOUT THE AUTHORS

Bruce A. Markell is the Doris S. and Theodore B. Lee Professor of Law at the William S. Boyd School of Law at the University of Nevada, Las Vegas, where he teaches Contracts, Secured Transactions, Sales, Payment Systems, Securitization, and Bankruptcy. He is also Of Counsel to the Los Angeles law firm of Stutman, Treister & Glatt.

Professor Markell is the author of numerous articles on bankruptcy and commercial law. He is a member of the editorial board of *Collier on Bankruptcy*, and contributes several chapters to that publication. He recently published a Contracts casebook, *Making and Doing Deals: Contracts in Context*, with David Epstein and Lawrence Ponoroff, and will soon publish, with John Dolan and Lawrence Ponoroff, a new casebook involving secured transactions, *Core Commercial Law Principles: Past, Present, and Future*. He is also the author of the forthcoming *Questions & Answers: Bankruptcy* (LexisNexis 2004).

Professor Markell is a member of the American Law Institute, a conferee of the National Bankruptcy Conference, a fellow of the American College of Bankruptcy and a charter member of the International Insolvency Institute. He has been a consultant to the United Nations on secured transactions issues, and to the Republic of Indonesia on reform of its secured transactions laws.

Timothy R. Zinnecker is a professor at South Texas College of Law, where he teaches Secured Transactions, Payment Systems, and Consumer Bankruptcy. Professor Zinnecker graduated with honors from the J. Reuben Clark Law School, Brigham Young University, in 1986, where he served as lead note and comment editor of the law review and was a member of the Order of the Coif. He then served as a judicial clerk for the Hon. Frank X. Gordon, chief justice of the Arizona Supreme Court, and the Hon. Edith H. Jones, United States Court of Appeals for the Fifth Circuit.

Professor Zinnecker practiced commercial law in Dallas and Houston for five years before joining the faculty at South Texas College of Law in 1994. He has been a visiting professor at Samford University's Cumberland School of Law and will be a visiting professor at Florida State University College of Law during fall 2003. His scholarship has appeared in *Tennessee Law Review, Missouri Law Review, Richmond Law Review, Kansas Law Review, Arizona State Law Journal*, and *The Business Lawyer*. He also is the author of *The Default Provisions of Revised Article 9 of the Uniform Commercial Code* (ABA 1999), the co-author of *Payment Systems, Banking and Documentary Transactions* (Carolina Academic Press 2003), and the co-author of the forthcoming *Questions and Answers: Payment Systems* (LexisNexis 2003).

PREFACE

The primary source of law for Secured Transactions is Article 9 of the Uniform Commercial Code. This study guide uses multiple-choice and short-answer questions to test your knowledge of Article 9 and its occasional intersection with other sources of law (e.g., the Federal Tax Lien Act [part of the Internal Revenue Code], and the Bankruptcy Code). These materials are based on the uniform version of Article 9 (as adopted by all states no later than 2001, and often referred to as "Revised Article 9") found in the softback statutory books used in most law schools. The materials do not reflect non-uniform amendments enacted by any particular state.

The short-answer questions should be answered in no more than eight sentences and under fifteen minutes. We believe that you will better understand the materials if you prepare your own answer before peeking at the model answer. Also, although some questions involve dates before July 1, 2001 (the effective date of Revised Article 9), you should answer all questions in this study guide as if Revised Article 9 applied at all times.

We love teaching Secured Transactions and are delighted that you are using our study guide to supplement your understanding of this challenging subject. We invite you to contact us with your questions and comments.

Professor Bruce A. Markell
bmarkell@unlv.edu
Las Vegas, Nevada
April 2003

Professor Timothy R. Zinnecker
zinneck@stcl.edu
Houston, Texas
April 2003

TABLE OF CONTENTS

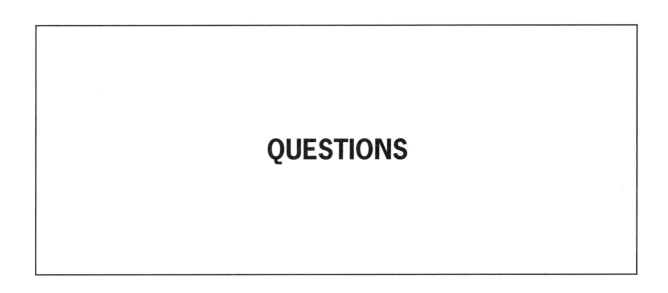

QUESTIONS

1. Article 9 applies to all of the following, except

    (A) commercial, purchase-money, real estate mortgages.

    (B) consignments of jet engines to a seller of used aircraft parts.

    (C) sales of chattel paper.

    (D) sales of credit card receivables

Alberto wants to borrow $2,000 from Lender to upgrade the kitchen in his residence. Lender insists on collateral. Alberto offers his savings account maintained with Lender, his rights as a beneficiary under a life insurance policy, and his rental income from his garage apartment.

2. Article 9 will cover Lender's property interest in

    (A) none of the collateral.

    (B) only the savings account.

    (C) only the savings account and the rental income.

    (D) only the savings account and the rights under the life insurance policy.

3. Which of the following transactions is within the scope of Article 9?

    (A) To secure repayment of a $1 million loan that will be used to renovate numerous units, Galleria Apartments offers as collateral its monthly rents payable by its tenants.

    (B) FinCo purchases and takes delivery of various furniture leases from the lessor, Office Products, Inc., a company that sells and leases furniture in several states.

    (C) To secure repayment of a $10,000 loan, Meredith Ruiz offers a collateral her $75,000 claim against her neighbor for an unprovoked assault and battery.

    (D) Connie Nguyen collateralizes a $25,000 loan with a $40,000 court judgment for trade libel recently entered in her favor.

Marcella Lopez desires to buy a piano on credit from Dealer so her three children can take piano lessons. Marcella has offered as collateral not only the piano, but also a non-negotiable, non-transferable certificate of deposit issued in writing by Providence Savings.

4. Can Dealer take a UCC Article 9 security interest in the certificate of deposit?

ANSWER:

Frank goes to Tania's Mobile Homes to buy a mobile home. He is looking to pay something close to $50,000 for a mobile home. He knows he has to finance the purchase, and he is confused by the financing options. Tania then tells Frank that he can lease a mobile home for five years, just like he could lease a spot in the trailer park. Frank inquires about what happens at the end of five years, and Tania tells Frank that he could then buy the mobile home for $1, even though it will likely be worth $5,000 at that time; for that privilege, however, Frank will have to agree not to terminate the lease before the end of five years. Frank then inquires about the payments, and he is told that a five-year lease on a $50,000 mobile home will cost about $1050 per month. "Why, that's the same as your five-year financing option at 10%!", exclaims Frank. "I'll take it!"

Tania files no financing statements, and mobile homes are not subject to a certificate of title statute in any applicable state. Two years after Frank entered into the lease, Frank defaulted on his payments. Joe, who had loaned Frank $2,000 after Frank leased the mobile home, reduces his claim to judgment about the same time. When Tania sends out some workers to hitch up and take back the mobile home, they are interrupted by the sheriff who seizes the mobile home under a valid writ of execution, issued in connection with Joe's judgment.

5. As between Frank, Joe, and Tania,

   (A) Frank is entitled to the mobile home because of the confusion.

   (B) Joe is entitled to the mobile home because he is a judgment lien creditor.

   (C) Tania is entitled to the mobile home because she owned the mobile home, and Frank was only a lessee.

   (D) Tania is entitled to the mobile home because her debt arose before Joe's.

6. In which of the following transactions is the secured creditor most likely to be said to hold a purchase-money security interest?

    (A) On August 1, Katherine Hodges borrows $20,000 from her parents and buys a Steinway grand piano. The piano dealer delivers the piano that same day. Two weeks later, Katherine borrows $20,000 from SmallBank and uses the money to repay the unsecured loan to her parents. SmallBank secures repayment of its loan by taking an enforceable security interest in the piano.

    (B) Bill Baxter buys 100 shares of capital stock of Pegasus Corp. on credit, as permitted by his brokerage agreement with Provident Securities. Under that agreement, the 100 shares secure repayment of the loan.

    (C) Esther Johnson buys a new Jaguar automobile from Hollywood Motors, which retains an enforceable security interest in the vehicle to secure its unpaid purchase price. Through a paperwork mix-up, however, Hollywood Motors never perfects its security interest.

    (D) Gordon Smith borrows $35,000 from Freemont Finance to purchase a boat. To secure repayment of the loan, Gordon grants to Freemont Finance a security interest in the boat. Freemont Finance issues the $35,000 check to Gordon, who deposits it in his savings account. A week later, he purchases the boat by issuing a $35,000 check drawn on his checking account.

Mary borrows $5,000 from Bank and executes a promissory note. Fran, Mary's sister, co-signs the note and also grants to Bank a security interest in her car. Bill, the father of Fran and Mary, guaranties repayment of the loan.

7. Which statement is TRUE?

    (A) Mary and Fran are debtors and Bill is an obligor.

    (B) Mary is a debtor and Bill is a secondary obligor.

    (C) Mary is a primary obligor and Bill is a debtor.

    (D) Fran is an obligor and Bill is a secondary obligor.

Karen sold Diana a car for $8,000. Some documents were signed at the time of sale. Diana still owes Karen $3,000. Karen wants to use this right to payment as collateral on a loan from Bank.

8. As collateral, this right to payment could be any of the following <u>except</u> a(n)

    (A) chattel paper.

    (B) payment intangible.

    (C)   account.

    (D)   instrument.

Bank has agreed to lend $50,000 to Gary. To secure repayment of the loan, Gary has offered as collateral some or all of the following investments that he owns:

100   shares in the Argus Large Cap Growth Fund (a stock mutual fund that does not issue certificates but provides Gary with periodic performance statements);

200   shares of Enterek stock issued in certificated form to (and possessed by) Gary; and

500   shares of Scantronix stock purchased by Gary's investment broker, Providence Securities, for Gary's account (Gary owns other investments in his Providence account, but these will not serve as collateral for the loan).

  9. Which statement is FALSE?

    (A)   Gary's ability to liquidate the Scantronix stock without Bank's consent effectively prevents Bank from obtaining control of the Scantronix stock.

    (B)   The Argus Large Cap Growth Fund shares are uncertificated securities.

    (C)   The Scantronix stock is a security entitlement.

    (D)   Bank can control the Scantronix stock without becoming the registered owner.

Baxter Boats sold a boat to Gordon on credit. Under its standard written installment sales contract executed by Gordon, Baxter Boats retained title to the boat until Gordon repaid the purchase price.

Later, Baxter Boats borrowed $250,000 from Lender, offering as collateral several of its standard written installment sales contracts executed by its customers (including the contract executed by Gordon).

  10. Gordon wants to use the boat as collateral for a loan from Bank. Using Article 9 terminology, what type of collateral is the boat?

ANSWER:

  11. Using Article 9 terminology, what type of collateral are the installment sales contracts?

ANSWER:

12. Which of the following debtors is not a registered organization (assuming that each debtor has the organizational form indicated in its name)?

    (A) Wallace Corporation.

    (B) Newman & Sloane, L.L.C.

    (C) Palmer, McCall, and Crain, L.P.

    (D) Ethan Gentry d/b/a "Pop's Grocery Shoppe."

Wellington Corporation intends to grant a security interest in its current and future accounts to Lender.

13. Which of the following payment receivables (which are not evidenced by an instrument or chattel paper) is not an account?

    (A) an IRS tax refund.

    (B) an annual software licensing payment.

    (C) credit card receivables.

    (D) monthly equipment lease payments.

Lender has an enforceable security interest in Dealer's current and future "accounts." Dealer's customers often pay by using a credit card.

14. These credit card receivables are part of Lender's collateral as

    (A) accounts.

    (B) accounts, but only if the rights to payment are not evidenced by chattel paper.

    (C) accounts, but only if the rights to payment are not evidenced by instruments.

    (D) accounts, but only if the rights to payment are not evidenced by chattel paper or instruments.

Lender has an enforceable security interest in the current and future inventory of Merchant, a dealer of electronic entertainment equipment (e.g., televisions, stereo components, DVD players, etc.). A few of Merchant's customers pay with cash, while others tender a personal check. But most customers pay with a credit card.

15. Which forms of payment create "cash proceeds"?

    (A) cash, checks, and credit cards.

    (B) only cash and checks.

    (C) only cash and credit cards.

    (D) only cash.

16. All of the following are "goods" except

    (A) grain growing in a field.

(B)　a microwave oven that is a "fixture" under local real estate law.

(C)　a stock certificate, in registered form, evidencing ownership of 100 shares of a publicly-traded company.

(D)　an unborn calf.

Frank wants to sell his house. Betty wants to buy it. Frank and Betty agree on terms, and reduce their agreement to writing on June 1. Under this document, Betty will pay Frank a non-refundable deposit of $5,000 within five days of signing, and will pay an additional $145,000 upon closing, scheduled to occur on July 15. The closing is subject to Betty obtaining acceptable financing.

Before signing the contract, on May 1, Frank had entered into a security agreement with his brother Harry. That agreement secured a $50,000 loan Harry had made to Frank on February 1, as well as any other obligations Frank owed Harry. The security agreement described the collateral as "all accounts, now owned or hereafter acquired." On May 15, Harry filed an adequate and complete financing statement with the applicable secretary of state against Frank. It contained an identical collateral description to that used in the security agreement.

On June 3, Frank defaults under the security agreement with Harry, just after Betty made her $5,000 payment by check. Frank has other financial problems, but he has not filed (and does not wish to file) bankruptcy.

17.　Harry may pursue

(A)　nothing described in this question, since it is all real estate related and Article 9 only covers personal property.

(B)　nothing, because Harry perfected his security interest more than ten days after attachment, and thus all of his security is a preference.

(C)　Betty's check only, since Betty's obligation to pay the $145,000 is contingent.

(D)　both the check and Betty's obligation to pay the $145,000.

18.　A secured party may obtain a purchase-money security interest in each of the following assets except

(A)　an antique motor vehicle.

(B)　a baseball card collection.

(C)　a stock certificate evidencing 100 shares of General Motors capital stock.

(D)　a rare bottle of wine.

19. A debtor must authenticate a security agreement to create an enforceable security interest in its

    (A) deposit accounts.

    (B) tangible chattel paper.

    (C) general intangibles.

    (D) equipment.

Elaine Johnson recently graduated from college and for the first time is living alone in an apartment. To furnish the apartment, she borrowed $5,000 on June 1 from her sister, Laura. To secure repayment of the loan, Laura insisted that Elaine execute a promissory note and a security agreement that granted to Laura a security interest in the furnishings acquired with Laura's funds. The security agreement, dated June 4, included an after-acquired property clause and otherwise reasonably described the collateral. Elaine used Laura's money to purchase the following:

bedroom furniture	June 3
television	June 8
sofa	June 12
dining room table w/ chairs	June 16

20. Under Article 9, Laura has an enforceable security interest in

    (A) all items.

    (B) only the sofa, television, and bedroom furniture.

    (C) only the television and bedroom furniture.

    (D) only the bedroom furniture.

Graham Excavation Corporation ("GEC") builds roads and clears land for governmental, commercial, and private parties. In February, Hoover Finance loaned $1 million to GEC. To secure repayment of the loan, GEC granted to Hoover Finance a security interest in its excavation equipment. During the year, Hoover Finance funded additional advances to GEC. Also during the year, GEC bought additional excavation equipment. A summary of the activity follows:

February	Hoover Finance advances $1 million
	Value of existing excavation equipment is $1.2 million
April	Hoover Finance advances $250,000
May	GEC buys road grader for $250,000
June	GEC buys bulldozer for $300,000
August	Hoover Finance advances $250,000

In November, GEC defaulted on its obligations to Hoover Finance, having repaid none of the loans. A review of the security agreement revealed that it included a future advance clause but not an after-acquired property clause.

21. Ignoring any effects of market changes in the value of the equipment, Hoover Finance is

(A) undersecured by $350,000.

(B) undersecured by $300,000.

(C) oversecured by $200,000.

(D) oversecured by $750,000.

22. Assume that a review of the security agreement revealed that it included after-acquired property clause but not a future advance clause. Ignoring any effects of market changes in the value of the equipment, Hoover Finance has unsecured debt of

(A) 0.

(B) $200,000.

(C) $300,000.

(D) $500,000.

Travis borrowed $100 from his neighbor, Earl, in February. Travis and Earl orally agreed that Travis's lawnmower would serve as collateral for the loan. Earl had no room in his garage to keep the lawnmower, so Travis and Earl agreed that Travis's daughter, Sharon, would keep it at her place three blocks away. Sharon stored the lawnmower in her garage after making room for it.

23. Does Earl have an enforceable security interest in the lawnmower?

ANSWER:

Rachel Ramirez operates a landscaping business as a sole proprietorship. She recently borrowed $3,000 from Cumberland Credit Union. To secure repayment of the business loan, the Credit Union insisted on taking a security interest in Rachel's personal savings account maintained with the Credit Union. Rachel orally agreed to this arrangement, which was never memorialized in a writing or otherwise authenticated.

24. Which statement is TRUE?

(A) Article 9 does not permit the Credit Union to take a security interest in Rachel's personal savings account.

(B) Article 9 permits the Credit Union to take a security interest in Rachel's personal savings account, but the security interest will not attach until Rachel executes a written security agreement that reasonably identifies the account.

(C) Article 9 permits the Credit Union to take a security interest in Rachel's personal savings account, but only if the savings account is maintained with a financial institution other than the secured party.

(D) The Credit Union has an enforceable security interest in Rachel's personal savings account.

Montgomery Motors sells automobiles. Its customers include organizations that will use the vehicles in their business and individuals who will use the vehicles for personal use. Belmont Bank intends to make a $2 million loan to Montgomery Motors, taking a security interest in the automobiles.

25. If the parties desire to use Article 9 terminology when describing the collateral, the security agreement should describe the collateral as

(A) inventory.

(B) inventory and equipment.

(C) inventory and consumer goods.

(D) inventory, equipment, and consumer goods.

On May 1, Clinic executed a written security agreement granting to Bank a security interest in Clinic's existing and future equipment to secure repayment of a loan in an amount not yet agreed upon by the parties. On May 3, Clinic bought a new X-ray machine. Loan negotiations concluded on May 7, when Bank executed a binding commitment to lend up to $150,000 to Clinic in one or more advances. On May 9, Clinic requested the initial advance of $45,000. Bank funded the $45,000 advance on May 11. On May 13, Bank filed its financing statement against Clinic's equipment. On May 15, Clinic bought a new kidney dialysis machine.

26. Bank's security interest in the X-ray machine attached on

(A) May 3.

(B) May 7.

(C) May 9.

(D) May 11.

27. Bank's security interest in the kidney dialysis machine attached on

(A) May 7.

(B) May 11.

(C) May 13.

(D) May 15.

On July 1, Elliott sold a baseball autographed by Babe Ruth to his neighbor, Marcus, for $5,000. Marcus did not have that amount of cash, so he paid $1,000 at the time of sale and executed a short-term promissory note that stated: "In consideration for a baseball autographed by Babe Ruth, I promise to pay $4,200 to Elliott on December 1." Marcus also signed a financing statement that described the baseball. Elliott filed the financing statement on July 3. The parties did not execute any other documents.

28. Does Elliott have an enforceable security interest in the baseball?

ANSWER:

29. A security interest will not attach under an after-acquired property clause to

    (A) electronic chattel paper.

    (B) a deposit account.

    (C) a commercial tort claim.

    (D) a letter-of-credit right.

Dealer intends to sell some equipment on credit to Debtor, an Illinois corporation, for everyday use at Debtor's plant in Chicago.

30. To create an enforceable security interest in the equipment, the security agreement must be authenticated by

    (A) Dealer and Debtor.

    (B) only Dealer.

    (C) only Debtor.

    (D) neither Dealer nor Debtor.

31. Furthermore, for attachment purposes, the security agreement

    (A) can, but need not, be memorialized on paper or other tangible medium.

    (B) should use the word "equipment" when describing the collateral.

    (C) should include Debtor's organizational identification number if Debtor has one.

    (D) should include an address for the Chicago plant.

32. If the parties are relying on a written security agreement to create an enforceable security interest, the agreement must include a real estate description if the collateral includes

    (A) mobile goods.

    (B) timber to be cut.

    (C) crops.

    (D) as-extracted collateral.

Lender intends to secure repayment of a $15 million loan to Debtor, a Texas corporation, by taking a security interest in all of Debtor's personal property.

33. When describing the collateral in the security agreement, Lender may not rely solely on an Article 9 "type" of collateral when describing

   (A) investment property.

   (B) commercial tort claims.

   (C) letter-of-credit rights.

   (D) deposit accounts.

In July, Computronics borrowed $50,000 from Bank. Repayment of the loan was secured by an enforceable security interest in Computronic's current and after-acquired inventory of computers and peripherals (e.g., printers). Bank perfected its security interest by filing a proper financing statement with the appropriate clerk.

On August 1, Computronics changed its legal name to Quest Systems.

On September 1, Quest Systems took computers and peripherals with an aggregate value of $12,000 from its inventory and used them to upgrade its internal computer system.

On October 1, Quest Systems moved its operations from the east side of town to the west side of town.

34.   Article 9 dictates that Bank should file an amended financing statement to reflect

(A)   only the name change.

(B)   only the name change and change in use of some of the collateral from inventory to equipment.

(C)   only the name and address changes.

(D)   all three changes.

Garza Graphics borrowed $5,000 from Essex Financing and signed a security agreement adequately describing some of Garza's personal property. Essex filed a financing statement with the appropriate clerk against that personal property. The clerk recorded the financing statement in its records.

35.   Essex is not perfected if

(A)   Garza failed to authenticate the financing statement.

(B)   Garza failed to authorize the filing.

(C)   the financing statement omitted the mailing address of Essex.

(D)   the financing statement failed to indicate whether Garza is an individual or an organization.

Last year, a group of banks (Bank One, Bank Two, and Bank Three) made a $1 million loan to Allied Corporation. The loan was secured by an enforceable security interest in Allied's accounts, inventory, and equipment. The security agreement included an after-acquired property clause. The three banks agreed that Bank Four would serve as the collateral agent for the group.

A loan officer for Bank One has asked you to review the financing statement that was filed. You have done so, noting that the financing statement (i) fails to mention the after-acquired property clause, (ii) is not signed, executed, or otherwise authenticated by Allied, and (iii) lists the secured party of record simply as "Bank Four."

36.   Should Bank One be concerned?

ANSWER:

Robert W. Zimmer lives in Kansas City, Missouri (Jackson County). Zimmer operates a consulting service (RWZ Consulting) as a sole proprietorship across the state line in Kansas, in the more affluent Johnson County. Yesterday Zimmer bought a new computer system on credit from Bradford Computer Co. To secure repayment of the loan, Bradford retained an enforceable security interest in the computer system (which Bradford installed at Zimmer's business location).

37.   To perfect its security interest Bradford should file its financing statement with

   (A)   the county clerk of Jackson County, Missouri.

   (B)   the county clerk of Johnson County, Kansas.

   (C)   the central filing office in Missouri.

   (D)   the central filing office in Kansas.

Wallace Office Equipment sells photocopiers, fax machines, computer hardware, and other office equipment. Many of its customers buy office equipment on credit, executing a single-page contract that bears the heading "PROMISSORY NOTE." Wallace often sells these contracts to Finance Company for a discounted price.

38.   How should Finance Company perfect its interest in the contracts?

ANSWER:

On May 1, Debtor (a retail bookseller) executed a written security agreement granting to Bank a security interest in Debtor's existing and future equipment to secure repayment of a loan in an amount not yet agreed upon by the parties. That day, Bank filed a proper financing statement against "equipment" with the proper official. On May 3, Debtor bought two new cash registers. Loan negotiations concluded on May 7, when Bank executed a binding commitment to lend up to $500,000 to Debtor in one or more advances. On May 9, Debtor requested the initial advance of $100,000. Bank funded the $100,000 advance on May 11. On May 13, Debtor bought a new office chair.

39.   Bank's interest in the two cash registers became perfected on

   (A)   May 1.

    (B)   May 3.

    (C)   May 7.

    (D)   May 11.

40.   Bank's interest in the office chair became perfected on

    (A)   May 1.

    (B)   May 7.

    (C)   May 9.

    (D)   May 13.

41.   A secured party must file a financing statement in order to perfect a security interest in

    (A)   a security entitlement.

    (B)   a commercial tort claim.

    (C)   electronic chattel paper.

    (D)   a letter-of-credit right.

Bank takes an enforceable security interest in Borrower's "accounts, chattel paper, deposit accounts, documents, equipment, general intangibles, instruments, inventory, and investment property." The security agreement executed by Borrower (a corporation) includes an after-acquired property clause and a future advance clause. Bank submits a financing statement, with the appropriate fee, to the proper filing office.

42.   The filing officer may legitimately reject the financing statement if it

    (A)   is not authenticated by Borrower.

    (B)   describes the collateral as "all personal property."

    (C)   fails to provide a mailing address for Bank.

    (D)   fails to reasonably describe the debt.

Maria Garza, a resident of Dallas, Texas, intends to borrow $25,000 from SmallBank. The loan will be secured by the following collateral:

> 10 shares of 3X stock, represented by a certificate in Maria's possession;
> 200 shares of the Franklin Large Cap Fund (the Fund is organized under Delaware law; the account agreement is governed by New York law); and
> all of the investments in her brokerage account managed by the Houston, Texas, office of Providence Securities, an entity organized under Delaware law (the account agreement is governed by New York law).

43.   Assume SmallBank will perfect its security interest by filing. In which state(s) should SmallBank file a financing statement?

ANSWER:

44. Three months after funding the loan, SmallBank learns that Maria recently moved to New Orleans, Louisiana, and mailed the 3X stock certificate to her father in Philadelphia, Pennsylvania (solely for safekeeping purposes). Should either of these events concern SmallBank?

ANSWER:

45. Assume that Maria continues to live in Dallas, Texas, and retains possession of the 3X stock certificate. Knowing that a security interest perfected by control will enjoy priority over a security interest perfected by filing (*see* section 9-328(1)), SmallBank has decided to perfect its security interest in all of the collateral by control. SmallBank should comply with the perfection rules of which state(s)?

ANSWER:

Lender desires to perfect an enforceable security interest in Borrower's inventory, accounts, equipment, investment property, and deposit accounts. Borrower does business in Texas, Oklahoma, and Louisiana. Its chief executive office is located in Texas.

46. Which statement is TRUE?

   (A) If Borrower is a corporation organized under Delaware law, then Lender should file in Delaware to perfect its security interest in inventory and equipment and in Texas to perfect its security interest in accounts and investment property.

   (B) If Borrower is a general partnership, then Lender should file in each state where inventory and equipment is located to perfect its interest in that collateral and in Texas to perfect its interest in accounts and investment property.

   (C) Lender should control the deposit account in accordance with the law of Borrower's jurisdiction.

   (D) Borrower's relocation of its chief executive office to Oklahoma has no impact on the continued effectiveness of Lender's financing statement if Borrower is a registered organization.

47. In which type of collateral is a security interest perfected exclusively by control?

   (A) Investment property.

   (B) Deposit accounts.

   (C) Commercial tort claims.

   (D) Electronic chattel paper.

On August 1, Lauren borrowed $8,000 from her parents and bought a new bedroom suite from Dealer for her home. Dealer delivered the bedroom suite two days later. On August 13, Lauren borrowed $8,000 from Finance Company and used the money to repay the unsecured loan to her parents. Finance Company secured repayment of its loan by taking a security interest in the bedroom suite.

When Lauren files a bankruptcy petition seven months later, the trustee challenges the perfection of Finance Company's security interest because Finance Company never filed a financing statement. Finance Company contends that it did not have to file a financing statement because its security interest was automatically perfected on attachment.

48. Who is right?

ANSWER:

Amanda operates a music studio, where she gives voice and piano lessons to neighborhood residents. In July, Amanda bought a new keyboard for her studio on credit from Dealer. To secure repayment of the purchase price, Dealer retained an enforceable purchase-money security interest in the keyboard. Dealer never filed a financing statement.

49. Does Dealer have a perfected security interest in the keyboard?

ANSWER:

Lender desires to secure repayment of a $1 million loan to Debtor, a Florida corporation, with a perfected security interest in Debtor's copyrights, trademarks, and patents. Debtor has registered all of its copyrights, trademarks, and patents with the national registries in Washington, D.C.

50. Under present caselaw, Lender's financing statement filed in Florida will perfect its security interest only in Debtor's

   (A) patents.

   (B) patents and trademarks.

   (C) trademarks and copyrights.

   (D) copyrights and patents.

51. In which of the following situations should Lender perfect its security interest by, among other things, filing a financing statement in California?

   (A) Debtor is a Delaware corporation with all of its tangible assets located in San Francisco.

   (B) Debtor is a Texas corporation with its chief executive office located in San Diego.

(C)   Debtor is a general partnership that manages, from offices in both New York City and Los Angeles, most of its multi-state business operations.

(D)   Debtor is a Chicago resident who will offer, as collateral, a stock certificate kept in a safety deposit box in Oakland.

Bank makes a $10,000 loan to Baxter Corporation (a Delaware corporation) in January. The loan is secured by a security interest in Baxter's current and after-acquired equipment. Bank promptly files a proper financing statement with the appropriate Delaware clerk.

52.   Baxter Corporation changes its name to "Westex Inc." on February 1. Westex acquires a piece of equipment in April (Item #1), and another piece of equipment in July (Item #2). Does Bank have a perfected security interest in Item #1 and Item #2?

ANSWER:

53.   Assume that Baxter Corporation does not change its name. Instead, in August, Baxter sells a piece of equipment (Item #3) to Calvert Industries, Inc. (also a Delaware corporation) without Bank's knowledge. Does Bank have a perfected security interest in Item #3 after the sale?

ANSWER:

54.   Would your analysis to the preceding question change if Bank knew of and consented to the sale of Item #3?

ANSWER:

55.   Assume that Bank does not consent to the sale of Item #3. What advice would you give Bank if Calvert Industries was incorporated under Texas, rather than Delaware, law?

ANSWER:

Brent Bliss owns and operates a chain of taco stands under the trade name of "Brent's Best Tacos." His business letterhead reads "Brent's Best Tacos, a division of Brent Enterprises." In fact, a separate legal entity named Brent Enterprises exists, but Brent has never followed through with the corporate formalities to complete the transfer of any property from himself to Brent Enterprises.

56.   Moron Savings wants to lend funds to Brent's Best Tacos on a secured basis. Its financing statement should describe the debtor as

(A) "Brent's Best Tacos."

(B) "Brent Enterprises, doing business as Brent's Best Tacos."

(C) "Brent Bliss, doing business as Brent's Best Tacos."

(D) "Brent Bliss" (with the financing statement also being indexed under "Brent's Best Tacos").

Sam Secured and Debra Debtor are in the middle of a divorce. As part of the property settlement, Debra will keep her law partnership interest, and Sam will keep the marital house. This division of property results in Debra owing Sam $100,000. She offers to pay this amount to Sam over time. She also offers to grant to Sam a security interest in her partnership interest in the firm (Sam, Debra, and the law partnership are all located in the same state). Sam looks at the agreement, sees no mention of the Uniform Commercial Code anywhere in it, and agrees to Debra's offer. Debra then signs an otherwise valid security agreement, which adequately describes the partnership interest.

57. To perfect his security interest in the partnership interest, Sam

(A) need not take any action because perfection is automatic.

(B) need not file any financing statement because the collateral is not subject to Article 9.

(C) should file a financing statement with the central filing office in the state where Debra resides.

(D) file a financing statement with the local county recorder in the county where Debra resides.

Jim's Confidential Dating Service, Inc. ("JCDSI") is in the business of matchmaking. It takes applications from customers and tries to match them with other customers of similar interests. JCDSI has a few employees, a few computers, some office furniture, and its customer list.

JCDSI wants to expand. It approaches Bad Boy Bank ("BBB") for a $1,000,000 loan. BBB agrees to the loan, and JCDSI signs a $1,000,000 note and a security agreement that describes the collateral as "all accounts, equipment, and general intangibles." BBB files in the appropriate place a financing statement that is otherwise adequate, but which describes the collateral as "all assets."

58. Upon filing the financing statement, BBB has a perfected security interest in

(A) nothing, since the description in the financing statement was inadequate.

(B) the computers and office furniture, but nothing else.

(C) all of JCDSI's accounts receivable, and all of its computers and office furniture, but nothing else.

(D) at least JCDSI's customer list.

Bubba, a lifelong resident of North Dakota, manufactures and sells bird cages. His birth certificate reads "David Michael Reed", his North Dakota driver's license reads "Bubba Reed," which is the name by which everyone knows him.

Bubba has never incorporated his business, and he approaches ZincBank for a $500,000 loan to expand. ZincBank, after consideration, tells Bubba that it will not loan to him unless he incorporates and transfers all his business assets to the corporation. ZincBank states that the reason for the move is that the Secretary of State's office (the proper place to file all financing statements) indexes and searches financing statements by placing the first name after the last name without any spaces (so that financing statement naming Bubba Reed would be filed and searched as "reedbubba," and a financing statement naming David Michael Reed would be filed and searched under "reeddavidmichael").

Incorporating will not cost Bubba anything but minor incorporation costs, but Bubba does not want to change if it is not necessary. Bubba consults you as to the reasonableness of the Bank's request.

59.   Which of the following is the best advice?

   (A)   ZincBank is being unreasonable since Bubba has lived in North Dakota all his life.

   (B)   ZincBank is being reasonable since the UCC filing system is only for businesses, and not for individuals.

   (C)   ZincBank is being unreasonable since transferring assets simply to obtain a loan is fraudulent.

   (D)   ZincBank is being reasonable if the Secretary of State's search system would not return a financing statement filed against Bubba Reed if the search request was for filings against David Michael Reed.

MegaCorp, a Delaware corporation, has its chief executive office in Detroit. MegaCorp owns 100% of the capital stock of Alamo, Inc., a Texas corporation. Alamo's capital stock is evidenced by a stock certificate that MegaCorp keeps in a safety deposit box in Chicago. MegaCorp has granted an enforceable security interest in the stock certificate to Fidelity Finance. Fidelity Finance has decided to leave the stock certificate in Chicago and perfect its security interest by filing a financing statement.

60.   Fidelity Finance should file its financing statement in

   (A)   Delaware.

   (B)   Illinois.

   (C)   Michigan.

   (D)   Texas.

On July 7, Midway Bank obtained an enforceable security interest in the current and after-acquired inventory of Odyssey Furniture, a business that sells home furnishings. Midway Bank filed its financing statement in the appropriate place against Odyssey's inventory on July 13.

On September 4, Customer bought a sofa on credit from Odyssey Furniture. Customer executed a document, entitled "PROMISSORY NOTE," that called for full payment in six months. Under the terms of the promissory note, Odyssey retained a security interest in the sofa until the promissory note was paid in full.

On September 8, Purchaser bought a kitchen table, using cash as payment. That afternoon, Odyssey used the actual cash paid by Purchaser to acquire some computer hardware for in-store use.

61. As of October 1, does Midway Bank have a perfected security interest in the promissory note?

ANSWER:

62. As of October 1, does Midway Bank have a perfected security interest in the computer hardware?

ANSWER:

Debtor is in the business of selling furniture. Bank obtains an enforceable security interest in Debtor's "inventory." The security agreement includes an after-acquired property clause. Bank files a proper financing statement with the appropriate filing office. Later, Debtor sells two sofas to an entity in exchange for a new photocopier and $1,000 cash. Debtor takes the cash and buys a very nice microwave oven for the employee lounge. Assume that Bank can satisfy any tracing burden. Also assume that any period of automatic perfection has passed.

63. Bank has

(A) a perfected security interest in the photocopier and the microwave oven.

(B) an unperfected security interest in the photocopier and the microwave oven.

(C) a perfected security interest in the photocopier and an unperfected security interest in the microwave oven.

(D)   an unperfected security interest in the photocopier and a perfected security interest in the microwave oven.

Lender has a perfected security interest in Debtor's inventory and accounts. Contrary to the terms of the security agreement, Debtor deposited cash proceeds in a bank account in April that contained deposits of non-proceeds. Evidence reveals the following activity during April:

> the opening balance on April 1 was $5,000 ($1,000 of which is proceeds)
> Debtor deposited cash proceeds into the account as follows:
>> $7,000 on April 5
>> $2,000 on April 24
> Debtor deposited non-proceeds into the account as follows:
>> $6,000 on April 15
>> $3,000 on April 28
> Debtor made the following withdrawals from the account:
>> $8,000 on April 7
>> $7,000 on April 20

64.   Under the lowest intermediate balance rule, Lender can claim a security interest in

(A) $5,000.

(B) $6,000.

(C) $8,000.

(D) $10,000.

Bank has an enforceable security interest in a CAT-scan machine owned by Clinic. The security interest is unperfected because Bank filed its financing statement in the wrong state. Without Bank's consent, Clinic sells the machine to Dealer, who pays for the machine by delivering to Clinic a $25,000 cashier's check made payable to the order of Clinic.

65.   If the check is traceable as proceeds of the CAT-scan machine, Bank has

(A)   no security interest in the check.

(B)   an unperfected security interest in the check.

(C)   a security interest in the check that is automatically, but temporarily, perfected for 20 days upon Clinic's receipt.

(D)   a perfected security interest in the check; the perfected status is not temporary because the check is "cash proceeds."

Bill Hood operates Bill's Used Car Lot. BigBucks Bank ("BBB") finances Bill's Used Car Lot. BBB has a properly perfected security interest in all of Bill's inventory and accounts, and in all proceeds thereof. BBB's filed financing statement claims a security interest in "inventory and accounts."

One slow day, Bill leases one of his cars to Larry Lugnut. Leasing cars otherwise offered for sale is a default under BBB's security agreement. The lease is in writing and provides that Larry will rent the car for one month. The total rent is $500, payable on termination of the lease.

The day after this transaction, Larry wrecks the car. The insurance proceeds, in the form of an uncashed check from the insurance company made payable to Bill's Used Car Lot, are $5,000. Under the terms of the lease, Larry is still responsible for the $500 lease payment. At all relevant times, Bill's Used Car Lot owes BBB more than $10,000. Bill files a Chapter 7 bankruptcy petition.

66. BBB is entitled to

    (A) the insurance check and the $500 due and owing from Larry.

    (B) the insurance check and the $500 due and owing from Larry, but only if BBB files a financing statement covering the lease within twenty days after the date the lease is signed.

    (C) the insurance check, but not the lease proceeds under any circumstances.

    (D) neither the insurance check nor the lease proceeds.

Acme Manufacturing ("Acme") manufactures widgets and sells them to retailers. It sold 1,000 widgets to Bill's Widget Shop, Inc. ("BWSI"), an Arizona corporation with retail stores in Nevada, Idaho, and Arizona (its main office is in Las Vegas, Nevada, which is where all corporate records are kept, where all executives have their office, and where all major corporate decisions are made). BWSI sells widgets to the public. In the contract for sale to BWSI, Acme agreed that BWSI could pay for the widgets within thirty days of delivery. In addition, Acme insisted on the following term: "Acme reserves title in all widgets sold to secure payment of the purchase price."

Before shipment, Acme filed an otherwise valid financing statement, which described the collateral as "all assets" with the Secretary of State of Arizona. Acme shipped the widgets to a BWSI retail outlet in Nevada.

Two months after delivery, BWSI files for bankruptcy without paying Acme's bill. After investigation, it appears that 250 of the widgets are still in the Nevada store. Of the remaining 750 widgets, BWSI has checks from consumers for 200 of them that have not yet been deposited (all of which are dated more than twenty days ago). BWSI is owed $5,000 from X Corp., who bought 500 of the widgets on unsecured credit from BWSI. There is no trace of what happened to the remaining 50 widgets.

67. As against BWSI's trustee in bankruptcy, Acme can recover

    (A) none of the widgets, none of the customer checks, and none of the $5,000 debt from X Corp.

    (B) the 250 widgets and the checks from the consumers only.

    (C) the checks from the consumers and the $5,000 debt from X Corp. only.

    (D) the 250 widgets, the checks from the consumers, and the $5,000 debt from X Corp.

Greg lives in California. He is an independent software developer. He has borrowed $100,000 from Silicon Valley Savings. Silicon Valley, at the time of the loan, had Greg sign a security agreement securing the loan. The security agreement described the collateral as "all general intangibles, now owned or hereafter acquired." Silicon Valley filed an accurate and complete financing statement against Greg with the California Secretary of State. It contained the same collateral description as the security agreement. Silicon Valley dids not file anything with the Copyright Office in Washington, D.C.

One day, Greg decides to retire to Pago Pago. To raise money for this, he sells "all of his right, title, and interest" in all the software he is in the process of developing to Amanda. Amanda pays Greg with a $50,000 check, and Greg hands over to Amanda all his coding sheets and electronic media containing his work. Greg has never copyrighted any of his work.

Greg takes the check and deposits it in his bank account (which at the time had a $100 balance). He buys a first-class ticket to Pago Pago with a $1,400 check written on this account, and then has the bank issue to him a cashier's check for the balance.

Silicon Valley learns of the sale just before Greg departs for Pago Pago.

68. If Silicon Valley acts quickly enough, it may replevy

   (A) the tickets to Pago Pago, the cashier's check, and all the materials sold to Amanda.

   (B) only the cashier's check and all the materials sold to Amanda.

   (C) only the materials sold to Amanda.

   (D) nothing.

Lender has a perfected security interest in the inventory and accounts of Debtor, a merchant that sells bridal gowns. Lender's security agreement (which includes an after-acquired property clause) and financing statement each describe the collateral as "inventory and accounts." The loan papers do not mention "proceeds."

On June 1 (several months after Debtor and Lender had entered into their contractual relationship), Debtor sold a bridal gown to Heather, who sold and leased office equipment (e.g., photocopiers and fax machines). Debtor agreed to sell the bridal gown to Heather in exchange for a new desktop photocopier. Debtor documented the sale in its records to reflect the exchange.

69. On July 1, Lender has

   (A) no interest in the photocopier because the collateral description in its security agreement does not mention "equipment."

   (B) no interest in the photocopier because the collateral description in its security agreement does not mention "proceeds" of inventory.

   (C) an unperfected security interest in the photocopier because its financing statement mentions neither "equipment" nor "proceeds."

   (D) a perfected security interest in the photocopier.

Assume that Heather paid cash for the bridal gown on June 1. That afternoon, Debtor took most of Heather's cash, walked next door to another merchant, and bought a new desktop photocopier. Debtor's records detail the sale of the bridal gown and the subsequent purchase of the photocopier with Heather's cash.

70. On July 1, Lender has

    (A) a perfected security interest in the photocopier.

    (B) an unperfected security interest in the photocopier.

    (C) no interest in the photocopier because the collateral description in its security agreement does not mention "equipment."

    (D) no interest in the photocopier because the collateral description in its security agreement does not mention "proceeds" of inventory.

Debtor is granting to Bank a security interest in its current and after-acquired equipment. Bank intends to perfect its security interest by filing a financing statement with the applicable filing office. Bank is concerned that some of the equipment could be deemed a fixture, so Bank also intends to file a fixture filing.

71.   Unlike the financing statement, the fixture filing must

(A)   be authenticated by the owner of the real estate on which the fixture is or may be located.

(B)   provide a description of the real estate on which the fixture is or may be located.

(C)   summarize the secured debt.

(D)   describe, with detailed particularity, the equipment that is or may become a fixture.

Norman Bates owns and operates The Bates Motel. Hitchcock Finance Corp. holds a mortgage on the motel, on "all fixtures now or hereafter affixed thereto," and on the underlying real estate. The mortgage (which is not a construction mortgage) was filed in the appropriate real property records in January. On April 5, Norman purchased a new central air conditioning unit on credit from Balsam Heating and Air Conditioning (with Balsam retaining an enforceable security interest in the unit). Balsam installed the unit (a "fixture" under applicable law) on April 11. In July, Norman defaulted on his obligations to Hitchcock and Balsam.

72.   Which statement is FALSE?

(A)   Balsam's interest in the unit enjoys priority if Balsam recorded a proper fixture filing in the right place on April 27.

(B)   Hitchcock's interest in the unit enjoys priority if Balsam neither filed a financing statement nor made a fixture filing.

(C)   If Balsam enjoys priority and removes the unit, Balsam must reimburse Hitchcock for any diminution in the motel's value caused by the absence of the unit.

(D)   To be effective, any fixture filing filed by Balsam must describe the real estate on which the motel is built.

Meredith bought her first home in March of this year. Fidelity Finance financed the purchase and holds the mortgage on the home, "all fixtures now or hereafter affixed thereto," and the underlying real estate. The mortgage (which is not a construction mortgage) was filed in the appropriate real property records in March.

On October 1, Meredith purchased four large trees on credit from Walker Nursery, which retained an enforceable security interest in the trees. Walker Nursery planted the four large trees (each a "fixture" under applicable law) on October 8. Walker Nursery filed a fixture filing with the appropriate official on October 25.

In December, Meredith lost her job and shortly thereafter defaulted on her obligations to Fidelity Finance and Walker Nursery.

73. Which creditor's interest in the four trees enjoys priority?

ANSWER:

Carl Creditor sold Dick Debtor an elevator and installation accessories on credit, taking back a security interest to secure the deferred portion of the purchase price. Dick signed a valid security agreement, and Carl filed valid and complete financing statements with the appropriate central filing authority before Dick took delivery of the goods. Carl did not, however, make any fixture filings.

Dick bought the elevator for his new office building. Before Dick bought the elevator and accessories, Vicious Bank had agreed to lend Dick up to $5,000,000 to enable Dick to buy the land for the building and to pay for its construction. To secure repayment of this amount, Vicious had Dick sign a valid and complete mortgage encumbering the land and any buildings constructed thereon. This mortgage contained an adequate real estate description, indicated it was to be a fixture filing and a construction mortgage, and also contained language granting to Vicious a security interest in all of Dick's inventory and equipment used in the building. The mortgage was filed with the local county recorder, the appropriate place to file a real estate mortgage. Vicious did not, however, file any other document with any other state official.

The mortgage creates a valid and perfected lien on the land and buildings under local real estate law, and it contains a valid and customary clause that states that "all appurtenances thereto and fixtures thereon, including without limitation elevators and light fixtures" are subject to the lien of the mortgage.

Under applicable local law, installed elevators in a building are fixtures. They are not readily removable from the building under any standard.

Carl delivers the elevator (in several large crates) to the building site as agreed. Before installation, however, Dick defaults on all loans and files a Chapter 11 petition in bankruptcy.

74. In a priority contest between Carl and Vicious concerning the elevator,

   (A) Carl will win because he filed a financing statement with the appropriate central filing authority, and Vicious did not.

   (B) Vicious will win because Carl did not make a fixture filing.

   (C) Vicious will win only if a court would hold that Vicious' mortgage was a construction mortgage.

(D)   Carl will win because he has a purchase-money security interest in the elevator.

Assume the same facts, except now assume that Dick installs the elevator in the building before filing his Chapter 11 bankruptcy petition.

75.   In a priority contest between Carl and Vicious concerning the elevator,

(A)   Carl will win because he filed a financing statement with the appropriate central filing authority, and Vicious did not.

(B)   Vicious will win because Carl did not make a fixture filing.

(C)   Vicious will win only if a court holds that Vicious' mortgage was a construction mortgage.

(D)   Carl will win because he has a purchase-money security interest in the elevator.

Assume the original facts, except now also assume that Dick installs the elevator in the building before filing his Chapter 7 bankruptcy petition.

76.   In a priority contest between Carl and the bankruptcy trustee, which of the following best states the most likely result?

(A)   Carl will win because he filed a financing statement with the appropriate central filing authority.

(B)   The trustee will win because Carl did not make a fixture filing.

(C)   The trustee will prevail since it has the standing of a bona fide purchaser of real estate.

(D)   Carl will win because he has a purchase-money security interest in the elevator.

Fred sells lights and light fixtures. He finances his inventory with Blot Bank, Inc. ("BBI"). BBI has a valid security agreement with Fred and has filed an accurate and complete financing statement against Fred in Nebraska, his home state, with the appropriate official (the Nebraska Secretary of State). Both the security agreement and the financing statement describe the collateral as "inventory."

Fred sells $10,000 worth of lighting and light fixtures to Acme Manufacturing, Inc., a California corporation ("AMI"). The terms of the sale are that AMI will pay Fred the entire $10,000 thirty days after delivery and installation of the lights. Fred's contract also says that he retains title to the lights until paid in full.

Fred delivers the lights to AMI on October 1, and he files a financing statement with the California Secretary of State on the same day. AMI will use the lights and light fixtures in a building that it is constructing for itself. The lights and light fixtures are actually installed on October 15 and become fixtures in the building under local law on that date.

AMI never pays for the lights and files a Chapter 7 bankruptcy petition on December 1.

77.   In a dispute between Fred and AMI's Chapter 7 bankruptcy trustee over priority to the lights,

(A) Fred wins because his interest is attached and perfected.

(B) Fred loses because his interest is attached but not perfected.

(C) Fred loses because he no longer has any interest in the lights.

(D) Fred loses because although he still has an interest in the lights, that interest is now governed solely by real estate law, and Fred did nothing to perfect his interest under such real estate law.

On March 24, First Finance obtained an enforceable security interest in the existing and future accounts of Odyssey Furniture, a business that sells home furnishings. First Finance filed its financing statement against the accounts on March 29.

On July 7, Midway Bank obtained an enforceable security interest in the current and after-acquired inventory of Odyssey Furniture. Midway Bank filed its financing statement against the inventory on July 13.

On September 6, Buyer bought a bedroom suite, using a credit card as payment.

    78.   As of October 1, whose interest in the credit card receivable (and any cash payments thereon) enjoys priority?

ANSWER:

On June 1, Supplier obtained an enforceable security interest in Debtor's current and after-acquired inventory. Supplier filed its financing statement with the appropriate filing officer on June 4.

On September 1, Bank obtained an enforceable security interest in Debtor's deposit account maintained with Bank. Bank never filed a financing statement.

On December 1, Debtor deposited $4,000 into its deposit account maintained with Bank. The deposit represented identifiable proceeds from the sale of Debtor's inventory.

    79.   Whose interest in the $4,000 enjoys priority?

ANSWER:

On May 15, Debtor borrowed $50,000 from Lender. To secure repayment of the loan, Debtor granted to Lender a security interest in its current and after-acquired equipment. The security agreement was executed that day.

On May 20, Lender filed a financing statement against Debtor's "equipment."

On May 25, Debtor used its own money to buy a new lathe for internal use.

On May 30, Debtor borrowed $35,000 from Bank (who had prior knowledge of Lender's security interest and recorded financing statement). To secure repayment of the loan, Debtor granted to Bank a security interest in its inventory, equipment, and accounts. The security agreement was executed that day and included an after-acquired property clause. Loan negotiations had been going on for several days, and Bank had previously filed a financing statement against Debtor's "equipment" on May 10 with Debtor's permission.

A few months passed, and Debtor defaulted on both loans. The default triggered a priority dispute in the lathe.

80. Whose security interest enjoys priority?

   (A) Lender enjoys priority because its security interest attached first.

   (B) Lender enjoys priority because its security interest became perfected first.

   (C) Lender's security interest enjoys priority because Bank had prior knowledge of Lender's security interest and financing statement when Bank's security interest attached.

   (D) Bank's security interest enjoys priority.

First National Bank ("FNB") loaned $100,000 to Osgood Furniture Corp., an entity that sells home furnishings. The loan was secured by an enforceable security interest in Osgood's inventory. The security agreement included an after-acquired property clause. FNB filed its financing statement on February 15, three days after the loan was funded and the security agreement was authenticated.

In need of additional funding, Osgood Furniture sold numerous accounts and chattel paper contracts to Miller Finance in June for $14,000 (the accounts and chattel paper contracts resulted from inventory sales). Miller Finance, in the business of buying accounts and commercial paper, took possession of the chattel paper contracts. As part of its due diligence, Miller Finance ordered and received a UCC search report that revealed FNB's financing statement.

When FNB discovered what Osgood had done, it sued Miller Finance for conversion of the accounts and chattel paper contracts.

81. Will FNB win its lawsuit?
ANSWER:

On May 1, Bank obtained an enforceable security interest in Debtor's deposit account at Bank, pursuant to a security agreement authenticated by Debtor.

On September 1, Lender loaned $10,000 to Debtor, retaining an enforceable security interest in Debtor's "equipment, whether now owned or hereafter acquired." Lender filed a proper financing statement against "equipment" with the appropriate authority on September 10.

On October 1, Debtor wrote a $2,000 check drawn on its deposit account at Bank and tendered the check as payment for a new photocopier ("equipment" in Debtor's hands). Bank discovered the delivery of the $2,000 check and, with Debtor's permission, filed a proper financing statement against Debtor's "equipment" with the appropriate authority on October 15.

82. Debtor defaulted on both loans on December 1. On that date,

(A) Bank's security interest in the photocopier enjoys priority because Lender's security interest is unperfected.

(B) Lender's security interest in the photocopier enjoys priority because Bank's security interest is unperfected.

(C) Both Lender and Bank have a perfected security interest in the photocopier, but Lender's security interest enjoys priority.

(D) Both Lender and Bank have a perfected security interest in the photocopier, but Bank's security interest enjoys priority.

On February 1, 2001, Polk Finance obtained an enforceable security interest in the current and after-acquired equipment of Blocker Corp., a Delaware corporation. Polk Finance filed its financing statement in Delaware on February 4, 2001.

On June 4, 2002, Albany Bank obtained an enforceable security interest in the current and after-acquired equipment of Davidson, Inc., a Delaware corporation. Albany Bank filed its financing statement in Delaware on June 10, 2002. The security agreement prohibited any dispositions of the equipment.

On August 10, 2003, Davidson sold an item of equipment (the "Item") to Blocker, for use as equipment.

On September 1, 2003, Albany Bank seeks a declaratory judgment that its security interest in the Item enjoys priority over the competing security interest in the Item held by Polk Finance.

83. How should the judge rule?
ANSWER:

On August 1, Dekka Corporation executed a valid security agreement in favor of BigBank, granting a security interest in "100 shares of Segway capital stock" then owned by Dekka. BigBank did not give any value to Dekka until August 6.

On August 3, SmallBank advanced $5,000 to Dekka and obtained an enforceable security interest in Dekka's "investment property, whether now owned or hereafter acquired." SmallBank filed a proper financing statement with the appropriate authority on August 4, describing the collateral as "investment property."

A priority dispute arises on September 1.

84.   Which statement is TRUE?

(A)   If BigBank filed a proper financing statement with the appropriate authority on August 2, its security interest in the Segway shares was perfected as of that date.

(B)   If BigBank filed a proper financing statement with the appropriate authority on August 1, it enjoys priority in the Segway shares.

(C)   If BigBank perfected its security interest in the Segway shares by obtaining control on August 8, SmallBank enjoys priority in the Segway shares.

(D)   SmallBank does not have a perfected security interest in the Segway shares because its collateral description in the financing statement lacks the specificity required by statute.

The priority dispute between BigBank and SmallBank also concerns 50 shares of Herrick capital stock that Dekka acquired on August 15 with funds from a federal tax refund.

85.   Which statement is TRUE?

(A)   SmallBank's security interest in the Herrick shares became perfected on August 4, when SmallBank filed its financing statement.

(B)   BigBank enjoys priority in the Herrick shares if it filed its financing statement before August 4.

(C)   SmallBank will enjoy priority in the Herrick shares, regardless of when BigBank files its financing statement.

(D)   If the shares are classified as an uncertificated security, then SmallBank's financing statement is ineffective to perfect a security interest in the shares.

First Bank obtained an enforceable security interest in Debtor's current and after-acquired inventory in January 2000. First Bank filed its financing statement on January 10, 2000.

Second Bank obtained an enforceable security interest in Debtor's current and after-acquired inventory in August 2003. Second Bank filed its financing statement the same month. Second Bank had knowledge of First Bank's security interest and financing statement.

In March 2005, Second Bank files a motion, seeking a declaratory judgment on the priority of its security interest in Debtor's inventory. Evidence reveals that First Bank filed a continuation statement on July 7, 2004.

86.   How should the court rule on Second Bank's motion?

ANSWER:

On October 1, John obtained an enforceable security interest in 250 shares of Waldorf capital stock that is owned by Sharon. John perfected his security interest by filing a financing statement on October 7.

On November 1, Heather obtained an enforceable security interest in the same Waldorf shares. Heather perfected her security interest by taking possession of the stock certificate on November 3.

On December 1, Sharon defaulted on both loans.

87. Whose security interest in the Waldorf shares enjoys priority if the stock certificate was issued to Sharon in bearer form?

ANSWER:

88. Whose security interest in the Waldorf shares enjoys priority if the stock certificate was issued to Sharon in registered form but was not indorsed by Sharon or registered in Heather's name by Waldorf?

ANSWER:

In February, David borrowed $1,000 from Helen, his aunt. Repayment of the loan was secured by an enforceable security interest in all of the shares held by David in (and purchased directly from) the Templeton Mutual Fund (which issues quarterly performance statements but no share certificates). Helen perfected her security interest by filing a financing statement in the appropriate state on February 7.

In June, David borrowed $2,000 from Wallace, a co-worker. Repayment of the loan was secured by an enforceable security interest in the same Templeton Mutual Fund shares. Wallace never filed a financing statement. But with David's consent, Templeton Mutual Fund revised its books to reflect Wallace as the registered owner.

David defaults on both loans in September.

89. As between Helen and Wallace, whose security interest in the Templeton Mutual Fund shares enjoys priority?

ANSWER:

Lender holds an enforceable security interest in Borrower's inventory. The security agreement (executed on February 1) included an after-acquired property clause. Lender filed its financing statement against inventory with the proper official on February 3.

On March 1, Borrower leased a unit of inventory to Lessee. The lease described the unit and obligated Lessee to pay $150 per month for three years. On March 5, Borrower sold and delivered the lease to FinCo, an entity in the business of buying commercial paper (including leases). Before buying the lease, FinCo ordered a UCC search report against Borrower and discovered Lender's financing statement.

90.   Which statement is TRUE?

(A)   Lender's security interest does not extend to the lease.

(B)   Lender has an unperfected security interest in the lease.

(C)   Lender has a perfected security interest in the lease, but FinCo's interest in the lease enjoys priority.

(D)   Lender has a perfected security interest in the lease that enjoys priority over FinCo's interest.

In February, Julia Childress (a Houston resident) opened a local restaurant, "The Lucky Duck." She borrowed $500,000 from Lender. Lender took and perfected a security interest in the restaurant's equipment by filing a financing statement with the appropriate official against "Julia Childress d/b/a The Lucky Duck" on March 1. The security agreement included an after-acquired property clause.

On June 1, Julia incorporated her restaurant business as "Gourmet Enterprises, Inc.," under Texas law. Without Lender's approval, Julia transferred all of her restaurant assets to the new corporate entity, which became a "new debtor" under applicable law by assuming all of Julia's restaurant-related debts (including her obligations under the security agreement with Lender). Lender discovered the asset transfer but never filed a financing statement against Gourmet Enterprises.

On June 15, Gourmet Enterprises borrowed $750,000 from Bank. Bank took and perfected a security interest in the equipment of Gourmet Enterprises by filing a financing statement with the appropriate official on June 20. The security agreement included an after-acquired property clause.

On December 15, Bank filed a declaratory action against Lender to resolve a priority dispute in the equipment of Gourmet Enterprises, including the following:

Item   #1 (acquired by Julia on 2/1; transferred to Gourmet Enterprises on 6/1)

Item   #2 (acquired by Gourmet Enterprises on 8/1)

Item   #3 (acquired by Gourmet Enterprises on 11/1)

91.   As of December 15, Lender's security interest is

(A)   perfected in Items #1, #2, and #3.

(B)   perfected in Items #1 and #2 only.

(C)   perfected in Item #1 only.

(D)   unperfected in Items #1, #2, and #3.

92.   As of December 15, Lender has priority in

(A)   none of the Items.

(B)   Item #1 only.

(C)   Items #1 and #2 only.

(D)   Items #1, #2, and #3.

Clinic borrowed $80,000 from Bank on February 1. The loan was secured by an enforceable security interest in Clinic's equipment and accounts. The security agreement, dated February 1, included an after-acquired property clause. The security agreement also prohibited Clinic from incurring any future debt in excess of $8,000 without first obtaining Bank's written permission. Bank filed a proper financing statement with the appropriate filing office on February 4.

On July 1, Clinic bought a $10,000 computer system on credit from Dealer without obtaining Bank's prior written permission. Under the terms of the sale contract for the system executed on July 1, Dealer retained an enforceable security interest in the system to secure repayment of the purchase price. Dealer delivered and installed the system on July 8. Dealer filed a proper financing statement with the appropriate filing office on July 25.

93. If a priority dispute arises in the computer system,

    (A) Bank's security interest enjoys priority because Bank filed first.

    (B) Bank's security interest enjoys priority because Clinic's purchase of the computer system from Dealer violated Bank's security agreement.

    (C) Bank's security interest enjoys priority because Dealer filed its financing statement more than twenty days after Dealer's security interest attached.

    (D) Dealer's security interest enjoys priority.

Last year, Debtor borrowed $1 million from Lender. The loan is secured by an enforceable security interest in Debtor's equipment. The security agreement included an after-acquired property clause. Lender perfected its security interest by filing a financing statement shortly after extending credit.

On June 1 of this year, Debtor bought a new piece of equipment on credit from Dealer. Dealer retained an enforceable security interest in the equipment to secure repayment of its purchase price. Dealer delivered and installed the equipment at Debtor's plant on June 5 and filed its financing statement on June 27.

94. Which statement is TRUE?

    (A) Because Dealer did not file its financing statement within 20 days after the purchase date, Dealer's security interest is no longer a PMSI and does not enjoy priority.

    (B) Because Dealer did not file its financing statement within 20 days after the purchase date, Dealer's security interest does not enjoy priority, but it remains a PMSI.

(C) Because Dealer did not file its financing statement within 20 days after the installation date, Dealer's security interest is no longer a PMSI and does not enjoy priority.

(D) Because Dealer did not file its financing statement within 20 days after the installation date, Dealer's security interest does not enjoy priority, but it remains a PMSI.

Farmington Furniture borrowed $75,000 from Midtown Bank on March 1. The loan was secured by an enforceable security interest in Farmington's accounts, equipment, and inventory. The security agreement included an after-acquired property clause. Midtown Bank filed its financing statement on March 7.

On August 3, Farmington bought a new photocopier (for in-store use) from Dealer on credit. Under the sales contract executed that day by Farmington, Dealer retained an enforceable security interest in the photocopier. Dealer delivered the photocopier to Farmington on August 8 and filed its financing statement on August 25.

Later, Farmington defaults on both obligations.

95. Whose security interest in the photocopier enjoys priority?

ANSWER:

As of January 5, BigBank held an enforceable security interest in the current and after-acquired equipment of Smalltown College. BigBank filed a proper financing statement with the proper official on January 10.

On March 1, Smalltown College bought a grand piano from Dealer for $10,000. Dealer financed 20% ($2,000) and retained an enforceable security interest in the piano to secure repayment of the $2,000 credit. Dealer filed a proper financing statement with the proper official on March 24. Dealer delivered the piano on March 7.

Smalltown College financed the remaining 80% ($8,000) with funds borrowed from Lender. Lender, too, retained an enforceable security interest in the piano to secure repayment of its $8,000 loan. Lender filed a proper financing statement with the proper official on March 15.

Later, Smalltown College defaulted on its payment obligations to BigBank ($5,000), Dealer ($2,000), and Lender ($8,000).

96. If SmallTown College voluntarily sells the piano for $6,000, it should distribute

(A) $2,000 to Dealer and $4,000 to BigBank.

(B) $2,000 to Dealer and $4,000 to Lender.

(C) $5,000 to BigBank and $1,000 to Dealer.

    (D) $6,000 to Lender.

Assume the same facts as in the preceding question, except Dealer refused to extend any credit. Smalltown College then borrowed the $2,000 from ABC Finance, who retained an enforceable security interest in the piano to secure repayment of the $2,000 loan. ABC Finance filed a proper financing statement with the proper official on March 18.

Again, Smalltown College defaulted on its payment obligations to BigBank ($5,000), ABC Finance ($2,000), and Lender ($8,000).

   97. If Smalltown College voluntarily sells the piano (which Dealer had delivered on March 7) for $6,000, it should distribute

    (A) $2,000 to ABC Finance and $4,000 to BigBank.

    (B) $2,000 to ABC Finance and $4,000 to Lender.

    (C) $5,000 to BigBank and $1,000 to Lender.

    (D) $6,000 to Lender.

As of February 1, BigBank holds a perfected security interest in Debtor's equipment. The security agreement included an after-acquired property clause.

On March 1, Dealer agreed to sell several pieces of equipment from its inventory to Debtor during the next several months on credit. Dealer retained a security interest in all equipment that it sold to Debtor, and the security agreement included an after-acquired property clause and a future advance clause. The agreement also called for any payments made by Debtor to be applied to the oldest purchase price first. Dealer filed a proper financing statement with the appropriate official on March 6.

Dealer sold the following pieces of equipment to Debtor during the year:

          Item #1 ($50,000)
          Item #2 ($60,000)
          Item #3 ($40,000)

Debtor later defaulted, owing $100,000 to BigBank and $80,000 to Dealer.

   98. If Item #1 can be sold for $36,000, Dealer should receive

    (A) $0.

    (B) $16,000.

    (C) $20,000.

    (D) $36,000.

   99. If Item #2 can be sold for $45,000, Dealer should receive

    (A) $5,000.

    (B) $20,000.

    (C) $40,000.

    (D) $45,000.

100. If Item #3 can be sold for $42,500, Dealer should receive

    (A) $0.

    (B) $22,225.

    (C) $40,000.

    (D) $42,500.

Northwest Office Supplies ("NOS") needed a new computer network for in-store use. After shopping around, it decided to buy a computer network from CompuStore for $60,000. CompuStore agreed to a credit sale for 75% of the purchase price if NOS would make a 25% down payment. NOS did not have the necessary $15,000, so it borrowed that amount from its existing lender, Blumfield Bank, who held a perfected security interest in the current and after-acquired equipment of NOS. NOS used Blumfield Bank's money to make the down payment. CompuStore retained an enforceable security interest in the computer system to secure repayment of the $45,000 credit extension and filed a financing statement one week after the sale.

Later, NOS defaulted on its obligations to both CompuStore and Blumfield Bank, having paid only $10,000 to the former and $5,000 to the latter for the computer network financing.

101. The computer system has been sold for $30,000. Who is entitled to the proceeds?

ANSWER:

Assume that CompuStore refused to make a credit sale. Instead, NOS paid cash, using the $15,000 advanced by Blumfield Bank and $45,000 borrowed from Friendly Finance. To secure repayment of the $45,000, Friendly Finance obtained an enforceable security interest in the computer network and filed a financing statement two weeks after CompuStore delivered the computer network to NOS.

Later, NOS defaulted on its obligations to both Blumfield Bank and Friendly Finance, having paid only $5,000 to the former and $15,000 to the latter for the computer network financing.

102. The computer system has been sold for $30,000. Who is entitled to the proceeds?

ANSWER:

Frank Farmer has a purchase-money security interest in all eggs owned by David Debtor, a baker. The value of the eggs is $300. This security interest is properly perfected and secures a debt of $400. Cream Cheese, Inc., has a security interest in all of David's cream cheese. The value of the cream cheese is $500. Cream Cheese's security interest is properly perfected and secures a $700 debt.

David combines the cream cheese, eggs, and other ingredients to make 500 cheesecakes, which are worth $2 each.

103. Which of the following best describes the relative positions of Frank Farmer and Cream Cheese?

  (A) Neither has a security interest in the cheesecakes, since the ingredients were commingled and there is no way to determine what part of each cheesecake is attributable to eggs, and which is attributable to cream cheese.

  (B) Frank Farmer has priority since his security interest was a purchase-money security interest.

  (C) The two security interests rank equally and share in the ratio of 3:5.

  (D) The two security interests rank equally and share in the ratio of 4:7.

Flaming Factors has a perfected security interest in all air conditioners held for resale by Flakey Air Conditioning, Inc. Flakey signed a valid security agreement covering the air conditioners. Flaming Factors then took care to file the financing statement in all proper places. The financing statement describes the collateral as "all air conditioning units held for resale, and all proceeds thereof in whatever form."

Flakey wishes to buy air conditioners from AirCon, Inc. Flaming Factors refuses to extend any credit for this purchase. Undaunted, Flakey convinces AirCon to sell it air conditioners on a conditional sales basis; that is, AirCon will continue to hold title until Flakey pays for the goods. To be safe, however, AirCon has Flakey authorize the filing of a financing statement covering the shipment, and AirCon files this financing statement in all appropriate places before delivery. AirCon also telephones Flaming Factors and leaves a voice mail on its answering machine explaining the arrangement before AirCon delivers any air conditioners. There is no question Flaming Factors received this message.

After AirCon delivers the air conditioners, Flaming Factors notifies Flakey that the AirCon transaction violates the terms of the financing agreement between Flaming Factors and Flakey. It is correct in this regard. The notice also states that Flaming Factors is accelerating the debt. Flaming Factors then sends ten burly agents to Flakey to repossess all air conditioners found on the premises. Flakey consents to the repossession.

AirCon's units are among those repossessed. It is steamed, and makes demand upon Flaming Factors to return the units to AirCon or face a lawsuit.

104. In a priority dispute between Flaming Factors and AirCon concerning the repossessed AirCon units,

  (A) AirCon will win since it was not paid in full.

  (B) Flaming Factors will win because it did not breach the peace upon repossession.

  (C) AirCon will win because its interest was perfected upon delivery, and its notice to Flaming Factors was adequate.

(D) Flaming Factors will win because it filed first.

Jake operates a food cart in New York City. Last month he bought the cart from Beth, another food cart operator, when Beth decided to upgrade to a new cart.

Jake borrowed $2,000 from Henry to finance the purchase. Henry gave Jake a check for $2,000, made jointly payable to Beth and Jake. Henry and Jake also signed a valid security agreement, and Jake then filed an adequate and complete financing statement with the New York Secretary of State. Both the security agreement and the financing statement described the collateral as "one street cart."

Jake has not paid his federal taxes in a long time. One month after Jake's purchase, the IRS files a valid tax lien with the New York Secretary of State, the appropriate place under New York state law.

Jake then defaults on his debt to Henry and peaceably turns the cart over to Henry. Henry then advertises it for sale. The IRS notices the ad and makes demand on Henry for the cart. Albert also sees the ad and makes demand for the cart, showing Henry a valid security agreement and financing statement from Beth, under which Beth granted to Albert a security interest in the cart. Beth is now in default under her agreement with Albert.

105. If the IRS, Albert, Henry, and Jake are all joined in a lawsuit to determine possession of the cart, the party most likely to win is

(A) the IRS.

(B) Albert.

(C) Henry.

(D) Jake.

Sandra Chang bought a dining room suite on credit from Friendly Furniture for everyday use in her home. To secure repayment of the loan, Friendly Furniture retained a security interest in the furniture. Friendly Furniture never filed a financing statement, but its security agreement expressly prohibited Sandra from disposing of the furniture or using it as collateral to secure any other debt.

Several months later, and without the permission of Friendly Furniture, Sandra sold the dining room suite on an internet auction site to Jill Brunson for everyday use in her home. Friendly Furniture discovered the sale and insists that Jill surrender the furniture. Jill refuses.

106.   In a priority dispute between the two parties, Friendly Furniture

(A)   does not have priority because its security interest was never perfected prior to the internet sale.

(B)   does not have priority even though its security interest remained perfected after the internet sale.

(C)   does not have priority because it failed to file a financing statement against Jill within four months after the internet sale.

(D)   will enjoy priority because Sandra's sale violated the terms of her security agreement with Friendly Furniture.

107.   As a general rule, a purchase-money security interest in consumer goods is automatically perfected (a major exception being goods that are subject to a certificate-of-title registration scheme, such as automobiles). Nevertheless, the purchase-money creditor that is relying on automatic perfection should consider filing a financing statement in order to protect itself in a subsequent priority dispute with

(A)   a person who buys the collateral from the debtor and uses it primarily for a personal, family, or household purpose.

(B)   a future lien creditor of the debtor.

(C)   a party that buys the collateral from the debtor for the purpose of reselling it in the ordinary course of its business.

(D)   the bankruptcy trustee if the debtor later files a Chapter 7 petition.

Granite City Bank ("GCB") loaned $1 million to Warren County Music Company, a seller of musical instruments, songbooks, and sheet music. The loan was secured by an enforceable security interest in Warren County's inventory, equipment, and accounts. The security agreement included an after-acquired property clause and prohibited Warren County from selling any unit of collateral, except for inventory sales to customers who used cash or a credit card as a form of payment. GCB filed its financing statement with the appropriate official on March 1.

On June 1, Warren County Music Company sold a $20,000 grand piano to Ima Virtuoso. Ima executed a promissory note (an industry practice for such an expensive purchase), agreeing to make equal monthly payments for five years. Ima is a professional musician and will use the piano in a studio where she earns her livelihood by giving private lessons. Ima has knowledge of GCB's security interest.

On August 1, Warren County Music Company sold an in-house photocopier to an employee, Ingrid Mullins, for her personal use. Ingrid was not aware of GCB's security interest.

In October, GCB discovered these two sales and has sued both Ima and Ingrid for conversion of its collateral.

108.   Does Article 9 permit GCB to recover the piano from Ima?
ANSWER:

109.   Does Article 9 permit GCB to recover the photocopier from Ingrid?
ANSWER:

Bart goes to Fairway Chevrolet to buy a car. He sees a used Chevy Suburban that is right for him. He pays the $10,000 purchase price by check and drives the car off the lot.

During the negotiations, Fairway said that it would mail to Bart the "pink slip," the local jargon for the required certificate of title. Unbeknownst to Bart, the pink slip shows Harriet as owner, and SlowBank as a lienholder of record (which, under the local certificate of title statute, was all that SlowBank had to do to perfect a security interest in a car subject to the certificate of title). Fairway paid Harriet $8,000 for the car, and Harriet then endorsed the certificate of title in all appropriate places so as to effect a transfer of the Suburban to Fairway. Also unbeknownst to Bart, Fairway finances its cars with QuickBank. Fairway has signed a valid security agreement, and QuickBank has filed a financing statement with the appropriate official. The description of collateral in both documents is simply "inventory." QuickBank does not place any notation on Fairway's certificate of title.

SlowBank discovers that its debtor, Harriet, sold her Suburban to Fairway, and that Fairway sold it to Bart. Such a sale is a default under Harriet's valid security agreement with SlowBank under which she still owes SlowBank $10,000 (she did not pay to SlowBank the sales price paid to her by Fairway). Due to unrelated matters, Fairway is now in default on its loan from QuickBank.

110. In a replevin action among QuickBank, SlowBank, and Bart,

(A) Bart will prevail because he bought the car in the ordinary course of business.

(B) QuickBank will prevail because it had a perfected security interest in all cars on Fairway's lot, including all used cars.

(C) SlowBank will prevail because its name was noted on the certificate of title.

(D) SlowBank will prevail because Harriet did not turn over to QuickBank the sales price that Fairway paid to Harriet.

On February 1, Kirby Piano Corp. sold a piano on credit to Heather Cortez, a Chicago resident who earns her living by giving piano lessons. Heather used the piano in her private studio, not in her home. Kirby retained a security interest in the piano to secure payment of the unpaid purchase price. Kirby filed a proper financing statement with the appropriate Illinois official on February 4.

In April, Heather relocated her studio (and piano) to Los Angeles.

In October, Heather sold the piano to Greg Mendoza (a California resident) so Greg's twin daughters could take piano lessons. Greg had no knowledge of Kirby's interest.

In November, Kirby filed a proper financing statement with the appropriate California official.

111. Greg is most likely to win a priority dispute with Kirby that is resolved in December by invoking

(A) section 9-315(a).

(B) section 9-317(b).

(C) section 9-320(a).

(D) section 9-320(b).

Lender has a perfected security interest in the current and after-acquired inventory of Dealer, a merchant that sells appliances (*e.g.*, washer/dryer units, microwave ovens). The security agreement permits Dealer to sell or lease appliances to customers who pay with cash, a debit card, a credit card, or a check. Credit sales (excluding credit card transactions) are prohibited.

Last week, Edith bought a refrigerator from Dealer for her home. At Edith's request, Dealer allowed her to pay with her signed, 30-day, negotiable, unsecured promissory note for the purchase price. Use of such notes as payment devices is usual and customary in the industry.

Lender discovered the unauthorized sale and sued Edith for conversion. Edith responded by invoking the protection afforded by section 9-320(a) to buyers in the ordinary course of business.

112. Which statement is TRUE?

(A) Edith is not a buyer in the ordinary course of business because the sale violated Lender's security agreement.

(B) Edith is not a buyer in the ordinary course of business because the refrigerator is not inventory in her hands.

(C) Edith would not be a buyer in the ordinary course of business if she had knowledge of Lender's security interest in the refrigerator.

(D) Edith is a buyer in the ordinary course of business.

On September 1, Dealer sold a piece of equipment (the "Equipment") to Debtor on credit. To secure payment of the purchase price, Dealer retained an enforceable security interest in the Equipment pursuant to agreement. Dealer delivered the Equipment to Debtor on September 5.

On September 10, Mason acquired the status of "lien creditor" against Debtor under applicable law. Mason's lien encumbers the Equipment as of September 10.

On September 30, Dealer seeks a declaratory judgment that its security interest enjoys priority over Mason's lien.

113.   How should the judge rule, if evidence reveals that Dealer filed a financing statement on September 18 (or September 23 or September 28)?

ANSWER:

On March 1, Bank loaned money to Debtor. To secure repayment of the loan, Bank took an enforceable security interest in an item of equipment already owned by Debtor.

On March 5, the item of equipment was seized by the sheriff pursuant to a writ of execution obtained by Tim, a judgment creditor of Debtor.

On March 9, Bank discovered the seizure and immediately delivered its proper financing statement (together with the filing fee) to the appropriate official. Somehow the filing officer misplaced the financing statement, so it never appeared in the records.

114.   If Tim became a "lien creditor" under applicable law on March 5, then

(A)   Bank's security interest became perfected, but Tim's interest enjoys priority.

(B)   Bank's security interest has priority because it attached before Tim became a lien creditor.

(C)   Bank's security interest has priority because Bank perfected its interest within the applicable grace period.

(D)   Bank's security interest does not enjoy priority because the interest was never perfected.

On September 1, Debtor granted to Bank a security interest in equipment worth $100,000 (the "Equipment") to secure a $30,000 loan. The security agreement had a future advance clause, but Bank was not obligated to make any future advances. Bank filed its financing statement on September 5.

On September 10, Jeremy obtained a $60,000 judgment against Debtor. Jeremy became a "lien creditor" under applicable state law on September 15 when the sheriff seized the Equipment to satisfy the judgment.

Bank advanced another $20,000 on October 1, another $30,000 on October 28, and another $20,000 on November 4.

On November 7, the sheriff sold the Equipment for $100,000.

115.   How should the sheriff distribute the proceeds if evidence reveals that Bank was aware of Jeremy's lien and the property seizure as early as October 25?

ANSWER:

Assume that the security agreement between Bank and Debtor included the following statement:

"Secured Party agrees to loan $150,000 to Debtor in one or more advances; provided that secured Party may refuse to fund an advance if an Event of Default exists."

Assume that *"Event of Default"* is defined to include judgments against Debtor in excess of $5,000.

116.   Would these assumptions affect the sheriff's distribution of the $100,000?

ANSWER:

Jim takes his couch to Couches Revitalized ("CR") for re-upholstering. CR performs the services and charges Jim $250, which is a reasonable fee for the work performed.

Jim disagrees and refuses to pay. CR refuses to give up the couch, relying solely on the following statute enacted in the state where CR operates:

Every person who, while lawfully in possession of an article of personal property, renders any service to the owner thereof, by labor or skill, employed for the protection, improvement, safekeeping, or carriage thereof, has a special lien thereon, dependent on possession, for the compensation, if any, which is due to him from the owner for such service; a person who makes, alters, or repairs any article of personal property, at the request of the owner, or legal possessor of the property, has a lien on the same for his reasonable charges for the balance due for such work done and materials furnished, and may retain possession of the same until the charges are paid.

Jim had granted a valid security interest in the couch to FirstBank when he bought it using credit that FirstBank extended to enable him to acquire the couch. FirstBank, however, never filed a financing statement. Jim contacts FirstBank and tells them about CR's actions. FirstBank correctly tells Jim that non-payment of the repair bill is a default under the security agreement and phones CR itself. CR still refuses to relinquish possession of the couch until it is paid.

117. In a lawsuit over possession of the couch among Jim, FirstBank, and CR,

    (A) Jim will win.

    (B) CR will win.

    (C) FirstBank will win.

    (D) Jim will win, but he will immediately have to turn over the couch to FirstBank.

Jim lent $5,000 to Bob two years ago. Bob has not repaid it. Bob is being chased by other creditors. Jim is still fairly friendly with Bob.

When Jim asks Bob to repay the debt, Bob responds that he cannot do so. He tells Jim that he will give Jim a security interest in "all his assets." Jim quickly drafts an otherwise valid security agreement and several financing statements, each of which contains the following description of the collateral: "All assets except violins." Jim files the financing statements with the proper central filing officer and the appropriate local county recorder.

At the same time, Jim asks for and Bob agrees to let Jim hold his Stradivarius violin as collateral for his loan. No documents are signed with respect to this transaction, and Bob hands over the violin to Jim.

Crispen, a judgment creditor of Bob's, knows about the Stradivarius. When he sees Jim holding it, he causes the sheriff to levy upon it pursuant to a valid judgment that Crispen previously obtained against Bob.

118. In a lawsuit between Crispen and Jim concerning the Stradivarius violin,

    (A) Crispen will prevail since the "all assets except violins" description is invalid.

    (B) Jim will prevail since he had possession of the violin.

    (C) Crispen will prevail if Jim in bad faith left the violin's description out of the security agreement.

    (D) Jim will prevail because he filed a financing statement locally.

As a general rule, a creditor's security interest in collateral acquired after the IRS files its tax lien notice is subordinate to the tax lien. An exception exists for "commercial financing security" that is timely acquired by the taxpayer.

119. Which of the following types of Article 9 collateral is not "commercial financing security"?

(A) Accounts.

(B) Equipment.

(C) Inventory.

(D) Chattel Paper.

On May 1, Bank entered into a binding commitment to make advances to Fashions Group, at Fashions Group's request, in an aggregate amount not to exceed $2 million. Fashions Group, which operates several retail clothing stores, executed a security agreement the same day in which it granted to Bank a security interest in all of its inventory, accounts receivable, and equipment. The security agreement included an after-acquired property clause and a future advance clause. Bank filed a proper financing statement with the appropriate official on May 8. Pursuant to its binding commitment, Bank made the following advances to Fashions Group (none of which have been repaid):

DATE	AMOUNT
5/5	$200,000
7/15	$100,000
8/4	$300,000
9/7	$400,000
9/20	$300,000

On July 1, the IRS assessed a $700,000 tax lien against Fashions Group. The IRS filed a tax lien notice with the appropriate officials on August 1. Bank did not discover the tax lien notice until September 5.

120. Assuming that the type and value of collateral are adequate, the IRS lien will be subject to Bank's security interest that secures debt of

(A) $1,300,000.

(B) $1,000,000.

(C) $600,000.

(D) $300,000.

121. In a priority dispute concerning a shipment of dresses and shoes acquired by Fashions Group on September 9,

    (A) Bank's security interest enjoys priority.

    (B) the tax lien enjoys priority because the items are not "commercial financing security."

    (C) the tax lien enjoys priority because Fashions Group acquired the items after Bank discovered the tax lien notice.

    (D) the tax lien enjoys priority because Fashions Group acquired the items more than 45 days after the IRS assessed the tax lien.

122.   In a priority dispute concerning two stitching machines purchased by Fashions Group on July 20,

    (A) the tax lien enjoys priority because the stitching machines are not "commercial financing security."

    (B) the tax lien enjoys priority because Fashions Group acquired the stitching machines after the IRS assessed the tax lien.

    (C) the tax lien enjoys priority because Fashions Group acquired the stitching machines before Bank acquired knowledge of the tax lien notice.

    (D) Bank's security interest enjoys priority.

123. Lender has a perfected security interest in Debtor's accounts, equipment, and inventory. Debtor recently defaulted. Lender's counsel will be most concerned to learn that the loan documents

    (A) are silent on Lender's ability to repossess the collateral upon default.

    (B) fail to state that Debtor remains liable for any deficiency following a foreclosure sale.

    (C) are silent on whether Lender can apply foreclosure proceeds to pay its reasonable legal fees and expenses incurred in connection with any foreclosure sale.

    (D) fail to mention that Lender can contact Debtor's customers and request them to remit payment directly to Lender.

124. A secured party's duty to send a disposition notice to a debtor is not excused if

    (A) the collateral threatens to decline speedily in value.

    (B) the collateral is typically sold on a recognized market.

    (C) the collateral is the subject of widely distributed standard price quotations.

    (D) the debtor authenticates a post-default waiver.

Metropolis Orchestra borrowed $40,000 from the local branch of AmeriBank in February to purchase a concert grand piano. To secure repayment of the loan, AmeriBank obtained an enforceable security interest in the piano. The Orchestra defaulted on the loan in July, and AmeriBank repossessed the piano with the Orchestra's consent.

AmeriBank has scheduled a public auction of the piano for 10:00 a.m. on Friday, August 14. AmeriBank intends to use regular mail to send its disposition notice to the Orchestra.

125. To invoke Article 9's safe harbor on timeliness, the notice must be

    (A) sent by AmeriBank no later than August 7.

    (B) received by the Orchestra no later than August 7.

    (C) sent by AmeriBank no later than August 4.

    (D) received by the Orchestra no later than August 4.

Historically, Friendly Finance has made secured loans only to businesses. But in an effort to expand its customer base, Friendly Finance has decided to make secured loans to consumers. Being realistic, Friendly Finance expects some of its consumer debtors to default, after which Friendly Finance expects to sell, lease, or otherwise dispose of the collateral at a nonjudicial foreclosure. Friendly Finance knows that Article 9 normally requires it to send notice of the disposition to the debtor and, if appropriate, to other parties. Friendly Finance intends to use its existing standard form of notice for businesses as a model for its "consumer goods" disposition notice.

126. In doing so, Friendly Finance must amend its existing form to mention

   (A) the debtor's right to attend any public disposition and purchase the collateral.

   (B) the debtor's liability for any deficiency remaining after the foreclosure.

   (C) a description of the default.

   (D) the debtor's right to insist on a strict foreclosure.

ToyCo, Inc., a Delaware corporation, has defaulted on its $2 million secured loan from Bank. Bank desires to sell certain collateral in its possession or control in which it has a perfected security interest.

127. In which of the following post-default scenarios will ToyCo be able to successfully challenge Bank's compliance with the notice-of-sale requirements of Article 9?

   (A) Without notifying ToyCo, Bank sells two stock certificates to Purchaser for the current market price. The stock certificates evidence capital stock of two companies listed on the American Stock Exchange.

   (B) Bank, intending to sell certain equipment at a private sale to be held no earlier than three weeks from the date of the letter, mails a proper notice to ToyCo's correct address. Somehow the U.S. Postal Service temporarily misplaces the letter. By the time the letter to ToyCo is finally delivered, Bank has sold the equipment at a private sale four weeks after the date of the letter.

   (C) Bank mails the following notice to ToyCo (which ToyCo timely receives): "The undersigned, pursuant to its rights as a secured party under Article 9 of the Uniform Commercial Code, intends to sell your three drilling presses presently in our custody and control. Our agent, Bradford Auctioneers, will conduct the public sale at its place of business located at 3556 Merrick, Houston, TX 77025."

   (D) Bank's written notice fails to state that ToyCo will remain liable for any deficiency and does not include an address or telephone number from which ToyCo can obtain additional information concerning the disposition.

Debtor (a corporation) borrowed $1 million from BankOne, which perfected an enforceable security interest in Debtor's major asset (the "Asset") worth $3 million if unencumbered by any liens or security interests. Two months later, Debtor borrowed $750,000 from BankTwo, which perfected an enforceable security interest in the Asset. Six months later, Debtor borrowed $500,000 from BankThree, which perfected an enforceable security interest in the Asset.

Two years later, the Asset has declined in value and Debtor defaulted on its loan from BankTwo. BankTwo obtained possession of the Asset with Debtor's consent. Then, after complying with the statutory notice requirements of Article 9, BankTwo conducted a commercially reasonable foreclosure sale of the Asset. Buyer purchased the Asset for $2 million (its fair market value at that time, if unencumbered). At the time of sale, Debtor owed $500,000 to BankOne, $400,000 to BankTwo, and $300,000 to BankThree.

128. How should the sale proceeds of $2 million be allocated among the parties?

ANSWER:

129. What effect does the foreclosure sale have on the various property interests in the Asset?

ANSWER:

130. Did Buyer pay too much for the Asset?

ANSWER:

131. A debtor that has granted a security interest in its inventory and equipment

   (A) may never waive its right to redeem the collateral.

   (B) may never waive its right to receive any surplus proceeds from any disposition of collateral.

   (C) may waive, pursuant to agreement authenticated at any time, its right to receive notice of any disposition of collateral.

   (D) may waive, pursuant to agreement authenticated after default, its right to have any disposition of collateral conducted in a commercially reasonable manner.

Last year, Bank loaned $7,500 to Lisa to open a dance studio. To secure repayment of the business loan, Bank obtained an enforceable security interest in 100 shares of Bradford Corp. capital stock. Bank perfected its security interest by filing a proper financing statement with the appropriate filing office.

The dance studio has been a bust, and Lisa has defaulted on her loan. The unpaid principal is $2,500. Bank is contemplating a strict foreclosure of the collateral.

132. Which statement is TRUE?

   (A) Partial strict foreclosure is prohibited.

   (B) Lisa's silence can create an effective consent to a proposal of full strict foreclosure.

(C) Absent Lisa's effective waiver, Bank must dispose of the collateral because Lisa has repaid more than 60% of the loan.

(D) Bank does not need to send its proposal of full strict foreclosure to any secured creditor that filed a financing statement <u>after</u> Bank filed its financing statement.

Dealer is in the business of selling home entertainment systems. Historically, Dealer has extended unsecured credit to about a third of its customers (the remaining customers pay with cash or a credit card). But given the recent downturn in the economy and the increased number of bankruptcies, Dealer has decided that any credit sales over $1,000 must be secured. Dealer is aware that Article 9 permits a secured party to dispose of collateral after default, but every aspect of the disposition must be "commercially reasonable."

133. Which statement regarding the quoted phrase is TRUE?

(A) Dealer can waive its duty to dispose of collateral in a "commercially reasonable" manner by agreement with its customers, but only in a transaction other than a consumer transaction.

(B) Dealer can waive its duty to dispose of collateral in a "commercially reasonable" manner by agreement with its customers, but only if the waiver is unambiguous and conspicuous and the agreement is authenticated by the customer after default.

(C) Dealer and its customers can determine, by agreement, standards of "commercially reasonable" behavior, but those standards cannot be unreasonable.

(D) Dealer and its customers can determine, by agreement, standards of "commercially reasonable" behavior, but those standards cannot be manifestly unreasonable.

Dealer sold a photocopier on credit to Baxter Honeycutt III for use in his business. Dealer retained an enforceable security interest in the photocopier. Dealer repossessed the photocopier after Baxter defaulted under the terms of the promissory note and security agreement, owing $7,600. After giving timely notice to Baxter, Dealer sold the photocopier at a public auction to Buyer for $4,300. Dealer then initiated a deficiency action against Baxter for $3,300. Baxter responded with proof that several aspects of the auction were not commercially reasonable. Furthermore, Baxter's expert testified that the photocopier had a fair market value of $5,800 at disposition. Dealer responded with proof that, even if all aspects of the sale had been commercially reasonable, the photocopier would not have sold for more than $5,000.

134. Based on this evidence, the court should enter a deficiency judgment against Baxter for

(A) $0.

(B) $1,800.

(C) $2,600.

(D) $3,300.

135. If Baxter keeps the photocopier in his home for personal use by family members, the court is *least* likely to enter a deficiency judgment against Baxter for

   (A) $0.

   (B) $1,800.

   (C) $2,600.

   (D) $3,300.

Otto's Autos is in the business of selling new and used cars. A few customers pay with cash, but most take advantage of Otto's secured financing. With its eye on the possibility of post-default repossession, Otto's standard form of security agreement includes the following provision: *"Debtor agrees that Secured Party may, without notice to Debtor, repossess the Vehicle from Debtor's residential premises, place of employment, or any other location where the Vehicle may be found at any time without damage to any surrounding property."*

Following the default of one of its customers, Keith (who had authenticated the standard form of security agreement), Otto's Autos employed Towtruck Tim, an independent contractor, to repossess the vehicle. Towtruck Tim went to Keith's home in the middle of the night and determined, by looking through a window, that the vehicle was in the garage. Finding the garage door unlocked, Towtruck Tim opened the garage door, removed the vehicle, closed the garage door, and towed the vehicle away. Towtruck Tim was on Keith's property less than five minutes and neither the neighbors nor Keith heard any noise throughout the repossession.

Keith discovered the repossession in the morning. Being a litigious sort, Keith quickly initiated an action against Otto's Autos and Towtruck Tim for breaching the peace, seeking compensatory and punitive damages.

136. With respect to the lawsuit,

   (A) Otto's Autos will be liable for any breach of the peace, for which both compensatory and punitive damages may be awarded.

   (B) neither Otto's Autos nor Towtruck Tim will be liable for breaching the peace because of the provision, quoted above, in the security agreement authenticated by Keith.

   (C) neither Otto's Autos nor Towtruck Tim will be liable for breaching the peace because Towtruck Tim was on Keith's premises for such a brief period of time, during which neighborhood tranquility remained undisturbed.

   (D) Otto's Autos will not be liable for any breach of the peace because Towtruck Tim, an independent contractor, actually repossessed the vehicle.

Dave Debtor contracts to buy a laptop computer on credit from Fast Freddie's Mail Order Computers. The contract Dave signs reserves title in Fast Freddie until Dave pays all amounts due. Fast Freddie files no financing statement with respect to this transaction. When Dave ordered the computer, he intended to use it at home as an educational aid for his daughter.

Once the computer arrived, Dave becomes fascinated with it and discards all thoughts of his child's education. He takes it to work and uses it every day. He also defaults on his payments.

137.   When Fast Freddie attempts to repossess,

     (A)   Dave can defend successfully on the basis that he and Fast Freddie never signed a security agreement.

     (B)   Dave can defend successfully on the basis that Fast Freddie never filed a financing statement.

     (C)   Dave can defend successfully on the basis that he bought the computer in the ordinary course of Fast Freddie's business, for value, and in good faith.

     (D)   Dave cannot successfully defend.

GougeBank lent Frivolous Sales $1,000,000. Frivolous signed an otherwise valid security agreement which contained a clause allowing GougeBank to declare Frivolous in default, accelerate the debt, and demand payment "at any time it deems itself insecure" by giving Frivolous written notice. The security agreement and financing statement each described the collateral as "all assets of the debtor, including, without limitation, all inventory, accounts, equipment, general intangibles, instruments, chattel paper, and all proceeds thereof." GougeBank filed the financing statement with the appropriate filing authority.

Frivolous was a new snowmobile dealer. One day, on a whim, Frivolous's president, Fred Flake, accepted two first-class airplane tickets to Bora Bora for one of its snowmobiles.

GougeBank's loan officer, Ima Tightwad, visited Frivolous the next day. Upon hearing Flake's tale, and seeing the tickets, Ima snatched the tickets from the desk and ran out of the dealership. Flake remained still, but yelled at Ima to stop. The state where Frivolous operates does not have a certificate of title system for snowmobiles.

138.   In a lawsuit by Frivolous against GougeBank to recover the tickets,

     (A)   Frivolous will win since GougeBank converted the tickets.

     (B)   GougeBank will win since it could accelerate the loan under the circumstances.

     (C)   Frivolous will win since GougeBank did not have a perfected security interest in the tickets.

     (D)   GougeBank will win since it was not required to make a demand upon Frivolous under the circumstances.

139.   Which of the following best describes the most likely result if GougeBank validly declares a default, accelerates the debt, and then attempts to recover the snowmobile Flake traded for the tickets?

     (A)   GougeBank will lose because it already has a security interest in the tickets, and to allow it to recover the snowmobile would be double recovery.

     (B)   GougeBank will win because the transaction involving the snowmobile was not in Frivolous's ordinary course of business.

(C) GougeBank will lose because its financing statement does not name the individual who now owns the snowmobile.

(D) GougeBank will win because the individual who traded for the snowmobile was on notice of GougeBank's security interest because of the filed financing statement.

Karen recently filed a Chapter 7 bankruptcy petition. BigBank holds a perfected purchase-money security interest in her 2002 Lexus sport utility vehicle to secure an unpaid debt of $18,000. Appraisers estimate the fair market value of the vehicle as low as $16,500 and as high as $19,000. BigBank intends to file a motion to lift the automatic stay, hoping that it can take possession of the vehicle and conduct a nonjudicial foreclosure as permitted by Article 9.

140. With respect to BigBank's motion,

(A) Karen has the burden of proof on the issues of adequate protection and her equity in the vehicle.

(B) BigBank has the burden of proof on the issues of adequate protection and Karen's equity in the vehicle.

(C) Karen has the burden of proof on the issue of her equity in the vehicle, and BigBank has the burden of proof on the issue of adequate protection.

(D) BigBank has the burden of proof on the issue of Karen's equity in the vehicle, and Karen has the burden of proof on the issue of adequate protection.

On July 1, Bank made a $150,000 loan to Clinic, repayment of which was secured by an enforceable security interest in all of Clinic's equipment, whether then owned or thereafter acquired. Bank perfected its interest on July 7 by filing a proper financing statement with the appropriate authority.

On August 1, MedCo sold a $100,000 kidney dialysis machine on credit to Clinic under a retail installment contract. MedCo retained an enforceable security interest in the machine. MedCo delivered the machine to Clinic on August 9 and filed a proper financing statement in the proper place on August 25.

On December 1, Clinic filed a Chapter 7 bankruptcy petition. As of that date, Clinic owed $120,000 to Bank and $80,000 to MedCo (all loan repayments had been made outside the preference period). Also as of December 1, Clinic's equipment had a fair market value of $140,000 (which included $90,000 attributable to the kidney dialysis machine).

141. If the trustee cannot set aside the security interests of the two creditors, which of the following statements best states their respective claims to Clinic's equipment?

(A) Bank has a $60,000 secured claim and a $60,000 unsecured claim, and MedCo has an $80,000 secured claim.

(B) Bank has a $90,000 secured claim and a $30,000 unsecured claim, and MedCo has a $50,000 secured claim and a $30,000 unsecured claim.

(C)   Bank has a $120,000 secured claim and MedCo has an $80,000 secured claim.

(D)   Bank has a $120,000 secured claim, and MedCo has a $20,000 secured claim and a $60,000 unsecured claim.

On June 1, Dealer sold a freezer on credit to Restaurant Corp. Under terms of the contract executed by both parties on that date, Dealer retained an enforceable security interest in the freezer to secure repayment of the purchase price. Dealer delivered the freezer to Restaurant on June 10. Dealer filed a proper financing statement with the appropriate official on June 18. Unknown to Dealer, Restaurant had filed a Chapter 7 bankruptcy petition on June 12.

142.   Which statement is TRUE?

(A)   Dealer's interest in the freezer was automatically perfected as a purchase-money security interest.

(B)   The freezer may be "exempt property" in the bankruptcy.

(C)   Dealer did not violate the automatic stay by filing a post-petition financing statement.

(D)   By filing its petition under Chapter 7, Restaurant is seeking reorganization.

Bank made a $2 million loan to Debtor on February 1. To secure repayment of the loan, Bank obtained an enforceable security interest in Debtor's inventory and accounts. The security agreement, also dated February 1, included an after-acquired property clause. Bank filed a proper financing statement with the appropriate official on February 10.

Debtor filed a Chapter 11 bankruptcy petition on July 1. On that date, Debtor owed $1 million to Bank. On August 1, Debtor still owed $1 million to Bank. Information on Debtor's inventory and accounts as of that date follows:

Inventory:

Existed as of July 1	$300,000
Purchased after July 1 with cash received from:	
accounts existing as of July 1	$100,000
accounts generated after July 1	$ 50,000
sale on July 15 of IBM stock purchased last year	$ 50,000

Accounts:

Existed as of July 1	$250,000
Generated after July 1 from credit sales of:	
inventory existing as of July 1	$100,000
inventory acquired after July 1	$ 50,000
equipment donated to Debtor last year	$ 50,000

143.   Ignoring voidable preference or fraudulent conveyance concerns, Bank can claim a perfected security interest in collateral worth

(A) $550,000.

(B) $750,000.

(C) $750,000 -$850,000.

(D) $800,000 -$900,000.

144. The "strong arm clause" permits the bankruptcy trustee to avoid

(A) an unperfected security interest.

(B) a property transfer made by the debtor "with actual intent to hinder, delay, or defraud" a creditor.

(C) a property transfer made by the debtor who "received less than a reasonably equivalent value in exchange for such transfer."

(D) a judicial lien that impairs an exemption.

145. Debtor, a Delaware corporation, filed a Chapter 11 bankruptcy petition on September 13. Under which of the following situations is Secured Party most vulnerable to an attack by the bankruptcy trustee under the "strong arm clause"?

(A) Secured Party's security interest in Debtor's equipment (located at a Delaware plant) attached on February 1, and Secured Party filed its financing statement with the appropriate Delaware official on February 7. On May 1, Debtor closed the Delaware plant and relocated the equipment to an Illinois plant. Secured Party never refiled a financing statement with the appropriate Illinois official.

(B) Secured Party's security interest in Debtor's investment property (a stock certificate held by Debtor in a safety deposit box in Atlanta) attached on July 2, and Secured Party filed its financing statement with the appropriate Georgia official on July 6.

(C) Secured Party's purchase-money security interest in Debtor's inventory (located in Texas) attached on September 8; Secured Party never filed a financing statement with the appropriate Texas official and did not file a financing statement with the appropriate Delaware official until three days after the petition date.

(D) Secured Party's security interest in Debtor's bank account (maintained with Secured Party) attached on July 20; Secured Party took no action to perfect its security interest.

146. Sally gives her daughter a birthday gift of a new car on her daughter's sixteenth birthday. Two weeks later, when one of Sally's judgment creditors seeks to levy execution on the car to satisfy the judgment owed.

(A) Sally's daughter will retain possession of the car so long as it is titled in her name.

(B) the judgment creditor will prevail if he can show that Sally is not generally paying her debts as they become due, and Sally does not offer any additional evidence at trial.

(C) Sally's daughter will retain possession of the car if she (the daughter) can prove that she is solvent.

    (D)   the judgment creditor will prevail only if Sally did not file a financing statement against her daughter describing the car as collateral.

Fred is the sole owner of all of the common stock issued by Gadgets, Inc., a Delaware corporation ("GI"). GI is a family business located in Kentucky that Fred incorporated for tax reasons several years ago. GI's general manager, Alice, knows that Fred wants to retire, and Fred has no sons or daughters who want to continue the business. Alice approaches Fred and offers to buy the business for $350,000. Fred agrees, and Alice and Fred agree that the purchase price will be paid by a downpayment of $50,000 at the closing on March 1, and then by the payment of four equal installments of $75,000 on each July 1 following the sale. Alice will sign a note to evidence the deferred portion of the purchase price.

Fred also wants collateral for the note. To accommodate his desires, at the closing, simultaneously with the transfer of the stock in GI from Fred to Alice, Alice (as the new GI chairperson of the board and president) will sign a security agreement on behalf of GI under which GI will grant an interest in "all inventory, accounts, equipment, general intangibles, instruments, investment securities, and deposit accounts, in each case whether now owned or hereafter acquired." The security agreement will secure the note and all of Fred's enforcement costs under the security agreement.

The closing goes as planned, and Fred files an accurate and complete financing statement with the Delaware Secretary of State that describes the collateral as "all assets."

Running the business, however, does not go as planned. It is a disaster. Alice tries to raise new equity capital, but she cannot do so. She tries to borrow money but is told that the presence of Fred's senior security interest makes any loan to GI risky. Both Alice and GI file a Chapter 7 bankruptcy petition on June 30.

Fred claims a security interest in all of GI's assets to secure the unpaid portion of the note. You represent GI's trustee in bankruptcy.

147.   You should

    (A)   do nothing; Fred is right and should get all the assets.

    (B)   bring an action against Fred alleging that the grant of the security interest in the assets of the business was an avoidable preference.

    (C)   bring an action against Fred alleging that the grant of the security interest in the assets of the business was a fraudulent transfer.

    (D)   bring an action against Fred alleging that the grant of the security interest in the assets of the business was both an avoidable preference and a fraudulent transfer.

Darren Debtor, a lifelong resident of Carson City, Nevada, runs a printing business. On June 1, Darren entered into negotiations with First Bank for a loan of $5,000,000. When Darren signed the letter of intent for the loan, First Bank had Darren sign the following: "I authorize First Bank to file an 'all assets' financing statement with the Nevada Secretary of State." First Bank then filed an otherwise accurate and complete financing statement with the Nevada Secretary of State naming Darren as the debtor and describing the collateral as "all assets." On June 15, Darren signed a security agreement granting a security interest to First Bank.

The collateral description in the security agreement is stated as "all equipment." The security agreement described the secured obligation as "that certain loan in the amount of $5,000,000 made by First Bank to Darren Debtor, all obligations under this security agreement (including all attorneys' fees), and all advances made by First Bank to Darren Debtor hereafter."

After the security agreement is signed, First Bank lends Darren $5,000,000. First Bank does not amend its financing statement.

On July 1, as anticipated in the security agreement with First Bank, Darren purchased a new printing press for $1,000,000, using a portion of the $5,000,000 loan proceeds. On August 15, Darren sells some surplus ink and paper to Seraph Printing, Inc. ("SPI"), another printing business. SPI gives Darren a check for the purchase price of $5,000. On September 30, Darren sells a used printing press to SPI for $500,000, with SPI giving Darren a check for $100,000, and its written promise to pay the balance by December 1.

Darren defaulted under the security agreement on October 1 and filed a Chapter 11 bankruptcy petition on October 15. It is now October 16. No purchases or sales of any of Darren's property other than completed printing jobs occurred between June 15 and October 15 except as stated above. Darren has not cashed, and still holds, the $5,000 and the $100,000 checks from SPI.

148. If the bankruptcy court determines that the value of all collateral in which First Bank has a perfected security interest is $6,000,000, the amount of First Bank's secured claim in bankruptcy is

   (A) less than $5,000,000.

   (B) $5,000,000.

   (C) $5,000,000 plus any of First Bank's attorneys' fees, but in no event more than $6,000,000.

   (D) $6,000,000.

149. If the bankruptcy court determines that the value of all collateral in which First Bank has a perfected security interest is $4,000,000, the amount of First Bank's secured claim in bankruptcy is

   (A) less than $5,000,000.

   (B) $5,000,000.

   (C) $5,000,000 plus any of First Bank's attorneys' fees, but in no event more than $6,000,000.

   (D) $6,000,000.

Debtor borrowed $100,000 from Bank on June 1. To secure repayment of the loan, Debtor granted to Bank a security interest in its current and future equipment. The security agreement was executed on June 1. On June 4, Bank filed a proper financing statement against Debtor's equipment with the appropriate filing officer. On June 8, Debtor used its own funds to buy a new piece of equipment (the "Item") from Seller, who placed a "sold" sticker on the Item. At Debtor's request, Seller did not deliver and install the Item at Debtor's office until June 12.

Debtor fell on hard times and filed a bankruptcy petition in late August. The trustee has challenged Bank's property interest in the Item as a voidable preference.

150. Under applicable bankruptcy law, the "transfer" took place on

(A) June 1.

(B) June 4.

(C) June 8.

(D) June 12.

On March 1, Kirk borrowed $5,000 from a co-worker, Robert. Kirk executed an unsecured promissory note with a maturity date of June 30. Kirk was unable to pay the note at maturity and requested a six-month extension. Robert agreed, provided that Angela (Kirk's sister) guarantee repayment of the loan and Elliott (Kirk's brother) collateralize the loan with a security interest in his investment portfolio. Angela obliged by executing a guaranty on July 10. Elliott obliged by creating an enforceable security interest in the investment portfolio on July 12. Robert perfected the security interest on July 25.

Alas, Kirk's financial situation did not improve, and he filed a Chapter 7 bankruptcy petition on October 15. On that date, he owed $4,500 to Robert. Angela had paid $500 to Robert on the debt just three days before the bankruptcy petition was filed.

Evidence reveals that Kirk has been insolvent for five months, and his unsecured creditors will not be paid in full in the bankruptcy.

151. Ignoring any possible defenses, the bankruptcy trustee can attack as voidable preferences

(A) neither the $500 payment nor the security interest.

(B) the $500 payment and the security interest.

(C) the $500 payment but not the security interest.

(D) the security interest but not the $500 payment.

152.   In a voidable preference action, the trustee

   (A)   enjoys an irrebuttable presumption of insolvency during the 90-day preference period.

   (B)   bears the burden of proving nonavoidability of the transfer under any exception found in 11 U.S.C. § 547(c).

   (C)   can never prove that a security interest transfer was made for antecedent debt if the security interest is perfected within ten days of attachment.

   (D)   cannot recover loan repayments from a non-insider creditor that were received by that creditor outside the 90-day preference period, even if the one-year preference period applies (e.g., when the debt is guaranteed by an insider).

153.   Which of the following voidable preference exceptions preserves only payment transfers?

   (A)   The "substantially contemporaneous exchange" exception.

   (B)   The "ordinary course of business" exception

   (C)   The "enabling loan" exception.

   (D)   The "floating lien" exception.

Bank loaned $2 million to Debtor on July 15. To secure repayment of the loan, Bank obtained a non-purchase-money security interest in Debtor's existing and future inventory under a security agreement executed by Debtor at the time of the loan. Bank filed a proper financing statement in the right place on July 18. Debtor filed a bankruptcy petition on October 1. Debtor had not repaid any of the loan, and its inventory (which turns over every 15 days) had the following value on the stated dates:

July 1	$2.1 million
July 15	$1.7 million
August 1	$1.6 million
August 15	$1.5 million
September 1	$1.5 million
September 15	$1.6 million
October 1	$1.8 million

The trustee has attacked Bank's security interest in each item of inventory as a voidable preference and has proven all elements of its case under Bankruptcy Code § 547(b).

154.   Under the "floating lien" exception, Bank can preserve its security interest in inventory worth

   (A) $1.5 million.

   (B) $1.6 million.

   (C) $1.7 million.

   (D) $1.8 million.

Susan borrows $5,000 from Friendly Bank on January 1. She also signs a valid security agreement granting Friendly a security interest in her existing television set, a 57′, flat-screen wonder. She uses the loan funds to take a trip to Bermuda. Friendly Bank does not file any financing statement.

Susan defaults on her loan on May 1, and Friendly accelerates the debt. Friendly sends one of its collection agents to Susan's house on May 15 to repossess the television set. Susan allows the person to come into her house to take the set. She does not object to the repossession in any way.

The next day, on May 16, Friendly forecloses upon the television set by selling it to one of its tellers for $2,500, which is the fair market value of the used set. On May 17, Susan files a Chapter 7 bankruptcy petition. Susan's trustee in bankruptcy demands that Friendly Bank give the trustee the $2,500 proceeds of sale.

155.   Friendly Bank

(A)   can keep the $2,500.

(B)   must pay the trustee the $2,500 because the trustee has the status of a lien creditor under state law.

(C)   must pay the trustee the $2,500 because Friendly's repossession of the television set was a preference.

(D)   must pay the trustee the $2,500 because it breached the peace by entering Susan's house to repossess the set.

156.   Which of the following situations creates a voidable preference? (Assume that unsecured claims will not be paid in full and no creditor is an insider.)

(A)   On May 1, Debtor borrows $1,000 from Lender. The loan is unsecured. Debtor's brother repays the loan on June 1. Prior to that time, Debtor did not owe her brother anything. Debtor files a bankruptcy petition on July 1.

(B)   On June 1, Debtor buys a piece of equipment for $100,000 from Dealer. Debtor makes a $20,000 cash payment and finances the $80,000 balance with Dealer, who retains a security interest in the equipment. Dealer files its financing statement against the equipment on June 8. Debtor makes a $35,000 loan repayment to Dealer on July 15 and files a bankruptcy petition on August 7. At all relevant times the equipment had a value of at least $80,000.

(C)   On April 1, Debtor borrows $50,000 from Bank. The loan is unsecured. Debtor repays the loan on May 1 and files a bankruptcy petition on August 15.

(D)   On February 1, Debtor borrowed $10,000 from Finance Company. The loan is unsecured. On February 5, after Debtor releases a poor earnings report, Finance Company insists on collateral. On February 8, Debtor granted to Finance Company a security interest in its existing inventory and equipment (which at all relevant times had a value of at least $20,000). Finance Company filed its financing statement on February 9. Debtor filed a bankruptcy petition on April 25.

PRACTICE FINAL EXAM

Jeff's Hubcab's, Inc. ("JHI") applies to LargeBanc for a $100,000 loan. At the start of negotiations, on July 1, LargeBanc, with JHI's consent, files an otherwise complete financing statement with the secretary of state of the state in which JHI is incorporated, describing the collateral as "all assets."

JHI and LargeBanc conclude their negotiations on July 31. On that day, JHI and LargeBanc sign the following documents:

(1)   a loan agreement, obligating LargeBanc to lend JHI up to $250,000 (subject to no event of default existing at the time of request);

(2)   a valid security agreement securing JHI's obligations under the loan agreement and under the security agreement (which describes the collateral as "inventory and accounts" and provides that JHI will pay LargeBanc's costs, expenses, and attorneys' fees incurred in connection with the loan); and

(3)   an approval of a valid amendment to the existing financing statement (which amendment would change the description of the collateral to simply "inventory and accounts").

LargeBanc files the amendment to the financing statement (which is complete and in good form) and loans JHI the $100,000 on August 1. JHI files for bankruptcy on September 15, having made no payments on the loan.

On July 15, Crazy Creditor validly levied on JHI's entire supply of office computers.

157.   In a priority dispute between LargeBanc and Crazy Creditor in the office computers,

(A)   LargeBanc will win because its financing statement covered equipment on the day Crazy Creditor levied execution.

(B)   Crazy Creditor will win because JHI had not authenticated a security agreement on July 15.

(C)   LargeBanc will win because Crazy Creditor's levy was preferential under the Bankruptcy Code.

(D)   Crazy Creditor will win only if the collateral had not been moved into the state from another state within the four months prior to the levy.

158.   Within six months of JHI's bankruptcy filing, JHI's bankruptcy trustee succeeds in liquidating the inventory and accounts for $110,000. These assets are the only assets available for distribution to creditors. If Crazy Creditor's lien is avoided as a preference, LargeBanc is entitled to

(A) $100,000 plus all contractual interest and reasonable expenses whenever incurred, but no more than the $110,000 in proceeds.

(B) $100,000 plus any interest accrued pre-petition, but no amounts due to any interest that accrued after the filing.

(C)   its pro-rata share of the estate's assets based on a claim of $100,000 plus interest to the date of filing should the trustee bring and competently prosecute a preference action under Section 547 of the Bankruptcy Code against LargeBanc.

(D)   nothing.

BigBank contractually agreed to loan $250,000 to Ace Corp. in one or more advances under the terms of a loan agreement. Jill Smith, the majority shareholder of Ace, agreed to grant to BigBank a security interest in her entire investment portfolio to secure repayment of the loan. The loan agreement, promissory note, and the security agreement (which included an after-acquired property clause) -all in writing -were executed by the appropriate parties on September 1. BigBank filed its financing statement with the appropriate official on September 8. Ace requested a $100,000 advance on September 12, which BigBank funded on September 15.

159.   Identify the three parties using Article 9 terms and indicate, for purposes of attachment, what information the security agreement must provide.

ANSWER:

160.   When did BigBank's security interest attach to 100 shares of Zinnergy capital stock that Jill purchased on September 5?

ANSWER:

161.   When did BigBank's security interest become perfected in 200 shares of Markelli capital stock that Jill purchased on September 20?

ANSWER:

Providence Bank has an enforceable security interest in the accounts of Ed's Electronics, which sells televisions, VCRs, DVD players, and other electronic home entertainment devices. The security agreement includes an after-acquired property clause.

A few of Ed's customers pay cash, but most use a credit card or execute Ed's standard written installment sales contract (in which the customer promises to pay the full purchase price, plus interest, within three months).

162. Does Providence Bank have an enforceable security interest in the credit card receivables and the installment sales contracts?

ANSWER:

Hank is a salesperson who sells sewing machines. He wants to borrow $500 from Linda. Linda does not want to loan Hank anything, but she covets Hank's diamond pinkie ring. She tells Hank that she will buy the ring from Hank for $500. Hank tells her, truthfully, that the ring is worth $1,500. "That's okay," Linda responds, "I'll let you buy it back from me in a year for $550." Hank reluctantly agrees and signs an agreement to memorialize the deal. He hands the ring over to Linda.

A month later, Hank is about to meet George, a potential customer Hank has been trying to land for the last several months. During this period, George had commented on Hank's pinkie ring. Hank goes to Linda and asks if he can have it for a day so as to impress the customer. Linda agrees. Hank picks up the ring and wears it to the meeting.

At the meeting, George says he will buy sewing machines from Hank if Hank throws in the pinkie ring. Hank agrees, and he gives the ring to George as part of an overall deal in which George will buy a significant number of sewing machines from Hank.

Linda finds out and is hopping mad.

163. In a replevin action filed by Linda against George,

(A) Linda will obtain possession of the ring because she had a security interest in it.

(B) George will retain possession of the ring so long as he had no knowledge of Linda's security interest in the ring.

(C) George will retain possession of the ring because Article 9 does not apply to these facts.

(D) Linda will obtain possession of the ring because George was not a buyer in the ordinary course of business.

To secure repayment of a $250,000 loan, PhysiCare Inc. granted to Bank a security interest in its current and after-acquired equipment. To perfect its security interest, Bank filed a financing statement with the appropriate clerk on February 1.

On April 1, PhysiCare amended its articles of incorporation by changing its legal name to Southwest Physicians, Inc. Bank was aware of the name change but took no action in response to it.

As of October 1, Southwest Physicians owned three significant pieces of equipment purchased on the following dates:

Item #1	March 15
Item #2	July 15
Item #3	September 15

164.   As of October 1, Bank has a perfected security interest in

   (A)   Items #1, #2, and #3.

   (B)   Items #1 and #2 only.

   (C)   Item #1 only.

   (D)   none of the items.

Landmark Systems sold two photocopiers on credit last year to Aspen, Inc. The loan recently went into default and Landmark repossessed the photocopiers (in which Landmark held a perfected security interest). Aspen immediately filed a Chapter 11 bankruptcy petition with the short-term goal of blocking Landmark's scheduled foreclosure sale of the photocopiers. Without the photocopiers, Aspen's business will not survive. Aspen still owes approximately $18,000 on the photocopiers, which have an aggregate fair market value anywhere from $16,500 to $19,000. The monthly depreciation is $250.

165.   Landmark has filed a motion to lift the automatic stay and proceed with the foreclosure sale. Should the bankruptcy judge grant Landmark's motion?

ANSWER:

Henry has a signed security agreement granting a security interest in all presently owned and after-acquired inventory and equipment with a company that signs its name "Q Corp." Henry has filed with the appropriate filing office an otherwise valid financing statement listing "Q Corp." as the debtor.

Q Corp. owes Henry $20,000. Q Corp. is in default under its security agreement with Henry. With the aid of a sheriff acting under a writ of replevin, Henry repossesses Q Corp.'s inventory and equipment. He then schedules a public auction of the goods for next week. He does no advertising and sends no notice to Q Corp. or anyone else of the time or date of the auction.

One day before the scheduled auction, Henry meets with Beth, who produces a valid security agreement signed by "Q Corporation, Inc." It is signed by the same individuals who signed Henry's security agreement. It lists in one of its provisions that "Q Corporation, Inc." is the true name of the entity, and that the business has adopted the trade name of "Q Corp."

Moreover, Beth's financing statement is filed in the same place as Henry's. It bears a date earlier than Henry's financing statement. Finally, Beth tells Henry that "Q Corporation, Inc." is in default of a $15,000 loan she has made to that company. She asks Henry to turn over to her all collateral that he intends to sell at the auction.

Confused, Henry asks Beth to leave, after telling her that he does not believe that her interest is valid. Henry holds the sale the next day and winds up selling the goods to Sarah, who knows nothing of the discussions between Henry and Beth, for $10,000.

Assume that "Q Corp." and "Q Corporation, Inc." are just different names for the same legal entity, and that the appropriate filing office lists the entity's proper name as "Q Corporation, Inc." Assume further that a search for filings against "Q Corporation, Inc." would not disclose any filings made against "Q Corp."

166. After the sale,

   (A) Beth may sue Q Corporation, Inc. to recover no more than $5,000 and Sarah to recover the inventory and equipment.

   (B) Beth may sue Q Corporation, Inc. to recover $15,000, and sue Sarah to recover the inventory and equipment (subject to a maximum recovery of $15,000).

   (C) Beth may sue Henry for the $10,000 sale proceeds on a theory of conversion, and then proceed against Q Corporation, Inc. to recover any deficiency left owing.

   (D) Beth may sue Q Corporation, Inc. to recover $15,000, may sue Henry for the $10,000 sale proceeds on a theory of conversion, and may also sue Sarah to recover the inventory and equipment (subject to a maximum recovery of $15,000).

In 2000, Edgar lent $25,000 to David. At that time, David and Edgar signed a valid security agreement granting to Edgar a security interest in David's "inventory, accounts, equipment, general intangibles, and all proceeds thereof, whether now owned or hereafter obtained." This security interest secured "all debts now and hereafter owing to Edgar, without regard to whether such debts are contingent or absolute." Adequate and complete financing statements containing this collateral description were filed with the appropriate filing office, the Arizona Secretary of State. David paid off the loan in 2002, but he did not request termination of Edgar's financing statement.

After the payoff, David developed "Beanies," a collectible item. He sought financing for his idea. This search culminated in 2003, with David borrowing $100,000 from NewCap, Inc., and signing a security agreement in favor of NewCap that described the collateral as "inventory, equipment, accounts, and general intangibles, including, without limitation, all rights David may have in any copyrights related to David's ownership, sale, or use of Beanies." NewCap filed adequate and complete financing statements containing this description with the appropriate filing office, the Arizona Secretary of State.

In 2004, David approached Edgar seeking an additional loan.

167. If Edgar lends David $25,000 and David executes only a promissory note, and that note does not refer to any prior transactions, Edgar will have a senior perfected security interest in

(A) nothing.

(B) everything.

(C) all collateral except registered copyrights, in which it will have a junior unperfected security interest.

(D) all collateral except registered copyrights, in which it will have no security interest.

With Debtor's permission, Bank One filed a financing statement against Debtor's accounts, equipment, and inventory on March 2. Loan negotiations did not conclude until April 13, when Bank One made a $25,000 loan to Debtor and Debtor authenticated a security agreement that granted to Bank One a security interest in Debtor's "accounts, equipment, and inventory."

On March 21, Bank Two made a $15,000 loan to Debtor, and Debtor authenticated a security agreement that granted to Bank Two a security interest in Debtor's "current and after-acquired equipment." Bank Two filed its financing statement against Debtor's equipment on March 28.

In July, Debtor defaulted on both loans.

168. With respect to an item of equipment purchased on April 1 by Debtor with its own funds, whose security interest enjoys priority?

ANSWER:

Debbie Debtor and her pal, Connie Collusive, devise the following scheme. Debbie runs a stationary store financed by Poltroon Savings & Loan. Debbie has signed a security agreement with Poltroon under which Debbie has given Poltroon a valid security interest in her inventory and equipment. Poltroon has filed a valid financing statement with the appropriate filing officer describing the collateral as "all assets."

One day, Connie arrives at Debbie's store and buys the inventory at cost, giving Debbie her unsecured note as consideration. This manner of sale is a default under the security agreement between Debbie and Poltroon. Connie then hauls off all of the inventory, sells it, takes the cash to a bank, and buys a cashier's check with it. She then gives the check to Debbie's mother, Abbie. Connie then files a bankruptcy petition. Debbie sends Connie's note to Poltroon fifteen days after the sale, which is the first that Poltroon hears of the matter. Poltroon promptly sues Abbie.

169. In a priority dispute between Poltroon and Abbie over the cashier's check,

(A) Abbie wins because Poltroon lost its security interest when the inventory was sold to Connie.

(B) Abbie wins because the original financing statement did not specifically cover instruments, accounts, or general intangibles.

(C) Poltroon wins because the sale was in bulk and not in good faith.

(D) Poltroon wins because it proceeded against Abbie within four months of learning of the scheme.

Larry borrowed $50,000 from Vapid Bank to buy a diamond pinkie ring to wear on a daily basis. Larry signed a valid security agreement which described the collateral as a "diamond pinkie ring," but Vapid did not file any financing statements.

Larry uses the loan funds to buy the ring. He then immediately sells the ring for $40,000 to a diamond merchant, who intends to take the stone from its setting and sell it as an industrial stone.

Larry deposits the $40,000 in his bank account at Dumstruck State Bank. This account had a $10,000 balance before the $40,000 deposit. Larry then draws a check on this account for $20,000 to purchase a Bancpain watch.

It is now one month after Larry sold the ring to the diamond merchant, who has thus far kept the ring intact. Vapid discovers the transactions, and in its investigations learns that the lowest balance in the account after the time Larry deposited the $40,000 to the date of discovery was $0. The current account balance is $25,000. The relevant jurisdiction has adopted the lowest intermediate balance test for tracing proceeds. Larry has never shown any remorse in spending any of the funds, and, naturally, his actions in selling the ring constitute a default under the terms of the signed security agreement, as confirmed by the fact that yesterday he personally filed a Chapter 7 bankruptcy petition.

170. Vapid can assert a superior interest in

(A) the ring, the watch, and up to $20,000 of the account balance at Dumstruck.

(B) the ring and the watch, but not any positive balances in the account at Dumstruck.

(C) the ring, but not the watch or any positive balances in the account at Dumstruck.

(D) neither the ring, the watch, nor any positive balances in the account at Dumstruck.

On April 20, BigBank obtained a perfected security interest in a deposit account maintained by Debtor with BigBank.

On June 10, Debtor borrowed $15,000 from Alamo Finance. The loan was secured by an enforceable security interest in Debtor's current and after-acquired equipment. Alamo Finance filed a financing statement with the appropriate official on June 15.

On August 1, Debtor bought a new item of equipment (the "Item") by tendering a $3,000 check drawn on its deposit account at BigBank.

After learning that Debtor paid for the Item by drawing a check on the deposit account, BigBank filed a financing statement against the Item on September 1 with Debtor's permission.

On September 25, Debtor defaulted on its loan from Alamo Finance. When Alamo Finance repossessed the Item, BigBank charged Alamo Finance with conversion of its collateral.

171. As between Alamo Finance and BigBank, whose security interest in the Item enjoys priority?

ANSWER:

On April 1, Texas National Bank ("TNB") made a $500,000 loan to Houston Music Company, a corporation that operates a retail music store in Houston at which it sells and leases musical instruments and offers music lessons. To secure repayment of the loan, TNB obtained an enforceable security interest in Houston Music Company's inventory, accounts, and equipment. The security agreement included an after-acquired property clause. On April 2, TNB filed a proper financing statement with the appropriate official against the "inventory, accounts, and equipment" of the debtor. The financing statement failed to include the after-acquired property clause.

On June 1, Houston Music Company amended its articles of incorporation by changing its legal name to Southwest Music Company ("SMC").

On August 1, Steinmark Piano Company ("Steinmark") sold five Steinmark upright pianos and five Steinmark grand pianos to SMC. Steinmark shipped the upright pianos from its Chicago warehouse and delivered them to SMC on August 15. It shipped the grand pianos from its Denver warehouse and delivered them to SMC on August 22. Steinmark retained an enforceable security interest in the pianos and filed its financing statement with the appropriate official on August 19. On August 5, Steinmark sent a written notice of its security interest in the pianos to TNB; the contents of the notice satisfied the statutory requirements of UCC Article 9. TNB received the notice on August 12.

172. Which of the following statements regarding TNB's interest in the pianos sold by Steinmark to the debtor is TRUE?

(A) The absence of the after-acquired property clause from TNB's financing statement prevents TNB's interest from attaching to the Steinmark pianos.

(B) The absence of the after-acquired property clause from TNB's financing statement does not prevent TNB's interest from attaching to the Steinmark pianos, but it does prevent perfection of that interest.

(C) TNB's failure to file an amended financing statement to reflect the name change prevents its interest from attaching to the Steinmark pianos if the name change is "seriously misleading."

(D) TNB has an enforceable and perfected security interest in the Steinmark pianos.

Assume that a priority dispute between TNB and Steinmark arises in September over the pianos sold by Steinmark to the debtor in August.

173. Which statement is TRUE?

(A) Steinmark's security interest in all of the pianos enjoys priority.

(B) TNB's security interest in the upright pianos enjoys priority; whereas Steinmark's security interest in the grand pianos enjoys priority.

(C) TNB's security interest in the grand pianos enjoys priority; whereas Steinmark's security interest in the upright pianos enjoys priority.

(D) TNB's security interest in all of the pianos enjoys priority.

On November 5, SMC bought a computer system on credit from the seller, Quark Systems ("Quark"). Quark retained an enforceable security interest in the system to secure repayment of the purchase price. Quark delivered and installed the system on November 7, and filed a proper financing statement against the system with the appropriate official on November 29. Quark had knowledge of TNB's financing statement but Quark never gave notice of its interest to TNB.

174. A priority dispute between TNB and Quark arises in December over the computer system sold by Quark to the debtor in November. If the debtor's name change was "seriously misleading," then

(A) Quark does not have a purchase-money security interest in the computer.

(B) Quark's security interest in the computer enjoys priority.

(C) Quark has a purchase-money security interest in the computer but does not enjoy priority because it failed to timely file its financing statement.

(D) Quark's security interest does not enjoy priority because it knew of TNB's earlier filing and failed to send timely written notice of its security interest to TNB.

Harriet wants to buy a used car from Frank's Cars, Inc. ("FCI"), for personal use. She and FCI agree on a car and sign a valid sales contract. The contract calls for Harriet to deliver the $1,000 consideration for the purchase by 5:00 p.m. on the day following the signing of the contract. FCI will maintain possession of the car until then.

Unbeknownst to Harriet, FCI finances all of its automobiles with Nasty Bank, Inc. ("NBI"). FCI owes NBI over $1,000,000. After Harriet leaves the lot, an NBI representative makes a lot check and believes that FCI does not have two cars on its lot that it has reported to NBI that it has not yet sold. If true, this fact would be a default under the valid security agreement between FCI and NBI, which describes the collateral as "all inventory of new or used cars, now owned or hereafter acquired." NBI has filed an otherwise accurate and complete financing statement with the appropriate secretary of state listing FCI as the debtor (under its proper name), and listing the collateral as "all assets."

On the next morning, sixteen burly men from NBI show up at FCI's lot. They bar all FCI employees from entering the property, and they drive off all the cars on the lot to a secure location. The car described in Harriet's contract is one of those driven away.

175.   As between Harriet and NBI,

(A)   Harriet has a superior right of possession, because she was a buyer in the ordinary course of business from FCI.

(B)   NBI has a superior right of possession, because Harriet did not take immediate possession.

(C)   Harriet has a superior right of possession, because she was a good faith purchaser for value.

(D)   NBI has a superior right of possession because it was a good faith purchaser for value.

176.   If NBI's lot checker was incorrect, and the two cars were really on the lot but she just overlooked them, then

(A)   NBI may retain the cars because FCI owed NBI over $1,000,000.

(B)   NBI need only return the cars if its method of driving them off the lot breached the peace.

(C)   NBI committed conversion as to all cars taken.

(D)   NBI committed conversion as to all cars taken except the car that was described in the contract between Harriet and FCI.

On June 1, Bank took and perfected a security interest in Borrower's equipment. Bank advanced $25,000 on the same day. The security agreement included a future advance clause but did not obligate Bank to fund any additional advances.

On June 15, PramCo became a "lien creditor" under applicable law. Its lien (for $80,000) encumbers Borrower's equipment.

Bank funded the following advances to Borrower: $25,000 (June 30); $25,000 (July 10); $25,000 (July 20); and $25,000 (August 5). Bank discovered PramCo's lien on July 15.

The sheriff sold Borrower's equipment for $120,000 on August 10. Borrower has not repaid any of the advances or PramCo's lien.

177.   The sheriff should distribute

(A) $120,000 to Bank.

(B) $100,000 to Bank and $20,000 to PramCo.

(C) $75,000 to Bank and $45,000 to PramCo.

(D) $40,000 to Bank and $80,000 to PramCo.

178. If the security agreement obligated Bank to loan up to $150,000 in one or more advances in the absence of any default, the sheriff should distribute

(A) $120,000 to Bank.

(B) $100,000 to Bank and $20,000 to PramCo.

(C) $75,000 to Bank and $45,000 to PramCo.

(D) $40,000 to Bank and $80,000 to PramCo.

First Bank obtained an enforceable security interest in Debtor's current and after-acquired inventory in January 2000. First Bank filed its financing statement on January 10, 2000.

Tort Victim obtained a judgment against Debtor in March 2004 and a judgment lien on Debtor's inventory in December 2004. In March 2005, Tort Victim files a motion, seeking a declaratory judgment on the priority of its judgment lien on Debtor's inventory. Evidence reveals that First Bank filed a continuation statement on July 7, 2004.

179. How should the court rule on Tort Victim's motion?

ANSWER:

On March 1, Dealer sold a $60,000 boat on credit to Sally Garcia. Dealer retained an enforceable security interest in the boat under the contract executed that day but never filed a financing statement. Sally uses the boat for weekend recreational pleasure.

On July 1, Sally granted an enforceable security interest in the boat to First Bank to secure a $10,000 personal loan made the same day. First Bank perfected its security interest by filing a financing statement that day with the proper official (the boat is not subject to any certificate of title law or other registration scheme). Sally's sister, Mary, guaranteed repayment of the $10,000 loan.

On August 15, Sally granted an enforceable security interest in the boat to Second Bank to secure a $5,000 personal loan made the same day. Second Bank perfected its security interest by filing a financing statement that day with the proper official.

For reasons beyond her control, Sally defaulted on the loan from First Bank on September 1. Shortly thereafter, First Bank repossessed the boat with Sally's consent.

First Bank intends to sell the boat at a public sale. It has received written notice of Dealer's security interest, but it has not received any notice of Second Bank's security interest. It has ordered, and received, a UCC search report reflecting all financing statements filed against Sally through September 15.

180. In order to comply with the requirements of Article 9, First Bank must send its notice of sale to

(A) Sally.

(B) Sally and Mary.

(C) Sally, Mary, and Dealer.

(D) Sally, Mary, Dealer, and Second Bank.

After sending proper notice to the required party (or parties), First Bank sells the boat for $48,000 at a public sale (all aspects of which are commercially reasonable). First Bank has received a timely written demand for proceeds from Dealer but no demand from Second Bank. At the time of the sale, Sally owes $35,000 to Dealer, $8,000 to First Bank, and $5,000 to Second Bank.

181. After deducting $8,000 to satisfy its own debt, First Bank should distribute

(A) $40,000 to Sally.

(B) $35,000 to Dealer, followed by $5,000 to Sally.

(C) $35,000 to Dealer, followed by $5,000 to Second Bank.

(D) $5,000 to Second Bank, followed by $35,000 to Dealer.

182. In order to comply with the notice requirements of Article 9, First Bank must include each of the following pieces of information in its disposition notice except

(A) a description of the collateral.

(B) a statement that the recipient remains liable for any deficiency.

(C) the nature of the default.

(D) a telephone number that the recipient may call to determine the redemption price.

Assume that after repossessing the boat First Bank decides not to sell it. Instead, First Bank proposes a strict foreclosure.

183. Which statement is TRUE?

(A) First Bank may not propose a partial strict foreclosure.

(B) First Bank must send its proposal to Mary.

(C) Sally's prolonged silence cannot create an involuntary consent to First Bank's proposal.

(D) Its decision to propose a strict foreclosure, instead of a nonjudicial foreclosure sale, negates any need for First Bank to request a UCC search report against Sally.

Ed buys a television from Sears. On the charge slip, Sears has caused the printer to print the following: *"The undersigned hereby grants to Sears a security interest in all goods purchased hereby."* Ed signs the charge slip, which also contains a description of the TV by make and model, and he takes the television home so he can watch his favorite programs on it. Sears does not file any financing statement.

Later that same week, Ed wins a better television in a local raffle. He then sells for cash the television bought at Sears to Jane, his next-door neighbor and a junior high school teacher, who takes the television set to school to use in her classroom.

184. In a priority contest between Sears and Jane concerning the TV sold by Sears to Ed,

(A) Jane will prevail because she took delivery without notice of Sears' security interest.

(B) Sears will prevail because Jane took the television set to school and used it there in her work.

(C) Jane will prevail because Sears did not file a financing statement.

(D) Sears will prevail because it was not required to file a financing statement naming a subsequent purchaser of the collateral.

In June, Robby borrowed $5,000 from his brother, Wally. Robby used the money to purchase some expensive equipment for use in his unincorporated business that he operated under the trade name of "The Plumber's Helper." Knowing of Robby's past financial difficulties, Wally took an enforceable security interest in all of the current and after-acquired equipment of the business and filed his financing statement against "The Plumber's Helper" with the appropriate clerk.

In August of the following year, Robby filed a Chapter 7 bankruptcy petition, still owing $4,000 to Wally. The collateral is conservatively appraised at $11,000, so Wally is not too concerned that Robert's unsecured creditors will receive less than a 25% payoff.

185. Should Wally be concerned?

ANSWER:

186. The automatic stay will not block a secured party from

(A) filing a continuation statement to continue the effectiveness of a financing statement that was effective on the petition date.

(B) repossessing collateral following a pre-petition default.

(C) conducting a nonjudicial foreclosure sale of collateral seized pre-petition.

(D) commencing a lawsuit against the debtor for a pre-petition default.

187. In which of the following transactions can the bankruptcy trustee avoid the creditor's security interest under the "strong arm clause"?

(A)   Evelyn, an amateur astronomer, acquired a telescope on credit from Merchant on February 1. Merchant retained an enforceable security interest in the telescope to secure its purchase price. Merchant never filed a financing statement against the telescope. Evelyn filed a bankruptcy petition on August 15.

(B)   Lender obtained an enforceable security interest in Debtor's inventory on August 1. The security agreement included an after-acquired property clause. Debtor acquired additional inventory on September 15. Lender filed its financing statement with the appropriate official on December 20. Debtor filed a bankruptcy petition on December 31.

(C)   Nelson bought 1,000 shares of Zircon capital stock from his father on October 15. On that date, Nelson executed and delivered a promissory note payable to the order of his father. In the note, Nelson granted to his father a security interest in the Zircon capital stock. A week later, Nelson's father delivered the Zircon stock certificate to Nelson. Mindful that Nelson was acquiring the Zircon stock for personal use, Nelson's father never filed a financing statement. Nelson filed a bankruptcy petition on November 15.

(D)   Dealer sold a photocopier on credit to Merchant on July 1. Under the sales contract executed by both parties that day, Dealer retained an enforceable security interest in the photocopier to secure repayment of the purchase price. Dealer delivered and installed the photocopier on July 8. Dealer filed a financing statement against the photocopier on July 25, without knowledge that Merchant had filed a bankruptcy petition on July 22.

Bank made a $2 million unsecured loan to Debtor on August 1. The next day, Competitor sued Debtor for patent infringement, seeking damages of $5 million. Nervous that the lawsuit might have some merit, Bank insisted on collateral for its loan. On August 3, Debtor granted to Bank an enforceable security interest in its then-existing equipment. Bank filed its financing statement on August 4. At all relevant times, the collateral had a value significantly greater than the outstanding loan balance.

On October 10, a jury returned a verdict in favor of Competitor, awarding it damages of $3.8 million. The next day, Debtor filed a Chapter 7 bankruptcy petition, still owing Bank the full amount of its loan. Debtor's trustee has attacked Bank's security interest as a voidable preference. Evidence reveals that Debtor has been insolvent since July 15, and its unsecured creditors will not be paid in full in the bankruptcy.

188.   Which statement is TRUE?

(A)   Because the transfer occurred within ten days of the debt, the trustee will be unable to prove that the transfer was for antecedent debt.

(B)   Because the collateral had a value significantly greater than the outstanding loan balance at all relevant times, the trustee will be unable to prove that the transfer placed Bank in a better position that it would be without the transfer in a Chapter 7 liquidation.

(C)   The trustee can prove all elements of a voidable preference, but Bank can preserve its security interest under the "ordinary course of business" exception of 11 U.S.C. § 547(c)(2).

(D)   The trustee can prove all elements of a voidable preference, and Bank is unable to successfully invoke the "contemporaneous exchange" exception of 11 U.S.C. § 547(c)(1).

Darren Debtor, a lifelong Carson City, Nevada resident, runs a printing business. On June 1, Darren entered into negotiations with First Bank for a loan of $5,000,000. When Darren signed the letter of intent for the loan, First Bank had Darren sign the following: "I authorize First Bank to file an 'all assets' financing statement with the Nevada Secretary of State." First Bank then filed an otherwise accurate and complete financing statement with the Nevada Secretary of State naming Darren as the debtor and describing the collateral as "all assets." On June 15, Darren signed a security agreement granting a security interest to First Bank. The collateral description in the security agreement is stated as "all equipment." The security agreement described the secured obligation as "that certain loan in the amount of $5,000,000 made by First Bank to Darren Debtor, all obligations under this security agreement (including all attorneys' fees), and all advances made by First Bank to Darren Debtor hereafter."

After the security agreement was signed, First Bank loaned $5,000,000 to Darren. First Bank did not amend its financing statement.

On July 1, as anticipated in the security agreement with First Bank, Darren purchased a new printing press for $1,000,000, using a portion of the $5,000,000 loan proceeds. On August 15, Darren sells some surplus ink and paper to Seraph Printing, Inc. ("SPI"), another printing business. SPI gives Darren a check for the purchase price of $5,000. On September 30, Darren sells a used printing press to SPI for $500,000, with SPI giving Darren a check for $100,000, and its written promise to pay the balance by December 1.

Darren defaulted under the security agreement on October 1, and filed a Chapter 11 bankruptcy petition on October 15. It is now October 16. No purchases or sales of any of Darren's property other than completed printing jobs occurred between June 15 and October 15 except as stated above. Darren has not cashed, and still holds, the $5,000 and the $100,000 checks from SPI.

189.   First Bank has a perfected security interest in

(A)   the ink and paper sold to SPI.

(B)   both the ink and paper sold to SPI, and the used printing press sold to SPI.

(C)   the used printing press sold to SPI.

(D)   neither the ink and paper sold to SPI, nor the used printing press sold to SPI.

190.   First Bank has a perfected security interest in

(A)   all printing presses owned by Darren on October 15.

(B)   no printing presses owned by Darren on October 15.

    (C)   all printing presses owned by Darren on June 15, but no others.

    (D)   only those printing presses acquired by Darren after June 15.

191.   Assume the basic facts, but change only the following: Darren lives in and is a resident of South Lake Tahoe, California, and commutes to Reno, Nevada, where he conducts all of his business. Under these revised facts, First Bank has a perfected security interest in

    (A)   all printing presses owned by Darren on October 15.

    (B)   no printing presses owned by Darren on October 15.

    (C)   all printing presses owned by Darren on June 15, but no others.

    (D)   only those printing presses acquired by Darren after June 15.

192.   Assume the original facts. First Bank seeks to take control of some assets. Assuming that the bankruptcy court approves First Bank's request, but limits it to those assets in which First Bank had a perfected security interest on October 16, FirstBank may

    (A)   replevy the check for $5,000 and the check for $100,000, and it may notify SPI to pay to First Bank the $400,000 due under the contract to purchase the used printing press.

    (B)   replevy the check for $5,000 and may notify SPI to pay to First Bank the $400,000 due under the contract to purchase the used printing press.

    (C)   replevy the check for $100,000, and it may notify SPI to pay to First Bank the $400,000 due under the contract to purchase the used printing press.

    (D)   only notify SPI to pay to First Bank the $400,000 due under the contract to purchase the used printing press.

First Bank was sloppy in its checking of the Secretary of State's filing system. Had it checked carefully, it would have found an adequate and complete financing statement filed on April 1, listing the collateral as equipment, and listing the secured party as Mum's Financing, Inc. ("MFI"). Upon inquiry, it appears that MFI lent $5,000,000 to Darren on September 1.

193.   As between First Bank and MFI,

    (A)   MFI is junior in all respects to First Bank.

    (B)   First Bank is junior in all respects to MFI.

    (C)   First Bank is junior to MFI in all respects except as to the $100,000 check.

    (D)   First Bank is junior to MFI in all respects except with respect to the printing press acquired on July 1.

On October 15, 2001, First Church bought a concert grand piano for use in its sanctuary from Sounds Great, a retailer that sells and leases musical instruments. First Church agreed to pay the $50,000 purchase price over ten years. To secure repayment of the purchase price, Sounds Great retained an enforceable security interest in the piano. Sounds Great perfected its enforceable security interest in the piano by filing a financing statement, adequately describing the collateral, with the appropriate official on October 23.

In August 2006, vandals broke into the church and caused extensive property damage, including damage to the concert grand piano. As a result, First Church had to replace the piano's sound board. First Church paid for the sound board with a $14,000 loan from Salem Bank, which obtained an enforceable security interest in the sound board that First Church purchased from Stine Company on August 3. Stine Company delivered and installed the sound board on August 8. Salem Bank filed a financing statement, adequately describing the collateral, with the appropriate official on August 30.

On April 1, 2006, Sounds Great filed its continuation statement.

In August 2006 a tornado struck First Church. First Church received insurance proceeds of $40,000 for the total destruction of the concert grand piano.

194. In a priority dispute between Sounds Great and Salem Bank in the insurance proceeds,

    (A) Sounds Great is entitled to all of the proceeds because it filed its financing statement against the piano before Salem Bank filed its financing statement against the sound board.

    (B) Sounds Great is entitled to all of the proceeds because it perfected its security interest in the piano before Salem Bank perfected its security interest in the sound board.

    (C) Salem Bank is entitled to that part of the proceeds attributable to the sound board because Salem Bank holds a perfected purchase-money security interest in the sound board and Sounds Great holds only an unperfected security interest in the piano.

    (D) Salem Bank is not entitled to that part of the proceeds attributable to the sound board because its failure to timely file its financing statement prevents it from claiming a purchase-money security interest in the sound board.

Video Industries, LLC ("VILLC") produces and markets educational videotapes to the middle school market. It is financed by Rapacious Loan Company ("RLC"), and in this connection, VILLC has signed a complete and valid security agreement with RLC granting RLC a security interest in "all of VILLC's inventory and equipment, now owned or hereafter acquired." RLC has filed a complete and valid financing statement with this description of the collateral with the appropriate officials in the state in which VILLC is located.

The security agreement contains a clause declaring a default and immediate acceleration of the maturity date of all financing upon any non-payment of any funds due and owing under the terms of the security agreement. It also has the following clause:

10. **Remedies Upon Default**. In addition to any remedies it may have at law or equity or under the Uniform Commercial Code, upon default RLC may, in its sole and absolute discretion, send any of its repossession agents to VILLC's warehouse, and such agents may use any means necessary, including breaking locks, to gain access. Once access is obtained, such agents may take, transport, and use any and all collateral found there to such locations and for such uses as RLC may decide. VILLC specifically consents to this remedy and agrees not to oppose such actions. VILLC acknowledges that the rate on all loans hereunder has been reduced by one-half of one percent (½%) because of its consent to this provision.

On July 1, VILLC misses an interest payment due under the debt secured by the security agreement. As it was worried about the VILLC credit anyway, RLC then sends its repossession agents to the warehouse in the dead of night, and those agents bust down the doors with battering rams, and seize all the collateral. The agents take the collateral to another location that RLC uses to store repossessed collateral.

When VILLC's employees arrive at the warehouse the next morning, they find four walls and not much else. Deprived of its inventory, VILLC immediately files a Chapter 7 bankruptcy petition.

195. RLC files a $1 million proof of claim in VILLC's bankruptcy representing its deficiency claim after the collateral is sold. With respect to this proof of claim,

   (A) RLC will share as a regular unsecured creditor with an allowed claim of $1 million because VILLC consented to the form of repossession and received a benefit pre-petition for its consent.

   (B) The trustee will have standing to disallow all or a portion of RLC's claim on the basis that RLC's repossession was a breach of the peace, and thus RLC converted the collateral.

   (C) The trustee will have standing to disallow all or a portion of RLC's claim on the basis that the automatic default provision violated VILLC's due process rights, and thus RLC converted the collateral.

   (D) The trustee will have standing to disallow all or a portion of RLC's claim but only if the estate rebates to RLC the amount of interest reduction VILLC received.

Assume the same facts as in the preceding question, except assume now that RLC waits a day before taking any action, and then it enters into discussions with VILCC about repossession. At the end of those discussions, VILCC signs an agreement under which it consents to RLC's repossession of all collateral, and it waives any right to notice of the collateral's disposition and any right to redeem the collateral from and after the removal of that collateral from VILCC's warehouse. VILCC has no defense to formation of this agreement; that is, it would not be vulnerable to any claims of duress or unconscionability.

196. With respect to RLC's $1 million proof of claim under these revised facts,

   (A) RLC will share as a regular unsecured creditor with an allowed claim of $1 million because VILLC consented to the form of repossession.

(B)   The trustee will have standing to disallow all or a portion of RLC's claim on the basis that RLC's repossession breached the peace, and thus RLC converted the collateral.

(C)   The trustee will have standing to disallow all or a portion of RLC's claim on the basis that the automatic default provision violated VILLC's due process rights, and thus RLC converted the collateral.

(D)   The trustee will have standing to disallow all or a portion of RLC's claim but only if the estate rebates to RLC the amount of interest reduction VILLC received.

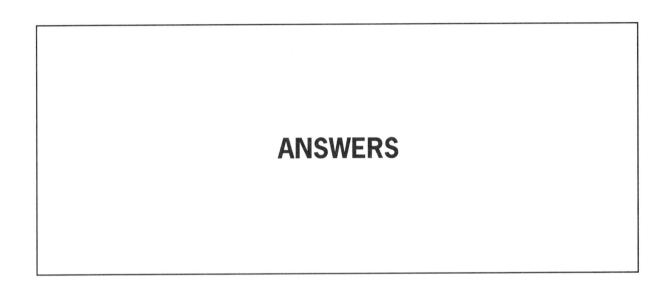

ANSWERS

1. **Answer (A) is correct.** Section 9-109 is the scope provision of Article 9. A consignment of the type described in the problem falls within the definition of "consignment" in section 9-102(a)(20) and, therefore, is covered by subsection (a)(4), **making Answer (B) an incorrect answer**. Sales of chattel paper and credit card receivables (which are "accounts" under section 9-102(a)(2)(vii)) are covered by subsection (a)(3), **making Answers (C) and (D) incorrect answers**. Perhaps of most importance, Article 9 covers "a transaction . . . that creates a security interest in *personal property* or fixtures by contract." § 9-109(a)(1). The emphasized language reveals that Article 9 does not apply to the transfer of realty interests. That suggestion is borne out by section 9-104(d)(11), which states that — subject to very limited exceptions — Article 9 does not cover "the creation or transfer of an interest in or lien on real property." Because Answer (A) describes a real estate transaction, the exclusion applies, **making Answer (A) the best answer**.

2. **Answer (A) is correct.** The scope provision of Article 9 is section 9-109. Subsection (a) states: "Except as otherwise provided in subsections (c) and (d), this article applies to: (1) a transaction . . . that creates a security interest in personal property or fixtures by contract. . . ." As a general rule, then, Article 9 applies to any voluntary transaction in which the collateral is not real estate (unless the real estate qualifies as a fixture). Under this general rule, Article 9 covers the savings account and Alberto's rights under the life insurance policy. It also covers the rental income unless rental income from real estate (the garage apartment) is treated as real estate instead of personal property. But even if the savings account, the rights under the life insurance policy, and perhaps the rental income are personal property, the general rule of section 9-109(a) is subject to exclusions found in subsections (c) and (d). And all three types of collateral offered by Alberto are excluded by subsection (d). Subsection (d)(8) excludes any transfer by Alberto of his rights as beneficiary under a life insurance policy, so **Answer (D) is incorrect**. Subsection (d)(11) excludes Alberto's rental income from the garage apartment, so **Answer (C) is incorrect**. And subsection (d)(13) excludes Alberto's assignment of his interest in the savings account in a "consumer transaction," so **Answers (B), (C), and (D) are incorrect**. This transaction is a "consumer transaction" as defined at section 9-102(a)(26) because Alberto incurred the debt to remodel a residential kitchen, creating an obligation incurred "primarily for personal, family, or household purposes."

Although Article 9 does not apply to any of the collateral, Alberto may still be able to use the savings account, the rights under the life insurance policy, and the rental income as security. But law other than Article 9 will govern the transaction. For example, the common law will govern Alberto's transfer of an interest in his savings account. And, under contract law, Alberto probably can assign his rights under the life insurance policy by a common law assignment consented to by the insurance company, or by requesting the insurer to name Lender as the loss payee. Finally, under real estate law, Alberto can assign his rental income to Lender by filing a transfer document (often called an "assignment of rents") in the real estate records in the county where the garage apartment is located.

3. **Answer (B) is correct.** Under the scope provision of section 9-109, subsection (a) states that Article 9 applies to "(3) a sale of accounts, chattel paper, payment intangibles, or promissory notes. . . ." The leases are "chattel paper" under section 9-102(a) because the writings ("records" under section 9-102(a)(69)) evidence both a monetary obligation (the lessee's contractual agreement to make periodic payments to the lessor) and a lease in specific goods (the office furniture leased by the lessor to the lessee). **Answer (A) is incorrect** because rental income from real estate (the apartment units) is excluded from the scope of Article 9 by section 9-109(d)(11). Local real estate law, rather than Article 9, governs the use of rental income from real estate as collateral. **Answer (C) is incorrect** because an assignment of a personal injury tort claim is excluded from the scope of Article 9 by section 9-109(d)(12). Common law governs the transfer of such a claim. And **Answer (D) is incorrect** because section 9-109(d)(9) excludes from the scope of Article 9 "an assignment of a right represented by a judgment, other than a judgment taken on a right to payment that was collateral." (An example that triggers the "other than" clause is a judgment on an unpaid account receivable that served as collateral.)

4. The certificate of deposit is a "deposit account" as defined at section 9-102(a)(29) unless the writing is an "instrument" under section 9-102(a)(47). The "non-negotiable" label prevents the certificate from being a "negotiable instrument" (see section 9-102(b), incorporating the definition of "negotiable instrument" from UCC Article 3, and section 3-104(d)), but the certificate may be an "instrument" if it "is of a type that in ordinary course of business is transferred by delivery with any necessary indorsement or assignment." § 9-102(a)(47). Because the certificate is "non-transferable," a court may conclude that the certificate falls outside the quoted language and is not an instrument; instead, the certificate is a deposit account. UCC Article 9 excludes from its coverage a security interest in a deposit account in a "consumer transaction" (see section 9-109(d)(13)). This transaction is a "consumer transaction" under section 9-102(a)(26) because the debt (the purchase price of the piano) was incurred, and the piano was acquired, for a personal, family, or household purpose. Therefore, unless the certificate is held to be an instrument, Dealer cannot take a UCC Article 9 security interest in the certificate.

5. **Answer (B) is correct.** First, you can **eliminate Answer (A)**; at a minimum, you are told that Joe has a valid judgment lien, and thus the sheriff, acting for Joe, will have priority. Of the remainder, you might very well ask yourself what does this question have to do with Article 9? It talks about leases. But section 9-109(a)(1) makes Article 9 apply to any "transaction, regardless of its form, that creates a security interest in personal property or fixtures by contract." So the form of the transaction as a lease is not determinative of scope; the import of section 9-109 is that we have to look through the form of the transaction to see if the contract at issue (which the parties have called a "lease") creates a "security interest in personal property."

In this regard, we look at the definition of "security interest," which is contained in section 1-201(b)(35). [Note: Article 1 was revised in 2000, and jurisdictions have begun to adopt Revised Article 1. Under former Article 1, all of the text discussed in this paragraph was found in section 1-201(37)). That section opens by stating that "'Security interest' means an interest in personal property or fixtures which secures payment or performance of an obligation." Leases are of particular concern under this section; so much so, that there is a separate section, 1-203, that speaks to the differentiation of "true" leases and security interests. That section begins by stating that "[w]hether a transaction in the form of a lease creates a lease or security interest is determined by the facts of each case." It then goes on to give certain presumptions and certain safe harbors. These can get complicated but boil down to essentially this: if the terms of the documents make it likely that the "lessee" will use the goods until they are no longer useful, or will buy the goods at some future time, the "lease" will be treated as a security agreement. That is, instead of a lease the transaction will be treated as a "sale" of the goods from the "lessor" to the "lessee."

In this case, section 1-203(b) parses as follows: "A transaction in the form of a lease creates a security interest if the consideration that the lessee is to pay the lessor for the right to possession and use of the goods is an obligation for the term of the lease and is not subject to termination by the lessee, and: . . . (4) the lessee has an option to become the owner of the goods for no additional consideration or for nominal additional consideration upon compliance with the lease agreement." We know that Frank cannot terminate the lease by himself; and we know that he will likely exercise the option at the end of five years (who wouldn't pay $1 for property worth $5,000?). Thus, this "lease" is likely a disguised sale, and would be held to be a "security agreement" in favor of Tania.

What are the consequences of this determination? First, note that if this were a "true" lease (think of renting a car for a week), the lessee/debtor's interest would be possessory only; the owner of the residual interest (who gets the use of the rental car after the week) would be the lessor (Hertz, Avis, etc.). That means, in the language of debtor/creditor relations, that creditors of the debtor/lessee would only be able to attach the debtor/lessee's one-week possessory interest, and that only creditors of the lessor/secured party could reach the "residual" interest.

If, as in the problem, the "lease" is really a disguised security agreement, these interests get reversed. Now, the lessee is a "debtor," and an "owner" of the residual interest; the lessor is a "secured party," albeit a purchase-money secured creditor. This means, to carry the observations in the last paragraph forward, that creditors of the lessee/debtor will now be able to attach or obtain a lien on the residual interest (that interest related to the time after the expiration of the lease's terms), and the creditors of the "lessor" get nothing.

It also means that Article 9 applies, and if the lessor/secured party wants to keep its interest senior, it must comply with Article 9. In the main, that means that it must file a financing statement to perfect its interest and comply with Part 6 of Article 9 with respect to enforcement of its interest on default. (In case of doubt, section

9-505 allows lessors to file "protective" filings without such a filing being an "admission" that the lease is a security agreement.)

Thus, Article 9 applies to this transaction. The "lease" is a security agreement, Frank is a "debtor," and Tania is a "secured party." There is no certificate of title issue here, so Tania had to perfect her interest by filing a financing statement. § 9-310(a). She did not. So under section 9-317(a), the general rule regarding priority between lien creditors and holders of security interests, a lien creditor such as Joe will prevail. That **eliminates Answer (C)** (and **Answer (D) is another red herring** — the date of creation of a debt never matters under Article 9 for purposes of determining priority). **Answer (B) is thus left as the correct answer.**

6. **Answer (C) is the best answer.** A purchase-money security interest (often referred to as a "PMSI" (pronounced by some as "pim-zee")) is defined at section 9-103(b)(1) as a "security interest in goods . . . (1) to the extent that the goods are purchase-money collateral with respect to that security interest. . . ." (Alternative methods of obtaining a PMSI are found in (b)(2) and (b)(3), which are irrelevant to this problem.) Under this definition, a creditor can claim a PMSI only in goods. This **eliminates Answer (B)** because capital stock is "investment property" under section 9-102(a)(49), which is excluded from the definition of "goods" under the last sentence of section 9-102(a)(44). But Answers (A), (C), and (D) remain viable answers because a piano, automobile, and boat are all examples of a "good." Continuing with the definition, the collateral (the goods) must be "purchase-money collateral," defined in section 9-103(a)(1) as "goods . . . that secures a purchase-money obligation incurred with respect to that collateral." A "purchase-money obligation" is defined at section 9-103(a)(2) as "an obligation of an obligor incurred as all or part of the price of the collateral [often referred to as seller financing] or for value given to enable the debtor to acquire rights in or the use of the collateral if the value is in fact so used [often referred to as third-party financing]." **Answer (A) is incorrect** because the SmallBank loan is not a "purchase-money obligation." SmallBank did not engage in seller financing, and its loan did not "enable the debtor to acquire rights in or the use of the collateral." Karen, the debtor, already owned the piano. **Answer (D) is not the best answer** because Freemont cannot be confident that its loan was a "purchase-money obligation." Freemont did not engage in seller financing. And because Freemont issued the check payable to the order of Gordon (rather than the seller (or to the seller and Gordon as co-payees)), who deposited it into his *savings* account, Freemont may have difficulty proving that its money was "in fact so used" when Gordon pays for the boat with a check drawn on his *checking* account. Depending on account balances, inter-account transfers, the activity in the accounts, and the applicable method of tracing (FIFO — funds first in are first out; LIFO — funds last in are first out), Freemont may or may not have a PMSI. But these issues do not exist under (C), which is the best answer. Hollywood Motors has engaged in seller financing, its extension of credit is a "purchase-money obligation," and the vehicle is "purchase-money collateral." Hollywood Motors' failure to perfect its security interest may result in losing a priority dispute with another creditor (or the loss of the security interest in a bankruptcy). But a creditor need not be perfected to claim a PMSI under section 9-103.

7. **Answer (D) is the correct answer**. Under section 9-102(a)(28)(A), Fran is a debtor because she is the party granting a security interest in her property. Mary and Bill are not granting a security interest in any property, so they are *not* debtors. Therefore, **Answer (A) is incorrect** because Mary is not a debtor. (But Fran is a debtor and Bill, a guarantor, is an obligor under section 9-102(a)(59).) And **Answer**

(B) is incorrect for the same reason: Mary is not a debtor (but Bill's obligation, as a guarantor, is secondary rather than primary). **Answer (C) is incorrect** because Bill is not a debtor (but Mary, as the borrower who executes a promissory note, is a primary rather than a secondary obligor). And **Answer (D) is correct** because Fran co-signed the note, making her an obligor, and Bill's obligation as a guarantor makes him a secondary (rather than primary) obligor.

Some helpful guidelines: an obligor can be primary or secondary; a party that signs a promissory note (often referred to as a "maker") is usually, but not always, a primary obligor; a maker may be a secondary obligor under section 9-102(a)(71)(b); a guarantor is a secondary obligor; and, as illustrated by this problem, the borrower is not always a "debtor" as defined by Article 9.

8. **Answer (B) is the correct answer.** If Diana's obligation is evidenced by a writing, the writing could be an instrument under section 9-102(a)(47) (Answer (D)), chattel paper under section 9-102(a)(11) (Answer (A)), or a promissory note under section 9-102(a)(65) (a type of "instrument," Answer (D)). So **Answers (A) and (D) are incorrect**. If the writing is not any of these, or if the obligation is not evidenced by a writing, then the obligation must be an account under section 9-102(a)(2) (Answer (C)) because the obligation arises from the sale of goods (the car is a "good" under section 9-102(a)(44)). So **Answer (C) is incorrect**. The obligation cannot be a payment intangible under section 9-102(a)(61) because payment intangibles and accounts are mutually exclusive. See §§ 9-102(a)(61) (defining "payment intangible" as a form of "general intangible"); 9-102(a)(42) (defining "general intangible" in a manner than excludes "accounts"). Because the right to payment cannot be a payment intangible, **Answer (B) is correct**.

9. **Answer (A) is the correct answer. Answer (A) is false** (and therefore correct because the question asks you to identify which statement is FALSE). Bank can have "control" of the Scantronix stock even if Gary has the ability to liquidate the stock without Bank's consent. See § 8-106(f). (Gary's continued ability to liquidate the stock without Bank's consent undermines Bank's purpose for obtaining control, so Gary, Bank, and Providence Securities should contractually agree that Providence Securities will not liquidate the stock at Gary's request without Bank's prior written consent. Appreciate, however, that while taking the steps necessary for exclusive control is a matter of good business judgment, it is not a legal requirement for control. One can have control without having exclusive control.) **Answer (B) is a true statement and therefore incorrect**. The facts indicate that Gary bought the mutual fund shares directly from Argus. If Gary had bought the mutual fund shares through a broker, the shares would represent a security entitlement. **Answer (C) is true (and therefore incorrect)** under section 8-102(a)(17). And **Answer (D) is true (and therefore incorrect)** because Bank can obtain "control" pursuant to a three-party agreement under section 8-106(d).

Although an oversimplification, investment property purchased directly from the issuer is a certificated or uncertificated security, and investment property purchased through and held by a broker is a security entitlement. If the collateral consists of every investment held by the broker, the collateral consists of a securities account and one or more security entitlements. If the collateral consists of some, but not all, investments held by a broker, the collateral consists of one or more security entitlements but not a securities account.

10. As the boat is a movable thing at the time of attachment, it is a "good" under section 9-102(a)(44). But the type of good cannot be determined with certainty because the problem does not reveal Gordon's primary use. If Gordon uses the boat primarily for personal, family, or household purposes (*e.g.*, weekend water-skiing), the boat is a "consumer good" under 9-102(a)(23). If Gordon is in the business of selling or leasing boats, or chartering this boat (*e.g.*, for midnight harbor cruises), then the boat is "inventory" under 9-102(a)(48). And if Gordon uses the boat in some other business manner (*e.g.*, as a commercial fishing vessel) the boat is "equipment" under 9-102(a)(33). Without additional information, any of those three labels are possibly correct collateral classifications.

11. The installment sales contracts are "chattel paper" as defined at section 9-102(a)(11). The contracts are written, so they are "records." The contracts evidence "a monetary obligation" of each customer to repay the purchase price of the boat. And the contracts evidence "a security interest in specific goods" (each customer's boat) because, under section 2-401 and section 1-201(b)(35), Baxter Boats' reservation of title in each boat "is limited in effect to a reservation of a security interest." As the installment sales contracts are in writing, a tangible medium, they also are "tangible chattel paper" under section 9-102(a)(78).

12. Answer (D) is the correct answer. As noted in section 9-102, cmt. 11, a registered organization includes a corporation (Wallace Corporation, Answer (A)), a limited liability company (Newman Sloane) (Answer (B)), and a limited partnership (Palmer, McCall, and Crain) (Answer (C)). So **Answers (A), (B), and (C) are incorrect**, since the question asks you to identify which entity is *not* a registered organization. A sole proprietorship (Pop's Grocery Shoppe) (Answer (D)) and a general partnership are two examples of business forms that are not registered organizations, so **Answer (D) is the correct answer**.

13. **Answer (A) is the correct answer**. The IRS tax refund does not fit within any of the eight categories of "account" in section 9-102(a). Therefore, it is a "general intangible" under section 9-102(a)(42). The other three answers fall within the definition of "account" and thus are incorrect answers. The annual software licensing payment (Answer (B)) and the monthly equipment lease payments (Answer (D)) are accounts under section 9-102(a)(2)(i) (a "right to payment of a monetary obligation . . . for property sold, leased, licensed, assigned, or otherwise disposed of"). So **Answers (B) and (D) are incorrect**. (These rights to payment would not be accounts if the monetary obligation was evidenced by an instrument or chattel paper (see first part of last sentence of section 9-102(a)(2)), but the facts indicate that is not the case.) And **Answer (C) is incorrect** because credit card receivables are accounts under section 9-102(a)(2)(vii). The credit card receivables are accounts even if the monetary obligation is evidenced by a writing because that writing cannot be "chattel paper" or an "instrument" as those two terms are defined in section 9-102(a)(11) and (47). Both definitions exclude writings "that evidence a right to

payment arising out of the use of a credit or charge card or information contained on or for use with the card."

14. **Answer (A) is the correct answer.** Section 9-102(a)(2) defines "accounts" as "a right to payment of a monetary obligation . . . (vii) arising out of the use of a credit or charge card. . . ." The definition goes on to say that the term "does not include (i) rights to payment evidenced by chattel paper or an instrument," which appears to make Answer (D) the correct answer. But both the definition of "chattel paper" in section 9-102(a)(11) and "instrument" in section 9-102(a)(47) expressly exclude records or writings that "evidence a right to payment arising out of the use of a credit or charge card. . . ." Therefore, credit card receivables cannot be chattel paper or an instrument, **making Answers (B), (C), and (D) incorrect answers**. They can only be accounts, **making Answer (A) the correct answer**.

15. **Answer (B) is the correct answer.** Section 9-102(a)(9) defines "cash proceeds" as "money, checks, deposit accounts, or the like." A credit card receivable is an "account" under section 9-102(a)(2)(vii), which is a type of collateral different from a "deposit account" (defined at section 9-102(a)(29)). An "account" is an example of "noncash proceeds" under section 9-102(a)(58) ("proceeds other than cash proceeds"). So **Answers (A) and (C) are incorrect**. Since "cash proceeds" includes checks, as well as cash, **Answer (B) is correct** and **Answer (D) is incorrect**. Ironically, a merchant may receive payment on a credit card receivable (a "noncash proceed") quicker than payment on a personal check (a "cash proceed").

Why is the classification important? Perhaps the most important reason is found in section 9-315(d)(2), which automatically extends the temporary 20-day perfection period applicable to proceeds if the proceeds are "identifiable cash proceeds." No such automatic extension applies to noncash proceeds.

16. **Answer (C) is the correct answer.** The definition of "goods" is found in section 9-102(a)(44), and includes "crops grown, growing, or to be grown" **(making Answer (A) an incorrect answer)**, "fixtures" **(making Answer (B) an incorrect answer)**, and "the unborn young of animals" **(making Answer (D) an incorrect answer)**. But the term "does not include . . . investment property. . . ." A stock certificate, in registered form, is an example of a "certificated security" under section 8-102(a)(4). And a certificated security is an example of "investment property" under section 9-102(a)(49). As investment property is excluded from the definition of "goods," **Answer (C) is the correct answer**.

17. **Answer (D) is the correct answer**. The question requires detailed knowledge of the definition of "accounts" in section 9-102(a)(3). First, examine the scope option. Answer (A) would be correct if the transaction was outside of Article 9. While security interests in real property are outside of Article 9, contracts for the sale of land are personal property subject to Article 9. The definition of "account" states that "'Account' . . . means a right to payment of a monetary obligation, whether or not earned by performance, (i) for *property* that has been or is to be sold, leased, licensed, assigned, or otherwise disposed of." This does not limit accounts to obligations to pay for goods or other personal property; it is broad enough to pick

up the obligations under a contract to sell realty. See § 9-102, cmt. 5.a. This analysis **eliminates Answer (A), and thus Answer (A) is incorrect**.

Of the remaining answers, we can also **eliminate Answer (B)**. While a preference analysis might be appropriate had Frank filed bankruptcy, he did not file. Thus, federal bankruptcy law is not applicable; indeed, you cannot even calculate the look back period, and thus **Answer (B) is incorrect.**

As between Answers (C) and (D), the question turns on whether the unearned amount under the contract is collateral. Again, the definition of account includes "a right to payment of a monetary obligation, whether or not earned by performance. . . ." So the contingent portion of the purchase price is collateral (although calling it collateral does not lessen Frank's obligations under the contract, or give Henry, as a secured party, any better rights than Frank had; in short, Betty will only have to pay under circumstances that would have caused her to pay before Frank had granted a security interest to Henry). The determination that a contingent obligation can be an account means that **Answer (D) is correct** and **Answer (C) is incorrect**.

18. **Answer (C) is the correct answer.** Under sections 9-103(a) and (b), a secured party can create a purchase-money security interest only in goods (or software integrated into the goods). The antique motor vehicle, baseball card collection, and rare bottle of wine are all goods under section 9-102(a)(44), so **Answers (A), (B), and (D) are incorrect**, since the question asks you to identify the asset in which a creditor *cannot* claim a purchase-money security interest. (Depending on the debtor's use, the items are a consumer good, a unit of inventory, or a piece of equipment.) The stock certificate is "investment property" (a certificated security) under section 9-102(a)(49). And under section 9-102(a)(2)(44), "goods" excludes "investment property." Therefore, a secured party may not obtain a purchase-money security interest in an asset that is not a "good," **making Answer (C) the correct answer**.

19. **Answer (C) is the best answer.** Section 9-203(b)(3) requires a debtor to enter into a security agreement in order to create an enforceable security interest. The statute offers the debtor four different options. Only the first option (section 9-203(b)(3)(A)) obligates the debtor to authenticate the security agreement. The second option (section 9-203(b)(3)(B)) requires the secured party to take possession of collateral (other than a certificated security) pursuant to the debtor's security agreement. That agreement may be oral and need not be authenticated (although the parties may wish to memorialize the understanding in writing for evidentiary purposes). This option is available (although not necessarily utilized) when the collateral is tangible. Chattel paper and equipment are examples of tangible collateral. Therefore, **Answers (B) and (D) are not the best answers** because the parties could rely on a security agreement that the debtor has not authenticated. The third option (section 9-203(b)(3)(C)) applies only if the collateral is a certificated security in registered form, and the security has been delivered to the secured party pursuant to the debtor's security agreement. As under the second option, the agreement need not be authenticated and can be oral. The fourth option (section 9-203(b)(3)(D)) requires the secured party to control the collateral pursuant to the debtor's security agreement, which need not be authenticated. This option applies only if the collateral is deposit accounts, electronic chattel paper, investment property, or letter-of-credit rights. Because this option is available when the collateral is deposit accounts, **Answer (A) is not the best answer**. The second, third, and fourth options are not available when the collateral is general intangibles. Instead, the parties must comply with the first option (section 9-203(b)(3)(A)), which requires the debtor to authenticate the security agreement (which must include a description of the collateral). Therefore, **Answer (C) is the best answer**.

Appreciate that the four options are not mutually exclusive. For example, the parties can rely on the debtor's authenticated security agreement (section 9-203(b)(3)(A)) or the secured party's control (section 9-203(b)(3)(D)) if the collateral is a deposit account. Also, the parties can rely on the debtor's authenticated security agreement (section 9-203(b)(3)(A)) or the secured party's possession (section 9-203(b)(3)(B)) if the collateral is equipment. And the parties can rely on the debtor's authenticated security agreement (section 9-203(b)(3)(A)), delivery to the secured party (section 9-203(b)(3)(C)), or the secured party's control (section 9-203(b)(3)(D)) if the collateral is a certificated security in registered form.

20. **Answer (C) is the correct answer**. As a general rule, Article 9 permits a debtor to grant a security interest in collateral that is acquired after the security agreement is in place by including in the agreement an after-acquired property clause. See § 9-204(a). But in an effort to discourage predatory practices, Article 9 renders ineffective an after-acquired property clause that attempts to encumber consumer

goods acquired by the debtor more than ten days after the creditor has given value. See §§ 9-204(a), (b).

Elaine's furnishings are consumer goods. Laura gave value on June 1, so the after-acquired property clause will not encumber furnishings that Elaine acquired after June 11 (notice that the ten-day period commences when the secured party gives value, not when the security agreement is finalized). Elaine acquired the sofa on June 12 and the dining room table and chairs on June 16. The after-acquired property clause will not reach these furnishings (even though Laura probably is not engaged in any predatory practice), **making Answers (A) and (B) incorrect answers**. But the bedroom furniture and television, acquired within the ten-day period, are collateral. Therefore, **Answer (D) is incorrect** because it fails to include the television. The **correct answer is Answer (C)**, which includes both the television and the bedroom furniture.

21. **Answer (B) is the correct answer**. To determine whether Hoover Finance is over-or undersecured, the secured debt must be compared to the value of collateral. If the secured debt exceeds the value of collateral, Hoover Finance is undersecured. But if the value of the collateral exceeds the secured debt, then Hoover Finance is oversecured.

Because the security agreement included a future advance clause (permitted by section 9-204(c)), the secured debt includes not only the initial loan of $1 million, but also the $250,000 advanced in April and again in August. Nevertheless, the security agreement did not include an after-acquired property clause, so the only collateral is the excavation equipment that GEC owned in February. The road grader acquired in May and the bulldozer acquired in June are not part of the collateral. The secured debt ($1.5 million) exceeds the value of the collateral ($1.2 million), so Hoover Finance is undersecured by the difference of $300,000 (**making Answer (B) the correct answer and Answers (A), (C), and (D) incorrect answers**).

22. **Answer (D) is the correct answer**. To determine the amount of unsecured debt, we simply determine how much of the total debt of $1.5 million is secured or unsecured. The security agreement failed to include a future advance clause, so the only debt that could be secured is the initial loan of $1 million. That debt is fully secured. The security agreement included an after-acquired property clause (permitted by section 9-204(a)), so the collateral includes the excavation equipment that GEC owned in February ($1.2 million), the road grader acquired in May ($250,000), and the bulldozer acquired in June ($300,000). Because the value of all of the collateral ($1.75 million) at least equals the amount of the initial loan of $1 million, that loan is fully secured. But the $250,000 advanced in April and again in August is unsecured debt because the security agreement did not include a future advance clause. Therefore, **Answer (D) is the correct answer** and **Answers (A), (B), and (C) are incorrect answers**. This unsecured debt of $500,000 is not secured by the $750,000 excess by which the collateral exceeds the initial loan. Instead, that excess is considered surplus and GEC's unencumbered equity.

Appreciate that if the value of collateral had been less than the initial loan of $1 million, the difference would have increased the amount of unsecured debt. For example, if all of the collateral was worth only $800,000 instead of $1.75 million, then the total amount of unsecured debt would be $700,000 ($1 million loan minus $800,000 collateral, plus $250,000 advanced in April, plus $250,000 advanced in August).

23. As Earl has given value of $100, and Travis has rights in the lawnmower, Earl will have an enforceable security interest in the lawnmower under section 9-203 if one of the four "security agreement" conditions of section 9-203(b)(3) is met. The third and fourth options (section 9-203(b)(3)(C) and (D)) are inapplicable because the lawnmower is not a deposit account, electronic chattel paper, investment property, or a letter-of-credit right, and the first option (section 9-203(b)(3)(A)) is not met because the parties are relying on an oral agreement rather than an authenticated agreement. The parties can rely on an oral security agreement under section 9-203(b)(3)(B) if the lawnmower "is in the possession of the secured party under Section 9-313. . . ." Earl, the secured party, can appoint an agent to take possession, but a court may conclude that Travis, the debtor, has retained effective possession if Sharon, the agent, is too closely connected with, or under the control of, Travis. (See § 9-313, cmt. 3.) A court just might reach that conclusion under these facts, where the agent is the debtor's blood relative. To avoid this possible adverse result (or the cost and time necessary to win a favorable ruling in litigation), Earl should take possession of the lawnmower or appoint someone other than Travis's relative as the custodial agent.

24. **Answer (D) is the correct answer**. Answer (A) would be correct under section 9-109(d)(13) if the transaction is a consumer transaction under section 9-102(a)(26). But because the loan is a business loan, the transaction is not a consumer transaction (**making Answer A incorrect**) and Article 9 permits Rachel to use her savings account as collateral. **Answer (B) is incorrect** because section 9-203(b)(3)(D) permits a security interest in a deposit account to attach by control, negating any requirement that Rachel authenticate a security agreement that describes the collateral (an option, but not a requirement, found at section 9-203(b)(3)(A)). **Answer (C) is incorrect** because Article 9 does not require the secured party to maintain the deposit account. See, e.g., section 9-104(a)(1) (secured party is bank that maintains deposit account), (a)(2)-(3) (secured party is not bank that maintains deposit account). **Answer (D) is correct**, as all elements of attachment under section 9-203 are present. The Credit Union has given value of $3,000 (section 9-203(b)(1)), Rachel has rights in the savings account (section 9-203(b)(2)), and the Credit Union has "control" of the savings account under section 9-104(a)(1) pursuant to Rachel's security agreement (section 9-203(b)(3)(D)).

25. **Answer (A) is the correct answer**. It is impractical, and — at least prior to a default — serves no commercial purpose, for Belmont Bank to take possession of the automobiles (permitted by section 9-203(b)(3)(B)). Instead, Belmont Bank will rely on a security agreement authenticated by Montgomery Motors that "provides a description of the collateral" as required by section 9-203(b)(3)(A). The collateral description turns on the debtor's use. The debtor is Montgomery Motors. In its hands, the automobiles are inventory under section 9-102(a)(48)(B) (goods held for sale or lease). It is irrelevant that Montgomery Motors sells the automobiles to

customers who may use them as equipment or consumer goods. Therefore, **Answers (B), (C), and (D) are incorrect**.

26. **Answer (B) is the correct answer**. A security interest attaches to collateral "when it becomes enforceable against the debtor. . . ." § 9-203(a). A security interest becomes "enforceable" when value has been given, the debtor has rights (or power to transfer rights) in the collateral, and a security agreement is in place between the parties. § 9-203(b). Notice that section 9-203(b) is a conjunctive statute; all three requirements must be satisfied. (The security agreement requirement can be satisfied in any of four ways; section 9-203(b)(3) is written disjunctively.) So the security interest in the X-ray machine attached when the last of the three requirements was met.

The earliest requirement occurred on May 1, when Clinic satisfied section 9-203(b)(3) by authenticating a security agreement that described the collateral. The next requirement was met on May 3, when Clinic acquired rights in the X-ray machine (section 9-203(b)(2)). The third requirement (value must be given) certainly occurred. It had yet to occur by May 3, so **Answer (A) is incorrect**. But was value first given on May 7 (when Bank committed to making the loan), May 9 (when Clinic requested a loan), or May 11 (when Bank funded the loan request)? The answer is found in section 1-204, which defines "value." Under subsection (1), Bank gave value when it entered into a "binding commitment to extend credit . . . whether or not drawn upon. . . ." (Alternatively, Bank's binding commitment satisfied subsection (4), which defines "value" as "any consideration sufficient to support a simple contract.") As Bank gave value on May 7, and the security agreement was previously authenticated and Clinic had already acquired the X-ray machine, Bank's security interest in the X-ray machine attached on May 7 (**making Answer (B) the correct answer** and **Answers (C) and (D) incorrect answers**).

27. **Answer (D) is the correct answer.** Borrowing from the previous answer, Clinic authenticated the security agreement on May 1 and Bank gave value on May 7. Clinic acquired the kidney dialysis machine later, on May 15. So Bank's security interest in the machine attached on that date (**making Answer (D) the correct answer**). **Answers (A), (B), and (C) are incorrect answers** because Clinic had not yet acquired rights in the machine by the dates mentioned in those answers.

Comparing the answers to this and the previous question reveals an important point: the three requirements of attachment under section 9-203(b) can occur in any order. But the security interest will not attach until all three requirements are in place.

One of your authors uses the following memory device to remember the elements of attachment: RAVE (R = rights in the collateral; A = agreement; and V = value; when all three are met, the security interest attaches, or becomes E-nforceable).

28. Although Elliott has given value (a credit extension), and Marcus has rights in the baseball, Elliott does not have an enforceable security interest in the baseball because Marcus never authenticated a security agreement that described the baseball. The language in the promissory note — "In consideration for a baseball autographed by Babe Ruth" — explains why Marcus has agreed to pay $4,200 to

Elliott, but the language falls far short of evidencing the creation of a security interest in the baseball. The financing statement contains the information required by section 9-203(b)(3)(A): authentication (*e.g.*, a signature) by Marcus and a description of the baseball. But because a financing statement can be filed before a security agreement is executed (section 9-502(d)), and since a financing statement "indicates merely that a person *may* have a security interest in the collateral indicated (section 9-502, cmt. 2, (emphasis added)), most courts have refused to hold that a financing statement alone can serve as the security agreement. *See, e.g., In re Bollinger*, 614 F.2d 924 (3d Cir. 1980). And absent any other executed documents, the "composite document rule" (a court-crafted rule that permits a judge to fashion a security agreement out of all of the documents executed by the parties) is of no help. So unless the financing statement satisfies the requirements for a security agreement, Elliott does not have an enforceable security interest in the baseball under section 9-203(b).

29. **Answer (C) is the correct answer.** As a general rule, Article 9 permits the use of after-acquired property clauses under section 9-204(a). But subsection (a) is subject to subsection (b). Subsection (b) states two situations in which the after-acquired property clause is ineffective. First, the clause will not encumber consumer goods acquired more than ten days after the secured party has given value. And second, the clause will not encumber a commercial tort claim (**making Answer (C) the correct answer**). (The limitations do not apply to electronic chattel paper, a deposit account, or a letter-of-credit right, so **Answers (A), (B), and (D) are incorrect answers**.) The effect of this exception is to require the parties to amend the original security agreement or authenticate another security agreement if they intend for the collateral package to include commercial tort claims that arise after the initial security agreement is authenticated.

Section 9-204, cmt. 4, discusses this exception but does not state a reason for it. Perhaps the unique nature of the asset, and its nontraditional use as collateral, justify the exclusion as an attempt to avoid inadvertent use of the claim as collateral. This explanation seems plausible in light of section 9-108(e)(1), which requires the security agreement to describe a commercial tort claim with particularity.

30. **Answer (C) is the correct answer.** Section 9-203(b)(3)(A) requires only the debtor to authenticate the security agreement, **making Answer (C) the correct answer**. A secured party also may authenticate the security agreement (particularly if the agreement obligates the secured party to take, or refrain from taking, certain action), but authentication by the secured party is not necessary for attachment purposes. Therefore, **Answers (A), (B), and (D)** (all of which include the Dealer as secured party) **are incorrect answers**.

31. **Answer (A) is the correct answer.** Under section 9-203(b)(3)(A), the security agreement must be "authenticated." The definition of "authenticate" in section 9-102(a)(7) reveals that the security agreement can (and, for evidentiary and other reasons, often will) be in writing. But it also can be in the form of a "record," defined at section 9-102(a)(69) as "information that is inscribed on a tangible medium or which is stored in an electronic or other medium and is retrievable in perceivable

form." For example, the security agreement could be drafted, and authenticated by the debtor, via e-mail. **Answer (B) is incorrect** because section 9-108 — which addresses the sufficiency of a collateral description — does not mandate the use of any particular terminology. The standard for a sufficient description is "reasonable identification." **Answer (C) also is incorrect**. Section 9-516(b)(5)(C)(iii) does permit a filing officer to reject a financing statement that omits a debtor's organizational identification number. But the security agreement need not reference that number in order to create an enforceable security interest in collateral. And **Answer (D) is incorrect** because section 9-203(b)(3)(A) requires the security agreement to include a location description only "if the security interest covers timber to be cut."

32. **Answer (B) is the correct answer**. Under section 9-203(b)(3)(A), the written security agreement must include a real estate description "if the security interest covers timber to be cut." Timber is mentioned in **Answer (B), making it the correct answer**. No other collateral (including, without limitation, mobile goods, crops, and as-extracted collateral) requires an accompanying real estate description in order to create an enforceable security interest, so **Answers (A), (C), and (D) are incorrect answers**.

33. **Answer (B) is the correct answer**. Section 9-108(a) states that a collateral description is sufficient if it "reasonably identifies what is described." Section 9-108(b) gives examples of reasonable identification, permitting descriptions by type of collateral, "except as otherwise provided in subsection (e)." Subsection (e) states: "A description only by type of collateral defined in [the Uniform Commercial Code] is an insufficient description of: (1) a commercial tort claim[.]" Thus, **Answer (B) is the correct answer**. (The limitation does not apply to investment property, letter-of-credit rights, or deposit accounts, so **Answers (A), (C), and (D) are incorrect answers**.) The policy is explained in cmt. 5: "Subsection (e) requires greater specificity of description in order to prevent debtors from inadvertently encumbering certain property." Comment 5 also notes that a description such as "all tort claims arising out of the explosion of debtor's factory" would be acceptable, "even if the exact amount of the claim, the theory on which it may be based, and the identity of the tortfeasor(s) are not described. (Indeed, those facts may not be known at the time.)"

34. **Answer (A) is the correct answer**. Section 9-507 addresses the effect of post-filing changes on the continued effectiveness of financing statements. Subsection (b) states the general rule: ". . . a financing statement is not rendered ineffective if, after the financing statement is filed, the information provided in the financing statement becomes seriously misleading. . . ." But this general rule is subject to two exceptions. A secured party may need to file a new financing statement if a "new debtor" (defined at section 9-102(a)(56)) becomes bound by the original debtor's security agreement. See §§ 9-507(b) and 9-508. The facts of this problem do not raise this concern as a mere name change does not create a "new debtor;" it is the *same* debtor merely with a new name. Second, a secured party needs to timely file an amendment to the original financing statement if the debtor so changes its name that the original financing statement becomes seriously misleading. See §§ 9-507(b), (c). In this problem, Computronics changed its name to Quest Systems. Has that name change rendered Bank's financing statement "seriously misleading"? The answer is found in section 9-506(c), which states that a financing statement is not seriously misleading if a search against the debtor's legal name (using the filing office's standard search logic) would disclose the earlier filing. It is almost a certainty that a search against "Quest Systems" would fail to disclose the earlier filing against "Computronics." The names are completely different. Therefore, the name change appears to be "seriously misleading." Thus, Bank should refile an amended financing statement that discloses the name change **(making Answer (A) the correct answer)**. To enjoy continued and uninterrupted perfection, Bank should file the amendment within four months after the name change. § 9-507(c). Section 9-507 does not mandate any amendment for an address change or change in use of the collateral, so **Answers (B), (C), and (D) are incorrect answers**.

35. **Answer (B) is the correct answer**. Section 9-502(a) states that a financing statement must provide three pieces of information: the name of the debtor, the name of the secured party or its representative, and a description of collateral. In a departure from previous law, the financing statement need not be signed, executed, or otherwise authenticated by the debtor. See § 9-502, cmt. 3. So **Answer (A) is incorrect**. It also would seem that Answers (C) and (D) are incorrect under section 9-502(a). But section 9-516 permits the filing officer to reject a financing statement that omits certain information, including the secured party's mailing address (section 9-516(b)(4)) and an indication that the debtor is either an individual or an organization (section 9-516(b)(5)(B)). And section 9-520(a) states that a filing officer "shall refuse to accept a record for filing for a reason set forth in Section 9-516(b). . . ." So both Answers (C) and (D) also appear to be correct. But notwithstanding the mandatory language of the statute ("shall refuse"), a filing clerk may (deliberately or unintentionally) file a financing statement that fails to contain the information described in section 9-516(b). In that situation, the filing is

effective under section 9-520(c). Therefore, **Answers (C) and (D) are incorrect** because the facts reveal that the clerk did file the financing statement. **Answer (B) is the correct answer** because section 9-509(a)(1) permits the secured party to file the financing statement only if the debtor authorizes the filing.

36. No, none of the three concerns renders the financing statement defective. First, a financing statement need not include an after-acquired property clause (or a future advance clause); those clauses need be mentioned only in the security agreement. § 9-204, cmt. 7; § 9-502, cmt. 2. Second, in a change from previous law (and in an attempt to accommodate electronic filing), Article 9 no longer requires the debtor to sign, execute, or authenticate a financing statement. § 9-502, cmt. 3. And third, the financing statement is effective to perfect the security interests of Bank One (and Bank Two and Bank Three), even though the financing statement does not indicate that Bank Four is acting as a representative or agent of an undisclosed party. § 9-503(d) and cmt. 3.

37. **Answer (C) is the correct answer.** Under section 9-301(a), Bradford should file its financing statement in the jurisdiction where the debtor is located. The law does not treat an individual and a sole proprietorship as two separate legal entities. In this problem, the debtor is an individual, Robert W. Zimmer ("RWZ"). Under section 9-307(b), an individual is located at his principal residence. Because RWZ lives in Missouri, Bradford should file somewhere in Missouri **(eliminating Answers (B) and (D) as possible answers)**. Absent any concerns that the computer has become a fixture, Bradford should file its financing statement with Missouri's central filing office, **making Answer (C) the best answer** under section 9-501(a), rather than the county clerk of Jackson County **(making Answer (A) an incorrect answer)**. If Bradford is concerned that the computer has become a fixture, it could file a second financing statement with the county clerk of Jackson County under section 9-501(a). But in a multiple choice problem, where you are asked to select the best answer, **Answer (C) is the best choice** (absent any facts suggesting that the computer has become a fixture and a real estate encumbrancer is challenging the priority of Bradford's security interest in the computer).

38. As the contracts evidence a monetary obligation to pay for a good, the contracts will fall within the definition of "account," "chattel paper," or "promissory note." The sale of each of these types of collateral is governed by Article 9 (see section 9-109(a)(3)). If the contracts are accounts, then Finance Company must perfect its interest by filing a financing statement (section 9-310(a)). If the contracts are chattel paper (i.e., the writing evidences not only the customer's payment obligation but also a security interest retained by Wallace in the office equipment sold on credit), or promissory notes (i.e., "negotiable instruments" under Article 3 or writings "that in ordinary course of business [are] transferred by delivery with any necessary indorsement or assignment" — section 9-102(a)(47)), then Finance Company can perfect its interest by filing a financing statement (section 9-312(a)) or taking possession of the contracts (section 9-313(a)). Appreciate that Finance Company will not be perfected if it takes possession of the contracts and they are deemed to be accounts, rather than chattel paper or promissory notes.

(Priority issue: If the contracts are chattel paper or instruments, then Finance Company should take possession of the contracts rather than rely on a financing statement if it wants to ensure priority over another "purchaser" (defined, in section 1-201, in a manner than includes a secured party). By taking possession, Finance Company eliminates the possibility that a subsequent purchaser of the contracts might enjoy priority over Finance Company under section 9-330.)

39. **Answer (C) is the correct answer.** A security interest becomes perfected "if it has attached and all of the applicable requirements for perfection [e.g., filing a financing statement] . . . have been satisfied. A security interest is perfected when it attaches if the applicable requirements are satisfied before the security interest attaches." § 9-308(a). So Bank's security interest became perfected upon filing, if the interest had previously attached; but Bank's security interest became perfected on attachment, if filing had previously occurred. Under section 9-203(a) and (b), Bank's interest attached on May 7. The security agreement was in place on May 1, Debtor acquired rights in the cash registers on May 3, and Bank gave value under section 1-204(1) on May 7 when it entered into a binding commitment to make a loan. The date on which the last of those three events occurs — May 7 — is the date of attachment. As Bank had previously filed its financing statement on May 1, attachment and perfection occurred simultaneously on May 7 **(making Answer (C) the correct answer** and **Answer (D) an incorrect answer). Answers (A) and (B) are incorrect** because the security interest had not yet attached (and therefore could not yet be perfected) on dates stated in those answers. **Answer (D) is incorrect** because the security interest had become perfected earlier, on May 7, for reasons already stated.

40. **Answer (D) is the correct answer.** As noted in the previous answer, Bank's security interest in the office chair became perfected upon filing, if the interest had previously attached; but Bank's security interest in the office chair became perfected on attachment, if filing had previously occurred. Under section 9-203(a) and (b), Bank's interest in the office chair attached on May 13. The security agreement was in place on May 1, Bank gave value on May 7, and Debtor acquired rights in the office chair on May 13. The date on which the last of those three events occurs — May 13 — is the date of attachment. As Bank had previously filed its financing statement on May 1, attachment and perfection occurred simultaneously on May 13 **(making Answer (D) the correct answer). Answers (A), (B), and (C) are incorrect** because they reflect dates on which the security interest had not yet attached (and therefore had not become perfected) because Debtor did not acquire rights in the office chair until a later date, May 13.

41. **Answer (B) is the correct answer.** A security entitlement is a form of investment property. See § 9-102(a)(49). A security interest in investment property can be perfected by filing (section 9-312(a)) or control (section 9-314(a)), **making Answer (A) incorrect. Answers (C) and (D) are incorrect** because a security interest in electronic chattel paper and a letter-of-credit right can be perfected by control. See § 9-314(a). A security interest in a commercial tort claim can be perfected only by filing a financing statement, **making Answer (B) the correct answer.** None

of the statutes mentioned in section 9-310(b) apply to commercial tort claims, leaving applicable subsection (a) — which requires a filed financing statement.

42. **Answer (C) is the correct answer.** A filing officer may legitimately reject a financing statement solely for reasons found in section 9-516. Subsection (b)(4) authorizes the filing officer to reject a financing statement that "does not provide a name and mailing address for the secured party," **making Answer (C) the correct answer**. **Answer (A) is incorrect** because (in a change from prior law) the debtor is not required to sign, execute, or otherwise authenticate the financing statement. See § 9-502, cmt. 3. **Answer (B) is incorrect** because (in a change from prior law) section 9-504 authorizes the use of supergeneric descriptions such as "all personal property" or "all assets" in a financing statement. (But supergeneric descriptions cannot be used in the security agreement. § 9-108, cmt. 2.) And **Answer (D) is incorrect** because Article 9 has never required a financing statement — a public record — to disclose the amount, or other payment terms, of the secured debt.

43. Section 9-301 provides rules that "determine the law governing perfection," but those rules are subject to sections 9-303 through 9-306. Because the collateral is investment property, one of the referenced sections — section 9-305 — applies. Section 9-305(a) provides general rules governing perfection, but subsection (a) is subject to subsection (c). And subsection (c) states: "The local law of the jurisdiction in which the debtor is located governs . . . perfection of a security interest in investment property by filing." Under section 9-307(b)(1), a debtor who is an individual is located at her principal residence. Because Maria is a Dallas resident, Texas law governs perfection by filing and is the state in which SmallBank should file its financing statement.

44. Under section 9-305(c), the law of the jurisdiction in which Maria is located dictates the place of filing. If Maria has moved from Dallas to New Orleans, then Louisiana law, rather than Texas law, has become the governing law. The effect of this change in jurisdictional law is that SmallBank will remain perfected only for four months after Maria's relocation. § 9-316(a)(2). To remain perfected thereafter, SmallBank must file a new financing statement in Louisiana within four months after the relocation. § 9-316(b). Otherwise, SmallBank will become unperfected prospectively (until it refiles in Louisiana) and is deemed unperfected retroactively against any "purchaser of the collateral for value" (which, under the definition of "purchaser" and "purchase" in section 1-201, includes other secured parties). § 9-316(b).

Because section 9-305(c) mandates a filing where the debtor is located, rather than where the collateral is located, SmallBank should not be concerned that Maria has mailed the 3X stock certificate to Pennsylvania.

45. The answer is found in section 9-305(a), which provides four different rules that vary with the nature of the investment property. With respect to the 3X stock certificate, SmallBank must comply with the law of the state in which the certificate is located: presently Texas. § 9-305(a)(1). For the shares in the Franklin Large Cap Fund (which are uncertificated securities), SmallBank must comply with the law of

the Fund's jurisdiction as specified in section 8-110(d). § 9-305(a)(2). Section 8-110(d) reveals that the Fund's jurisdiction is the jurisdiction under which it is organized: Delaware. And with respect to the investments in the Providence Securities account (a single "securities account" and a series of "securities entitlements"), SmallBank must comply with the law of Providence Securities' jurisdiction as specified in section 8-110(e). § 9-305(a)(3). Under section 8-110(e), which states a series of sequential tests, the applicable jurisdiction under the facts is the governing law stated in the account agreement: New York. § 8-110(e)(1).

46. **Answer (D) is the correct answer.** Under section 9-301(1), a secured party should file a financing statement in the jurisdiction where the debtor is located. If Borrower is a corporation, it is a "registered organization" under section 9-102(a)(70). Under section 9-307, a registered organization is located in its state of incorporation. A single filing will suffice, and the location of the collateral or chief executive office, and the places of business, are irrelevant. Therefore, **Answer (A) is incorrect**. If, as in Answer (B), Borrower is a general partnership, then it is not a "registered organization" and, under section 9-307(b)(2) and (3), is located at its single place of business or its chief executive office. Again, a single filing is sufficient, and **Answer (B) is incorrect**. When collateral consists of a deposit account (as in Answer (C)), Lender must perfect its security interest by control. § 9-312(b)(1). The governing law on control is the law of the bank's jurisdiction. § 9-304(a). So **Answer (C) is incorrect**. But **Answer (D) is correct**. As long as Borrower does not reincorporate under the laws of a different state, the location (or relocation) of its chief executive office (or collateral or places of business) remains irrelevant.

47. **Answer (B) is the correct answer.** Section 9-314(a) states that "a security interest in investment property, deposit accounts, letter-of-credit rights, or electronic chattel paper may be perfected by control. . . ." No other form of collateral can be perfected by control, **making Answer (C) an incorrect answer**. (A secured party must perfect a security interest in a commercial tort claim by filing a financing statement. § 9-310(a), (b).) But section 9-312(a) states that a security interest in investment property and chattel paper (which, by definition, includes both tangible and electronic forms) also can be perfected by filing, so **Answers (A) and (D) are incorrect** because control is not the exclusive method of perfection. Section 9-312(b)(1) states that "a security interest in a deposit account may be perfected *only* by control under Section 9-314" (emphasis added), **making Answer (B) the correct answer**.

48. The trustee is correct; Finance Company has an unperfected security interest (and, as a result, an unsecured claim in the bankruptcy). Finance Company can rely on automatic perfection only if its security interest is a PMSI in consumer goods (section 9-309(1)). The bedroom suite is a consumer good if Lauren is using it primarily for personal, family, or household use (section 9-102(a)(23)). But the security interest is not a PMSI under section 9-103 because the credit extended by Finance Company to Lauren is not a "purchase-money obligation" under section 9-103(a)(2). The credit given did not enable Lauren to acquire any rights in the bedroom suite; she already had acquired all of the rights in the furniture. (See § 9-103, cmt. 3, last paragraph.) As the security interest is not a PMSI, Finance Company cannot rely on automatic

perfection but instead must file a financing statement or take possession of the furniture.

49. No, Dealer does not have a perfected security interest in the keyboard. Dealer's reliance on any automatic perfection of its purchase-money security interest is misplaced. Only PMSI's in consumer goods are automatically perfected (section 9-309(1)). But Amanda is using the keyboard in her business, not primarily for personal, family, or household use. Therefore, the keyboard is "equipment" (section 9-102(a)(33)) and not a "consumer good" (section 9-102(a)(23)). Because the keyboard is not a consumer good, Dealer is not entitled to automatic perfection of its PMSI, but instead must file a financing statement (or take possession of the keyboard).

50. **Answer (B) is the correct answer.** Section 9-109(c)(1) states that Article 9 "does not apply to the extent that . . . a statute, regulation, or treaty of the United States preempts this article." Therefore, Lender must be concerned that federal law may require it to record its security interest in Debtor's registered copyrights, trademarks, and patents with the national registry. A financing statement filed in Florida may be insufficient. Under existing case law, Lender must record its security interest in Debtor's registered copyrights in the national registry (**making Answers (C) and (D) incorrect answers**) but may perfect its security interest in Debtor's registered patents and registered trademarks by filing a financing statement in Florida (as required by sections 9-301(1) and 9-307(e)) (**making Answer (B) the correct answer** and —). See, e.g., *In re Peregrine Entertainment, Ltd.*, 116 B.R. 194 (C.D. Cal. 1990) (copyrights); *Trimarchi v. Together Development Corp.*, 255 B.R. 606 (D. Mass. 2000) (trademarks); *In re Cybernetic Services, Inc.*, 252 F.3d 1039 (9th Cir. 2001) (patents). Also, emerging case law seems to indicate that a state filing under Article 9 is required to perfect a security interest in an *unregistered* copyright. *See In re World Auxiliary Power Co.*, 303 F.3d 1120 (9th Cir. 2002).

51. **Answer (C) is the correct answer.** As a general rule, a debtor's location dictates the place of filing. § 9-301(1). Under section 9-307(e), a registered organization, such as a corporation, is located in the state of incorporation. Therefore, **Answers (A) and (B) are incorrect answers**. Lender should file its financing statement against those Debtors in Delaware and Texas, respectively, rather than in the state where the tangible assets or the chief executive office are located. **Answer (D) is incorrect** because section 9-305(c)(1) requires Lender to file a financing statement in the state where the debtor is located under section 9-307(b)(1) (Illinois), rather than the location of the stock certificate (California). The Debtor in Answer (C) is a general partnership, an organization that is not a registered organization. And it has business operations in more than one location. Therefore, under section 9-307(b)(3), Debtor is located at its chief executive office. Section 9-307, cmt. 2, says that a chief executive office is "the place from which the debtor manages the main part of its business operations or financial affairs." Because Debtor's chief executive office appears to be in either New York City or Los Angeles, prudence suggests that Lender file in California (**making Answer (C) the correct answer**), as well as New York.

52. A search against the debtor's legal name of "Westex Inc.," using the filing office's standard search logic, is not likely to reveal the earlier filing against "Baxter Corporation." Therefore, under section 9-506(c), the name change has caused the earlier financing statement to become seriously misleading. Nevertheless, the filing against "Baxter Corporation" remains effective to perfect a security interest in equipment acquired by the debtor (i) prior to the name change and (ii) within four months after the name change (section 9-507(c)). Westex acquired Item #1 in April, within four months after the name change on February 1, so the original filing remains effective to perfect Bank's security interest in Item #1. But Westex acquired Item #2 in July, more than four months after the name change on February 1, so the original filing no longer perfects Bank's security interest in Item #2. To avoid this result, Bank should monitor its debtor for name changes and, in response thereto, file an amendment that describes the name change within four months after any such change.

53. Yes, Bank continues to have a perfected security interest in Item #3 after the sale. As a general rule (and no applicable exceptions apply in this case), a "security interest . . . continues in collateral notwithstanding sale . . . thereof unless the secured party authorized the disposition free of the security interest. . . ." (section 9-316(a)(1)). But this statute says only that the sale has not destroyed attachment; it does not address whether Bank must refile against Calvert Industries to remain perfected. The issue of perfection is addressed by section 9-507(a). Under that statute, Bank need not refile against Calvert Industries; instead, its financing statement filed against "Baxter Corporation" remains effective to perfect the security interest in Item #3 — even after the sale to Calvert Industries.

    (Because a financing statement filed against a seller [Baxter Corporation] can remain effective against a buyer [Calvert Industries] under section 9-507(a), a creditor of a buyer [Calvert Industries] "must inquire as to the debtor's [Calvert Industries'] source of title and, if circumstances seem to require it, search in the name of the former owner [Baxter Corporation]." § 9-507, cmt. 3.)

54. The answer depends on the nature of Bank's consent. Under section 9-315(a)(1), the security interest survives the sale unless Bank "authorized the disposition free of the security interest." If Bank gave this form of consent, then its security interest does not survive the disposition (and continued perfection under section 9-507 is irrelevant). But Bank may have consented to the sale, subject to continued retention of its security interest. If so, then Bank's security interest continues after the sale (section 9-315(a)(1)) and remains perfected by its original filing against Baxter (section 9-507(a)).

55. Even though the original filing remains effective to perfect Bank's security interest in Item #3 after its sale, that perfection will terminate much earlier than the normal five-year life of a financing statement because Baxter Corporation and Calvert Industries are incorporated under the laws of different states. Under section 9-316(a)(3), Bank's financing statement filed against Baxter Corporation in Delaware will remain effective until "the expiration of one year after transfer of collateral to a person that thereby becomes a debtor and is located in another jurisdiction."

Calvert Industries acquired a property interest in Item #3, which remains subject to Bank's security interest. Therefore, Calvert Industries is a "debtor" under section 9-102(a)(28)(A). And because Calvert Industries is incorporated under Texas law, rather than Delaware law, it is located in a jurisdiction different from Baxter Corporation's jurisdiction (see section 9-307(e)), where Bank filed its financing statement. Therefore, section 9-316(a)(3) applies, and Bank should file a new financing statement in Texas within one year after the sale.

56. **Answer (D) is the correct answer.** The key is to identify the debtor. Under Article 9, the debtor is the party who owns the collateral. § 9-102(a)(28). Here, we are told that Brent owns the property, despite the other entities involved. Thus, the financing statement should be against Brent and list his name as a debtor. That **eliminates Answers (A) and (B)**, since those answers list the incorrect party. **As between Answers (C) and (D), Answer (D) is preferable** because Answer (C) would mean that the entire quoted phrase, "Brent Bliss, doing business as Brent's Best Tacos" would be the name, and under section 9-503(a)(4)(A) the only property name is "the individual . . . name of the debtor," which stops after the word 'Bliss.' Were a financing statement filed under the name in Answer (C), a state's search logic might not return the whole phrase under a search of the proper, and shortened, name. Under Answer (D), the filing office will index the financing statement under both "Brent Bliss" and under the trade name, § 9-520(d), thus providing plenty of notice to future creditors.

57. **Answer (C) is the correct answer.** To answer this question, first try to determine what the collateral is in terms of the Article 9 categories provided in the definition section, § 9-102. The collateral is an interest in a general partnership, which is intangible personal property (so you do not have to examine any of the goods-related definitions). The basic classifications covering intangibles are accounts, deposit accounts (which we can exclude because no bank is involved), general intangibles (which includes payment intangibles and software), and in some cases investment property.

Is it an account? No, it is not really a right to payment; it is an ownership interest coupled with a right to receive a certain percentage of profits. Is it investment property? Investment property is defined in section 9-102(a)(49) as a "security," which in turn is defined in section 8-102 (incorporated via section 9-102(b)), as "except as otherwise provided in Section 8-103, . . . an obligation of an issuer or a share, participation, or other interest in an issuer or in property or an enterprise of an issuer. . . ." This looks like a general partnership interest might be a "security" (and hence investment property), but we have to check section 8-103. And that is where the maze stops: section 8-103(c) states that "[A]n interest in a partnership or limited liability company is not a security unless it is dealt in or traded on securities exchanges or in securities markets, its terms expressly provide that it is a security governed by this Article, or it is an investment company security." Debra's interest is not traded, and because it is a law partnership, it is not an "investment company security." Since there is no mention of the UCC in the partnership agreement, there is no "opt-in" to Article 8.

With accounts and investment property gone, what's left? The residual category of all types of Article 9 collateral is the "general intangible." The definition of "general intangible" in section 9-102(a)(42) defines by exclusion — once you eliminate every other form of collateral, anything left is a general intangible.

So how do you perfect a security interest in a general intangible? You must file a financing statement. § 9-310(a). With that knowledge, we can now examine the options. **Answer (A) is incorrect** since you must file a financing statement to perfect an interest in a general intangible. **Answer (B) is not correct** since a general partnership interest is personal property, and nothing in section 9-109 excludes it.

Answer (D) acknowledges a filing, but in the wrong place. All filings except for limited circumstances are now with the central filing office (under former Article 9, a local county or parish filing was appropriate in many states for interests in consumer goods). Thus, **Answer (D) is incorrect.**

That means that the default place of filing, the central filing office in the state in which the debtor is located, is the proper place. §§ 9-301; 9-307. That place is described in Answer (C), which means that **Answer (C) is the correct answer**.

58. **Answer (D) is the correct answer. Answer (A) is incorrect** since financing statements (but not security agreements) can use supergeneric descriptions such as "all assets" or "all personal property." § 9-504(2). The remainder of the question requires an examination of the use of definitions in Article 9.

We know that the security agreement covers "accounts, equipment, and general intangibles." Now let us take a look at the answers. Answers (B) and (C) refer to "computers and office furniture." Do these fit within any of the words used? We are aided in this inquiry by section 9-108(b)(3), which states that "a description of collateral reasonably identifies the collateral if it identifies the collateral by: . . . [¶] (3) . . . a type of collateral defined in [the Uniform Commercial Code]." This means that, in the security agreement, the presumption is that the parties used terms in their Agreement in the same way as the Uniform Commercial Code defines them. To complete the reasoning, this means that when the parties chose "equipment" as a definition, they adopted the definition set forth in section 9-102(a)(33).

"Equipment," as defined in section 9-102(a)(33), means "goods other than inventory, farm products, or consumer goods." It is a definition by exclusion, which is intended; "equipment" is the residual or default classification of goods. If it is tangible, and it is not something else, it is likely equipment. In the problem, the computers and office furniture would thus qualify as equipment. They are not inventory in that JCDSI does not hold them for resale, nor are they consumable supplies in the business. And they clearly are not farm products or consumer goods. So we cannot yet eliminate Answers (B) or (C).

We thus need to look at the intangible classifications. The security agreement covers "accounts." An "account" is defined in section 9-102(a)(2) as a "right to payment of a monetary obligation, whether or not earned by performance, (i) for property that has been or is to be sold, leased, licensed, assigned, or otherwise disposed of, (ii) for services rendered or to be rendered. . . ." That would seem to cover accounts receivable, the lay term for money owed to a business by its customers. This **eliminates Answer (B)** because it excludes anything but office furniture and computers.

As between Answers (C) and (D), we have to figure out how to classify the customer list. If it is covered by the security agreement, Answer (D) would be the correct answer. A customer list is both something tangible (piece of paper with writing on it) and intangible (a collection of names that has value). Since the primary value of the customer list is as a collection of names, or information, it will likely be treated as an intangible. The only part of the security agreement that could cover intangibles is "general intangibles." That term is defined in section 9-102(a)(42) as "any personal property, including things in action, other than accounts, chattel paper, commercial tort claims, deposit accounts, documents, goods, instruments, investment property, letter-of-credit rights, letters of credit, money, and oil, gas, or other minerals before extraction." It is the true residual category of Article 9 terms. Since the customer list is not a good (since its primary value is as intangible information), an account (it is not a right to the payment of money), or anything else mentioned, it is a general intangible. As such, it is covered by the security agreement, and **Answer (D) would be the correct answer**. Because it excludes the customer list (a general intangible covered by the security agreement), **Answer (C) is an incorrect answer**.

59. **Answer (D) is the correct answer.** We can get there by elimination. **Answer (B) is just silly.** Article 9 applies to consumers and businesses alike. While there may be different rules in different situations, there is no doubt as to coverage. Likewise, **Answer (A) is incorrect.** Where Bubba lives is not in doubt, and that only goes to where (or in which state) to file. If any financing statement is going to be filed, it will be filed in North Dakota.

Answer (C) is also incorrect. Transferring assets in bulk is only fraudulent if the transferor does so to avoid paying debts, or for some other fraudulent reason. The reason for the transfer here — to get a bank loan — would not be considered fraudulent.

That leaves Answer (D). We know that a financing statement must contain the name of the debtor, but what is that here? Is it the name on his birth certificate? Is it the name on his driver's license? Section 9-503 is not much help. It tells us with clarity what the name is of legal persons such as corporations and limited liability companies (the name on their incorporation or organizational papers), but with respect to individuals such as Bubba it simply says that a financing statement must "if the debtor has a name, . . . provide . . . the individual . . . name of the debtor." § 9-503(a)(4)(A). What is an individual name? Here, we rely on the common law. At common law a person's name is what they are generally known as for non-fraudulent purposes. That would seem to be Bubba Reed, but it is unclear under Article 9 whether the common law rule is adopted for individuals; in analogous situations for registered organizations, filing under trade names is specifically rejected. § 9-503(c). Especially because the search logic of the Secretary of State would not turn up a financing statement filed against Bubba Reed if the search request used David Michael Reed, it is possible that an incorrect filing might be misleading. § 9-506. Because none of this confusion occurs with registered organizations, the request to loan only to such a registered organization is not unreasonable, and thus **Answer (D) is the best answer**.

60. **Answer (A) is the correct answer.** The collateral, a stock certificate, is a form of investment property. Section 9-305 states some general rules regarding perfection of security interests in investment property. Subsection (a) states a general rule applicable to security certificates: a secured party should perfect its security interest under the law of the jurisdiction where the certificate is located. As the certificate is located in Chicago, Answer (B) appears to be the correct answer. But the rules of subsection (a) are subject to subsection (c). And that subsection states that if a secured party intends to perfect its security interest in investment property by filing (rather than some other method, such as control), then the creditor should file its financing statement in the jurisdiction where the debtor is located. In this problem, the debtor is MegaCorp, a Delaware corporation and, therefore, a "registered organization" under section 9-102(a)(70). A registered organization is located in the state of its incorporation. § 9-307(e). So Fidelity Finance should file its financing statement in Delaware, **making Answer (A) the correct answer**. A filing elsewhere (e.g., Michigan, Illinois, or Texas) would be an improper filing, **making Answers (B), (C), and (D) incorrect answers**.

61. The "promissory note" (which is "chattel paper" under section 9-102(a)(11) because it evidences Customer's payment obligations *and* a security interest in the sofa) represents "proceeds" of inventory under section 9-102(a)(64)(A) ("whatever is acquired upon the sale . . . of collateral"). Under section 9-203(f), Midway Bank's security interest in the inventory gives it "rights to proceeds provided by Section 9-315." Under that section, Midway Bank's security interest attaches to the promissory note because the note represents "identifiable proceeds" (i.e., proceeds that can be traced to the inventory). Under section 9-315(c), the security interest in the proceeds is perfected because the security interest in the original collateral — the sofa — was perfected (by a financing statement filed on July 13). This automatic perfection is only temporary for twenty days and terminates on September 25 unless perfection continues thereafter under subsection (d). Midway Bank enjoys continued perfection under (d)(1) because: Midway Bank filed a financing statement against inventory, the original collateral; the promissory note is a type of collateral (chattel paper) in which a security interest may be perfected by filing a financing statement in the same office as the inventory filing (sections 9-312(a), 9-301(1), and 9-307); and the promissory note was not acquired with cash proceeds.

62. As noted in the answer to the previous question, Midway Bank has an enforceable and perfected security interest in the computer hardware as "identifiable proceeds" of the inventory. But the automatic perfection terminates after twenty days unless perfection continues thereafter under subsection (d). Midway Bank cannot invoke (d)(1) because the computer hardware was acquired with cash proceeds. Subsection (d)(2) is inapplicable because the computer hardware does not fall within the definition of "cash proceeds" at section 9-102(a)(9). And because Midway Bank has not taken any other step to perfect its interest in the computer hardware (e.g., by filing a financing statement against "equipment" or "computer hardware"), subsection (d)(3) is inapplicable. Therefore, perfection lapsed on September 29, the twenty-first day after the security interest attached to the computer software on September 8.

63. **Answer (C) is the correct answer.** The facts state that Bank can satisfy its tracing burden, so the photocopier and the microwave oven are identifiable proceeds in which Bank has an enforceable security interest under sections 9-203(f) and 9-315(a)(2). Bank had a perfected security interest in the sofas, so its security interests in the photocopier and microwave oven were perfected for at least twenty days under section 9-315(c). But the problem assumes that the temporary perfection period has expired. For perfection to continue thereafter, Bank must successfully invoke section 9-315(d)(1), (2), or (3). Bank's interest in the photocopier remains perfected under (d)(1) because Bank's filed financing statement covered the sofas, Bank can perfect a security interest in the photocopier by filing a financing statement in the same office as its original filing (inventory and equipment filings are recorded

in the same office), and the photocopier was not acquired with cash proceeds. Because Bank's interest in the photocopier remains perfected, **Answers (B) and (D) are incorrect answers**. Bank's security interest in the microwave oven is unperfected. Bank cannot satisfy (d)(1) because the microwave oven was acquired with cash proceeds (notice that (d)(1) has three subparts, all of which must be met). Subsection (d)(2) does not apply because the microwave oven is not "cash proceeds." And (d)(3) offers no help because Bank has failed to take any other action to perfect its interest in the microwave oven (i.e., amending its original financing statement to mention the microwave oven or filing a new financing statement against the microwave oven). Because Bank's security interest in the microwave oven is not perfected after the automatic, but temporary, period of perfection expires, **Answer (A) is an incorrect answer and (C) is the correct answer**.

64. **Answer (A) is the correct answer.** The act of commingling proceeds with non-proceeds does not automatically destroy a secured party's ability to "identify" some or all of the assets as its collateral. Article 9 permits the secured party to identify the proceeds "by a method of tracing, including application of equitable principles, that is permitted under law other than this article with respect to commingled property of the type involved." § 9-315(b)(2). A common "equitable principle" is the "lowest intermediate balance rule." § 9-315, cmt. 3. Under the lowest intermediate balance rule, (i) the creditor can claim an interest in commingled assets identified as proceeds, (ii) non-proceeds are considered used before proceeds, and (iii) proceeds that are used by the debtor are not deemed replenished with subsequently commingled non-proceeds.

When the problem involves a bank account, it is helpful to run a daily balance and identify that part of the total balance that represents proceeds. The following is a summary of the bank activity:

Date	Balance	Proceeds
4/1	5,000	5,000
4/5	12,000	8,000
4/7	4,000	4,000
4/15	10,000	4,000
4/20	3,000	3,000
4/24	5,000	5,000
4/28	8,000	5,000

Because the ending number in the "proceeds" column is $5,000, **Answer (A) is the correct answer** and **Answers (B), (C), and (D) are incorrect answers**.

65. **Answer (B) is the correct answer. Answer (A) is incorrect** because sections 9-203(f) and 9-315(a)(2) give Bank an enforceable security interest in the check, even if the security agreement and the financing statement fail to describe the check or mention "proceeds." But under section 9-315(c), Bank's security interest in the check is perfected only if its interest in the CAT-scan machine was perfected. The facts state that Bank had an unperfected security interest in the machine, so its interest in the check also is unperfected. Therefore, **Answer (B) is the correct answer**. Because Bank's interest in the check is never perfected, **Answers (C) and (D) are incorrect answers**. If Bank's interest in the CAT-scan machine had been perfected, then Answer (D) would be the correct answer under section 9-315(d)(2).

66. **Answer (A) is the correct answer.** This problem involves proceeds. Consider the check from the insurance company first. The relevant portion of the definition of "proceeds" states that proceeds includes "to the extent of the value of collateral and to the extent payable to the debtor or the secured party, insurance payable by reason of the loss or . . . damage to, the collateral." § 9-102(a)(64)(E). The $5,000 check clearly satisfies this requirement. (Although Article 9 does exclude "a transfer of an interest in or an assignment of a claim under a policy of insurance," it also specifically states that "sections 9-315 and 9-322 apply with respect to proceeds and priorities in proceeds." § 9-109(a)(8). This conclusion **eliminates Answer (D)**, since Answer (D) does not include the insurance check.

What about the lease? Again, the definition of "proceeds" covers this situation. Under section 9-102(a)(64)(A), proceeds includes "whatever is acquired upon the sale, *lease*, license, exchange, or other disposition of collateral . . ." (emphasis supplied). As a consequence the lease is proceeds, and hence collateral. Payments on the lease are also proceeds (albeit "second generation" proceeds, but proceeds none the less). Section 9-102(a)(64)(B) states that "proceeds" includes "whatever is collected on, or distributed on account of, collateral. . . ." As a consequence, anything paid according to the terms of the lease will be proceeds and part of BBB's collateral. This **eliminates Answer (C)**, which does not include the payment on the lease.

That leaves Answers (A) and (B), which are the same except that Answer (B) seems to state that a new financing statement needs to be filed to continue perfection. That takes us to section 9-315. Under section 9-315(c), a proceeds interest is automatically perfected for twenty days. The need to file a further financing statement is in section 9-315(d). Under paragraph (1) of that rule, no new financing statement is necessary if: (i) a filed financing statement covers the original collateral (as it does under the facts here); (ii) the proceeds (the lease) are collateral in which a security interest may be perfected by filing in the office in which the financing statement has been filed (which is the case here; the lease is chattel paper under section 9-102(a)(1), and chattel paper is perfected by filing in the same office — the central filing office); and (iii) the proceeds (the lease) are not acquired with cash proceeds (they were not; Bill surrendered possession of the car for a month). As a consequence, BBB does not have to file a new financing statement to continue perfection in the lease, **making Answer (B) incorrect**.

67. **Answer (D) is the correct answer.** The question here requires you to categorize Acme's interest. It tried to reserve title; we know from sections 1-201(b)(35) and 2-401(1) that such a reservation is limited in effect to the taking of a security interest. Moreover, Acme filed in Arizona, which, given the fact that the debtor is an Arizona corporation (a registered organization under section 9-102(a)(70)), is the proper place to file regardless of where the assets may be. §§ 9-301; 9-307.

As a consequence, Acme had a perfected security interest in the original collateral. That interest remains in the 250 widgets in the Nevada store, thus **making Answers (A) and (C) incorrect**.

Answers (B) and (D) differ only with respect to the $5,000 debt owed by X Corp. The checks from the consumers are clearly proceeds under section 9-102(a)(64), in that they arose on the sale of the collateral, and clearly identifiable in the sense that they can be matched against sales of collateral, and thus Acme has a perfected security interest in them. § 9-315(d)(2).

What about the X Corp. debt? Is it proceeds? Yes. It arose upon the "sale . . . of collateral." § 9-102(a)(64)(A). Since more than 20 days have passed, however, we need to find a way that the interest is perfected. Otherwise the trustee in bankruptcy will prevail under the strong arm clause of 11 U.S.C. § 544(a)(1).

Perfection, however, is easy to show under section 9-315(d)(1). Under that paragraph, perfection continues beyond the 20 days if "the following conditions are satisfied: (A) a filed financing statement covers the original collateral (it does under the facts — the original filing in Arizona suffices); (B) the proceeds are collateral in which a security interest may be perfected by filing in the office in which the financing statement has been filed (they are; the debt owed is an "account" under section 9-102(a)(3), and accounts are perfected by filing in the same place as inventory — the debtor's location (Arizona)); and (C) the proceeds are not acquired with cash proceeds (which they were not; the debt owing arose under regular contract law without any cash exchanging hands)."

With an interest in the account of X Corp. thus perfected beyond the automatic, but temporary, 20-day period of sections 9-315(c) and (d), **Answer (D) becomes the better answer, rather than Answer (B)** (which fails to mention the interest in the account of X Corp.).

68. **Answer (A) is the correct answer.** This question turns on the status of unrecorded and unregistered copyrights under Article 9. The law as of mid-2003 is that, with respect to unregistered copyrights, federal law does not preempt Article 9, and thus perfection under Article 9 is the only way to obtain a security interest in such property. *See Aerocon Eng'g, Inc. v. Silicon Valley Bank (In re World Aux. Power Co.)*, 303 F.3d 1120 (9th Cir. 2002).

Under Article 9, it is most likely that the interest in the software under development would be classified as a general intangible. Under section 9-102(a)(75), "'Software' means a computer program and any supporting information provided in connection with a transaction relating to the program." The definition of "general intangible" in section 9-102(b)(42) includes the following sentence, at the end: "The term [general intangible] includes . . . software." A security interest in general intangibles is perfected by filing a financing statement. § 9-310. Because Silicon Valley filed a financing statement, it follows that it had a perfected security interest in the software under development.

Because Silicon Valley was perfected in the software, section 9-315(a)(1) combined with section 9-507(a) means that Silicon Valley still has a perfected security interest in the material Amanda bought. Because Greg was not in the business of selling software, Amanda cannot qualify as a buyer in the ordinary course of business, and thus cannot claim the protection afforded by section 9-320(a). Amanda thus took subject to Silicon Valley's security interest. §§ 9-210(a); 9-315(a). This conclusion thus **eliminates Answer (D)**.

The rest of the analysis turns on the proceeds analysis. We know that Amanda paid Greg $50,000 for his interest in the software. The check with which Amanda paid is proceeds; it is what was "acquired upon the sale . . . of collateral." § 9-102(a)(64)(A). Upon deposit and collection, the issue becomes whether the deposit account is "proceeds." Put another way, the issue is whether the commingling of the proceeds of the check with the money already on deposit (which was not collateral) destroyed the ability to attach the security interest to the deposit account. Section 9-315(a)(2) states that "a security interest attaches to any identifiable proceeds of collateral." Subsection (b) then goes on to say that "[p]roceeds that are commingled with other property are identifiable proceeds: . . . (2) if the proceeds are not goods, to the extent that the secured party identifies the proceeds by a method of tracing, including application of equitable principles, that is permitted under law other than this article with respect to commingled property of the type involved." Under the most commonly used version of equitable tracing, the lowest intermediate balance rule, Silicon Valley will be able to trace its interest into the account and to the items purchased from the account. Under the lowest intermediate balance rule, the presumption is that the funds first spent out of commingled fund are *not* proceeds; thus, the first $100 of the plane ticket are not proceeds, but since a ticket to Pago Pago costs $1,400, the ticket was purchased at least partially with proceeds. That makes the ticket proceeds as well. The same goes for the cashier's check: it is something that is purchased with proceeds, and thus is proceeds itself.

Thus, **Answer (A) is the correct answer** because all of those items are in that answer, and **Answers (B) and (C) are incomplete and incorrect answers**.

69. **Answer (D) is the correct answer.** Section 9-102(a)(64)(A) defines "proceeds" as "whatever is acquired upon the sale . . . of collateral." The photocopier represents "proceeds" from the sale of a bridal gown (a unit of inventory and, therefore, collateral). Debtor's documentation allows Lender to prove that the photocopier is an "identifiable" proceed (i.e., traceable to the bridal gown, a unit of inventory). When examined together, sections 9-203(f) and 9-315(a)(2) give Lender an enforceable security interest in the photocopier, even though neither its security agreement nor the financing statement mention "equipment" or "proceeds." Therefore, **Answers (A), (B), and (C) are incorrect.** Under section 9-315(c), Lender's interest in the photocopier initially is perfected because its interest in the bridal gown, a unit of inventory, was perfected. Under section 9-315(d), Lender's perfection continues beyond the automatic (but temporary) 20-day period under clause (1) because Lender's filed financing statement covered the bridal gown, Lender could perfect an interest in the photocopier by filing a financing statement in the same office as its original filing (inventory and equipment filings are recorded in the same office), and the photocopier was not acquired with cash proceeds (observe that (d)(1) has three subparts, all of which must be met). Lender has a perfected security interest in the photocopier, **making Answer (D) the correct answer**.

70. **Answer (B) is the correct answer.** Lender has an enforceable security interest in the photocopier on a proceeds theory for reasons stated in the previous answer.

So **Answers (C) and (D) are incorrect**. Under section 9-315(c), Lender's interest in the photocopier initially is perfected because its interest in the bridal gown, a unit of inventory, was perfected. But unlike the result in the previous question, Lender's perfection does not continue after June 21. Lender cannot satisfy the third requirement of subsection (d)(1) because the photocopier was acquired with cash proceeds. Subsection (d)(2) does not apply because the photocopier is not "cash proceeds" as defined at section 9-102(a)(9). And subsection (d)(3) offers no help because Lender has not taken any other action to perfect its interest in the photocopier (i.e., amending its original financing statement to mention the photocopier or filing a new financing statement against the photocopier). Because Lender's security interest in the photocopier is not perfected on July 1, **Answer (A) is incorrect** and **Answer (B) is correct**.

71. **Answer (B) is the correct answer.** The contents of an effective financing statement are summarized at section 9-502(b). A fixture filing must include the same information as a regular financing statement. It also must (i) state that it covers fixtures, (ii) state that it is to be filed in the real estate records, (iii) provide a description of the real estate, and (iv) provide the name of the record owner of the real estate if the debtor does not have a recorded interest. Only Answer (B) mentions information that the statute requires, so **Answer (B) is the correct answer**. Section 9-502(b) does not require the record owner of the real estate to authenticate the fixture filing, so **Answer (A) is incorrect**. Nor does section 9-502(b) require a description of the secured debt or a detailed description of the equipment that may be a fixture, so **Answers (C) and (D) are incorrect answers**.

72. **Answer (C) is the correct (i.e., false) answer.** Balsam has engaged in seller financing, so it can claim a purchase-money security interest in the unit under sections 9-103(a) and (b)(1). And Balsam's interest in the unit arose before the unit became a fixture on April 11. Therefore, Balsam's interest in the unit enjoys priority if it files a fixture filing no later than the twentieth day after April 11. § 9-334(d). So **Answer (A) is a true statement and, accordingly, an incorrect answer** (the problem asks which statement is FALSE). If Balsam never files a financing statement or a fixture filing, its security interest in the unit is never perfected (the unit is not a consumer good, so perfection is not automatic even though Balsam holds a purchase-money security interest). So Balsam cannot enjoy priority under sections 9-334(d) and (e). Instead, Hitchcock's interest has priority under the general rule of section 9-334(c), **making Answer (B) a true statement and an incorrect answer**. Because a fixture filing must include a description of the real estate under section 9-502(b), **Answer (D) is a true statement and an incorrect answer**. **Answer (C) is false, and therefore a correct answer**, under section 9-604(d). That section states that a secured party is liable for physical damage, but not economic loss, caused by removal.

73. The security interest held by Walker Nursery enjoys priority over the competing property interest of Fidelity Finance under section 9-334(d). That section states: "[A] perfected security interest in fixtures has priority over a conflicting interest of an encumbrancer [Fidelity Finance] . . . if the debtor [Meredith] has an interest of record in or is in possession of the real property and: (1) the security interest is a purchase-money security interest; (2) the interest of the encumbrancer [Fidelity Finance] [in the real estate] . . . arises before the goods [trees] become fixtures; and (3) the security interest [held by Walker Nursery] is perfected by a fixture filing before the goods [trees] become fixtures or within 20 days thereafter." Subsection (1) is met because Walker Nursery engaged in seller financing, so its interest is a purchase-money security interest under sections 9-103(a) and (b)(1). Subsection (2) is satisfied because Fidelity Finance acquired an interest in the real estate in

March, several months before the trees became fixtures in October. And Walker Nursery complied with subsection (3) by filing its fixture filing on October 25, no later than twenty days after the date on which the trees were planted (October 8). Having satisfied section 9-334(d), Walker Nursery's security interest in the trees enjoys priority over the competing property interest held by Fidelity Finance.

(Appreciate that the twenty days in section 9-334(d)(3) runs from the planting date [October 8], rather than the purchase date [October 1].)

74. **Answer (A) is the correct answer.** This problem seems to involve fixtures, but it does not. Therefore, **Answers (B) and (C) are incorrect answers**. The last paragraph states that "[b]efore installation," Dick defaults and files his bankruptcy petition. That means that the elevator has not been installed, and it still retains its character as personal property covered solely by Article 9. Thus, the contest is between Carl, a perfected purchase-money creditor and Vicious, who at most has an unperfected interest in the uninstalled elevator. This contest is really no contest, with Carl prevailing under section 9-322(a). **Answer (A) is a better answer than Answer (D)** because Carl's security interest enjoys priority from its perfection, not its purchase-money status.

75. **Answer (B) is the correct answer.** This problem now involves fixtures. As the problem states: elevators, once installed, are fixtures. We can first **eliminate Answer (A)**. Priority with respect to fixtures is determined by a "fixture filing," which is defined in section 9-102(a)(40) (and which incorporates parts of section 9-502), and which is perfected by filing with the filing office in which real estate interests are perfected (which is normally a county or parish recorder), section 9-501(a)(1)(B). Vicious' mortgage counts as a fixture filing. Under section 9-502(c), a mortgage, if it contains the requisite information, can serve as a fixture filing. Section 9-502 requires that the mortgage state the goods covered (the elevators), the real property affected, and contain the information otherwise required by a financing statement (the name of the debtor, the name of the secured party, and a description of the collateral). Because the mortgage does all of this, it is an appropriate fixture filing.

Because Carl did not file anything locally, and did not include a real estate description, his filing is not a fixture filing. Carl then loses under section 9-334(c), which makes an interest in fixtures subordinate to an interest of a real estate encumbrancer. That makes **Answer (B) correct**.

Because Answer (B) is correct, Answer (C) cannot be correct, because Vicious wins on grounds other than the fact that it does hold a construction mortgage. If Carl had made a fixture filing, Vicious would still prevail under section 9-334(h), because his mortgage has all the necessary requirements of a construction mortgage: it is a mortgage under section 9-102(a)(55) (a "consensual interest in real property"), and in conformity with section 9-334(h) it states that it is a construction mortgage. Construction mortgages have priority over purchase-money interests in fixtures under 9-334(h) on the theory that vendors such as Carl will be paid from a draw or advance under the construction loan (and people like Carl should know that and require a check from the construction lender).

Answer (D) is not correct because the purchase-money priority of section 9-334(d) requires a fixture filing and Carl did not make one. Moreover, even if he had, it would have been trumped by the construction mortgage.

76. **Answer (A) is the correct answer.** Note that although this question has more or less the same form as the prior two questions, it is not about priority; it is really about perfection. The trustee takes the status of a non-reliance judgment creditor under 11 U.S.C. § 544(a)(1). That means its interest arises as of the date of the bankruptcy filing, and it also means that anyone who is perfected under Article 9 as of that date has an interest that cannot be subordinated to the trustee's interest.

Was Carl perfected? Here is where it gets tricky. To the extent that Carl had a perfected security interest in the elevators, and to the extent the elevators are fixtures and not personal property (such as bricks, window panes, etc.) that are ordinary building materials incorporated into improvements, Carl's interest remains perfected. As we saw above, however, Carl's interest loses in priority to a fixture filing, but it is still perfected as against judgment creditors and bankruptcy trustees. Thus, section 9-334(e)(3) states that if the interest is "perfected by any method permitted under this article," the interest of the secured party is senior to the interest of a judgment creditor. See also § 9-334, cmt. 9. As a consequence, **Answer (B) is incorrect** because it is irrelevant for perfection that Carl make a fixture filing. **Answer (D) continues to be incorrect** because Carl has not filed a fixture filing as required by section 9-334(d); but for purposes of this question, filing a fixture filing would not add anything to perfection, however much it might add to the priority question.

Answer (C) draws on the trustee's status as a hypothetical bona fide purchaser of real estate under 11 U.S.C. § 544(a)(3). That section, however, only gives the trustee the status of a purchaser of real property "other than fixtures" from the debtor. Thus, bankruptcy law explicitly leaves the issue to state law (that is, Article 9), and as the above analysis shows, Carl would prevail under section 9-334. So **Answer (C) is incorrect**. Moreover, even if 11 U.S.C. § 544(a)(3) did not exclude fixtures, Carl would still win because (as is almost always the case) state law provides that a real estate purchaser takes subject to existing perfected liens. Carl's perfection would not be destroyed by a "purchase," be it real or hypothetical. Carl would thus prevail against a purchaser, and, accordingly, a bankruptcy trustee.

77. **Answer (A) is the correct answer.** The trustee in bankruptcy prevails if Fred's interest is vulnerable to a lien creditor under state law. Because the lights and light fixtures are "fixtures" under state law, the priority in those items of collateral will be governed by section 9-334. Specifically, under section 9-334(d), "[a] perfected security interest in fixtures has priority over a conflicting interest of an encumbrancer . . . if: . . . (3) the conflicting interest is a lien on the real property obtained by legal or equitable proceedings after the security interest was perfected by any method permitted by this article." This means that when Fred perfected in the items by filing with the California Secretary of State, he perfected by a "method permitted by this article." (Filing with the California Secretary of State is the appropriate place since AMI is located in California, as it is a California corporation, § 9-307(e), and

filings are appropriate in the state where the debtor is located, § 9-301.) That perfection allows Fred to have priority over an "encumbrancer," that is, a lien creditor. Thus, **the only correct answer is Answer (A)**. Because Fred has priority, **Answers (B), (C), and (D)** (each of which resolves the priority dispute against, rather than in favor of, Fred) **are incorrect**.

This is a little confusing. It means that you can perfect an interest in fixtures without the necessity of making a valid fixture filing. It also means that perfection alone does not help much with respect to priority. It will, as is the case here, assist in defeating involuntary lien creditors and bankruptcy trustees; it loses, however, to almost every other type of consensual real estate encumbrancer, such as mortgagors and the like.

The references to "not having any interest" are red herrings. So long as the property is classified as a "fixture," it will be governed by section 9-334. Only when collateral is "ordinary building materials incorporated into an improvement on land," § 9-334(a), does the property lose its characterization as personal property and become real property governed by law other than Article 9 (usually real estate mortgage law).

78.	The credit card receivable is an "account" under section 9-102(a)(2)(vii). Therefore, First Finance has a perfected security interest in the credit card receivable because its collateral includes accounts, its loan documentation includes an after-acquired property clause, and First Finance has filed a financing statement. Midway Bank has a perfected security interest in the credit card receivable on a proceeds theory under sections 9-315(c) and (d)(1). Both creditors enjoy a perfected security interest in any cash payments (on a proceeds theory) that are traceable to this particular account under sections 9-315(c) and (d)(2). The general priority rule of section 9-322(a)(1) (and, with respect to any proceeds, (b)(1)) will resolve this priority dispute. And under those rules, the security interest of First Finance enjoys priority because First Finance filed its financing statement on March 29, long before Midway Bank filed its financing statement on July 13.

79.	Supplier has an enforceable security interest in the deposited funds as identifiable proceeds from the sale of Debtor's inventory. §§ 9-203(f), 9-315(a)(2). That security interest in the proceeds is perfected under section 9-315(c) because Supplier's security interest in the inventory was perfected by the filed financing statement (and, if any of the proceeds resulted from a sale more than twenty days ago, the perfection continues after that 20-day automatic — but temporary — period under section 9-315(d)(2)). Bank's enforceable security interest in the deposit account is perfected by "control" under section 9-104(a)(1), since Bank is the financial institution that maintains the deposit account (and Bank's failure to file a financing statement is a red herring, since section 9-312(b)(1) states that "a security interest in a deposit account may be perfected only by control"). If the general priority rule used to resolve disputes between two perfected security interests (section 9-322(a)(1)) applied, Supplier would have priority because its filing date of June 4 is earlier than Bank's perfection date of September 1. But as noted in section 9-322(f)(1), the general priority rule of section 9-322(a) is subject to priority rules found elsewhere in part 3 of Article 9. One of those other rules is section 9-327. Under section 9-327(1), Bank's security interest in the $4,000 enjoys priority because, with respect to conflicting security interests in a deposit account, a security interest perfected by control enjoys priority over a competing security interest not perfected by control (e.g., filing).

80.	**Answer (D) is the correct answer.** The general priority rule used to resolve disputes between two secured creditors with perfected security interests is the "first to file or perfect, whichever is earlier" rule under section 9-322(a)(1). A creditor's knowledge is irrelevant (it is too difficult and costly to prove), so **Answer (C) is incorrect**. And both creditors have a perfected security interest, so the "first to attach" rule in section 9-322(a)(3) does not apply, **making Answer (A) an incorrect**

answer. Lender perfected its security interest on May 25, when Debtor acquired rights in the lathe (the security agreement was already in place on May 1, and Lender had previously given value on May 1 and filed its financing statement on May 20). Bank perfected its security interest on May 30, when the security agreement was executed and value was given (Bank had previously filed its financing statement on May 10 and Debtor had acquired rights in the lathe on May 25). Although Lender perfected its security interest five days before Bank, Bank's security interest enjoys priority because the date of its financing statement (May 10) is earlier than the date of Lender's perfection (May 25). Therefore, **Answer (D) is the correct answer and Answer (B) is an incorrect answer**. The result is justified because Bank was the first party to announce to the world (via its financing statement) that it might be claiming an interest in Debtor's equipment. Lender should have searched the relevant records and realized that its interest in Debtor's equipment would be junior to any competing security interest claimed by any party that had previously filed a financing statement against the collateral. Bank had done so on May 10, five days before Lender funded its loan on May 15.

81. FNB will win as to the accounts but lose as to the chattel paper contracts. Because the accounts and chattel paper contracts resulted from inventory sales, FNB can claim an enforceable security interest in them as proceeds under sections 9-203(f) and 9-315(a)(2) that is perfected under sections 9-315(c) and (d)(1). FNB's perfected security interest in the accounts enjoys priority over Miller Finance's unperfected security interest under section 9-322(a)(2) (Miller Finance also loses even if its security interest in the accounts is automatically perfected under section 9-309(2) because FNB's filing date of February 15 is earlier than Miller Finance's perfection date in June). But under section 9-330(a), Miller Finance, a purchaser of the chattel paper contracts, has priority over FNB's perfected security interest claimed merely as proceeds of inventory. Miller Finance acquired the contracts in the ordinary course of its business, took possession of the contracts, and gave "new value" under section 9-102(a)(57) in the form of $14,000. Furthermore, the facts do not indicate that the contracts included any type of legend indicating they had been assigned to FNB or any other party, and its knowledge of FNB's filed financing statement should not preclude Miller Finance from satisfying the requirement of good faith as defined in section 1-201(b)(20) (see section 9-330, cmts. 5 and 6).

82. **Answer (C) is the correct answer.** Lender's security interest in the photocopier became perfected on October 1, when Debtor acquired the photocopier (the security agreement was in place on September 1, Lender had given value on September 1, and Lender had filed its financing statement on September 10). Bank's security interest in the deposit account was perfected by control under section 9-104(a)(1) on May 1. Its interest in the photocopier (a "proceed" of the funds in the deposit account) was perfected for 20 days from the date of attachment under section 9-315(c) and thereafter under section 9-315(d) because Bank filed its financing statement against the photocopier on October 15. Because both Lender and Bank hold a perfected security interest in the photocopier, **Answers (A) and (B) are incorrect**. Even though Bank perfected its security interest in the deposit account on May 1, before Lender perfected its security interest in the photocopier on October

1, Lender's security interest enjoys priority under section 9-322(d) (**making Answer (C) correct** and **Answer (D) incorrect**). Under that section, a creditor's security interest in proceeds of a deposit account does not enjoy priority if another creditor filed first against those proceeds. To avoid this result, a party that takes a security interest in a deposit account should (i) promptly file a financing statement against any assets that the debtor might acquire by using funds in the deposit account and (ii) review the filing records to assure itself that no other creditor has filed a financing statement against the debtor. For additional reading, see section 9-322, cmts. 7, 8, and 9.

83. If the judge relies on the general priority rule of section 9-322(a)(1), then she should rule in favor of Polk Finance because Polk Finance filed its financing statement in 2001 and Albany Bank filed its financing statement in 2002. But if she does so, she would be wrong. Section 9-322(a) is subject to section 9-322(f), which states that priority rules found elsewhere in sections 9-301 through 9-342 (part 3 of Article 9, or "this part") may control. One of those rules is section 9-325, which states: "[A] security interest created by a debtor [Blocker] is subordinate to a security interest in the same collateral created by another person [Davidson] if: (1) the debtor [Blocker] acquired the collateral subject to the security interest created by the other person [Davidson]; (2) the security interest created by the other person [Davidson] was perfected when the debtor [Blocker] acquired the collateral; and (3) there is no period thereafter when the security interest is unperfected." Clause (1) is satisfied because Albany Bank's security interest survives the sale under sections 9-201 and 9-315(a), and Blocker's acquisition does not terminate the security interest under section 9-320(a) (Blocker is not a buyer in the ordinary course of business because the Item in Davidson's hands is equipment, not inventory) or section 9-320(b) (neither Blocker nor Davidson hold the Item as a consumer good, and Albany Bank has filed a financing statement). Clause (2) is met because Albany Bank's financing statement remained effective at the time of sale and, under section 9-507(a), thereafter. And section 9-325(b) applies to subordinate the security interest of Polk Finance to the security interest of Albany Bank because otherwise Polk Finance would enjoy priority under section 9-322(a).

The result should not be surprising. It is an instance of "nemo dat": a person can give only what it has. If Blocker acquires the Item subject to the security interest held by Albany Bank, then Blocker's creditors (e.g., Polk Finance) also take the Item subject to the security interest held by Albany Bank. Perhaps rephrased, a secured party can only take a security interest in the limited, and possibly encumbered, rights held by its debtor.

84. **Answer (B) is the correct answer. Answer (A) is false**. A security interest cannot be perfected before it attaches. § 9-308(a). And under sections 9-203(a) and (b), BigBank's security interest did not attach until BigBank gave value on August 6. **Answer (C) also is false**. Even though BigBank's control on August 8 comes after SmallBank's earlier filing on August 4, a security interest in investment property that is perfected by control always enjoys priority over a competing security interest perfected by filing, regardless of timing. § 9-328(1). And **Answer (D) is false** because "investment property" is an acceptable description under section 9-108(d)

(this is not a consumer transaction because the debtor is a corporation, so subsection (e) does not apply). **Answer (B) is true** under section 9-322(a)(1). BigBank filed its financing statement on August 1 and perfected its security interest on August 6. SmallBank filed its financing statement, and perfected its security interest, on August 4. SmallBank perfected its interest first, but BigBank had already filed its financing statement. So BigBank enjoys priority, **making Answer (B) the correct answer**.

85.   **Answer (C) is the correct answer. Answer (A) is incorrect**. SmallBank cannot perfect its security interest until the security interest attaches. § 9-308(a). Small-Bank's interest did not attach under sections 9-203(a) and (b) until Dekka acquired rights in the Herrick shares on August 15. **Answer (D) is incorrect**. SmallBank's financing statement provides a reasonable description of the collateral under section 9-108(d) and will perfect an interest in any type of investment property. **Answer (B) is incorrect** because BigBank has no security interest in the Herrick shares. The scope of its security interest is defined by the collateral description in the security agreement, and that description is limited to the Segway shares. It is irrelevant when BigBank files its financing statement (which cannot expand the collateral beyond the description found in the security agreement). SmallBank is the only party with an enforceable security interest in the Herrick shares, **making Answer (C) the correct answer**.

86.   The court should enter a declaratory judgment awarding priority to Second Bank. To continue its priority (under the general "first to file or perfect" rule of section 9-322(a)(1)) after January 10, 2005, First Bank needed to file a continuation statement within the six-month period ending on that date (section 9-515(d) (that is, the six-month period starting on July 10, 2004, and ending on January 10, 2005). But First Bank filed its continuation statement on July 7, 2004 — a date three days *before* the start of the six-month period that began on July 10, 2004 — so its continuation statement was ineffective (section 9-510(c)) even though the statement was recorded. As a result, First Bank's security interest became unperfected on January 10, 2005, and "is deemed never to have been perfected as against a purchaser of the collateral for value" (section 9-515(c)). Second Bank falls within the definition of "purchaser" (section 1-201) and presumably gave value (a loan). Therefore, Second Bank's perfected security interest enjoys priority over First Bank's unperfected security interest (section 9-322(a)(2)) as soon as the effectiveness of First Bank's original financing statement lapsed.

87.   John was the first party to file a financing statement and perfect his security interest, so he would seem to have priority under the general priority rule of section 9-322(a). But as noted in section 9-322(a) and (f), this general priority rule is subject to other priority rules, one of which is section 9-328(1). Under that rule, Heather enjoys priority because she has perfected her security interest by control and John has perfected his security interest solely by filing. Heather has control (see sections 9-106(a) and 8-106(a)) because the stock certificate, in bearer form, has been "delivered" to her. "Delivery" occurred under section 8-301(a)(1) when Heather took possession of the bearer certificate. Because Heather's security interest is

perfected by control, and John's security interest is perfected solely by filing, Heather's security interest enjoys priority under section 9-328(1).

88. For Heather to have control of a certificated security in registered form, she must have possession of the certificate and (i) the certificate must be indorsed by Sharon to Heather or in blank (that is, Sharon simply signed her name on the certificate), or (ii) Waldorf must register the shares in Heather's name. § 8-106(b). Because the certificate has not been indorsed by Sharon or registered by Waldorf in Heather's name, Heather has not perfected her security interest in the Waldorf shares by control. Nevertheless, under section 9-313(a), Heather perfected her security interest by taking "delivery" (i.e., possession) of the certificate under section 8-301. As noted in the previous answer, John appears to enjoy priority under the general rule of section 9-322(a), but that rule is subject to other priority rules. Heather does not have control, so she cannot invoke section 9-328(1) and enjoy priority. But she does enjoy priority under section 9-328(5), which states that a security interest in a certificated security in registered form that is perfected by delivery and not by control has priority over a competing security interest not perfected by control.

89. David purchased the shares directly from the issuer, rather than through a securities intermediary (such as a broker), so the shares are uncertificated securities (rather than a security entitlement). Because the Templeton Mutual Fund revised its books to reflect Wallace as the registered owner, the shares have been "delivered" to Wallace under section 8-301(b), which gives Wallace "control" of the shares under section 8-106(c)(1). And because Wallace has perfected his security interest in the shares by control and Helen is relying solely on her financing statement, Wallace enjoys priority under section 9-328(1) (control trumps non-control). Although Helen was the first creditor to file a financing statement and perfect her interest, she cannot claim priority under the general rule of section 9-322(a)(1). Under section 9-322(f), subsection (a) is subject to other priority rules in sections 9-301 through 9-342 (part 3 of Article 9, or "this part"), including section 9-328.

90. **Answer (C) is the correct answer.** The lease represents identifiable proceeds of the unit of inventory. Therefore, Lender has a security interest in the lease under sections 9-203(f) and 9-315(a)(2). So **Answer (A) is incorrect**. Lender's security interest is automatically perfected for twenty days from the date of attachment (March 1) under section 9-315(c). Perfection of the security interest in the lease continues thereafter under (d)(1) because Lender filed a financing statement against the inventory, the lease is chattel paper under section 9-102(a)(11) and a filing against inventory is made in the same office as a filing against chattel paper, and the lease was not acquired with cash proceeds. So **Answer (B) is incorrect**. But even though Lender's security interest in the lease is perfected, FinCo's interest enjoys priority under either section 9-330(a) (applicable if Lender claims an interest in the lease "merely as proceeds of inventory") or (b) (applicable if Lender claims an interest in the lease "other than merely as proceeds of inventory"). (For a discussion of the distinction, see PEB Commentary #8.) The lease is chattel paper, and FinCo is a "purchaser" under section 1-201(b)(30) (one who takes by "purchase" — a voluntary transaction — section 1-201(b)(29)). FinCo appears to have acted in good faith, has taken possession of the lease pursuant to a transaction in the

ordinary course of its business, and has given new value for the lease. The lease does not appear to "indicate that it has been assigned to an identified assignee [e.g., Lender] other than the purchaser," so FinCo enjoys priority if subsection (a) applies. And FinCo enjoys priority if subsection (b) applies because knowledge of Lender's financing statement does not give FinCo "knowledge that the purchase violates the rights of the secured party [Lender]." See § 9-330, cmt. 6. Because FinCo enjoys priority, **Answer (C) is correct** and **Answer (D) is incorrect**.

91. **Answer (B) is the correct answer.** Item #1 was an asset acquired by Julia and later transferred to Gourmet Enterprises, a separate legal entity. Lender did not authorize this asset transfer, so its security interest in the item continues under the general rule of section 9-315(a) (no exception applies). And the security interest remains perfected against Gourmet Enterprises under section 9-507 by the original financing statement filed against Julia. Because Lender's interest in Item #1 remains perfected, **Answer (D) is incorrect**. Julia did not transfer Items #2 and #3 to Gourmet Enterprises. Instead, Gourmet Enterprises acquired those items from another party. Therefore section 9-315(a) does not apply (it applies only to transferred assets). Because the facts state that Gourmet Enterprises is a "new debtor," Lender has an enforceable security interest in Items #2 and #3 under sections 9-203(d) and (e). Under section 9-508, the original financing statement filed against Julia is effective to perfect the security interest in assets acquired by Gourmet Enterprises, subject to a significant exception. If the difference between the name of the original debtor ("Julia Childress") and the new debtor ("Gourmet Enterprises, Inc.") is seriously misleading, then the original financing statement will not perfect a security interest in assets acquired by Gourmet Enterprises more than four months after it became bound under the original security agreement. The difference in names appears to be seriously misleading under section 9-506(c) because a search against "Gourmet Enterprises, Inc." is not likely to reveal the prior filing against "Julia Childress." Therefore, the original financing statement is ineffective to perfect a security interest in Item #3, which Gourmet Enterprises purchased on November 1, more than four months after Gourmet Enterprises became a new debtor in June. The original financing statement is effective, however, to perfect a security interest in Item #2, which Gourmet Enterprises acquired on August 1, within the four-month period. Because Lender has a perfected security interest in Items #1 and #2 but not Item #3, **Answer (B) is the correct answer**. **Answer (A) is incorrect** (the answer is overinclusive because it includes Item #3). And **Answer (C) also is incorrect** (the answer is underinclusive because it excludes Item #2).

92. **Answer (B) is the correct answer.** Lender's perfected interest in Item #1 enjoys priority over Bank's perfected interest under section 9-325 because Gourmet Enterprises acquired Item #1 subject to the security interest created by Julia (section 9-315(a)) and that security interest remained perfected when Gourmet Enterprises acquired Item #1 (section 9-507). So **Answer (A) is incorrect**. Lender and Bank each have a perfected security interest in Item #2. Because Bank has filed against Gourmet Enterprises and Lender has filed only against Julia, Bank's interest enjoys priority under section 9-326(a). Thus, **Answers (C) and (D) are incorrect. Answer**

(D) also is incorrect because Bank's perfected security interest in Item #3 enjoys priority over Lender's unperfected security interest under the general rule that a perfected interest trumps an unperfected interest. § 9-322(a)(2).

93. **Answer (D) is the correct answer.** Bank's security agreement included an after-acquired property clause, so its security interest in the computer system attached when Clinic acquired rights in the system on July 1. Because Bank had previously filed a financing statement, Bank's security interest also became perfected on July 1. Dealer's security interest in the computer system became perfected on July 25 when it filed its financing statement (the security agreement [the sales contract] was already in place, Dealer had previously given value in the form of credit, and Clinic had acquired rights in the computer system on July 1). In a priority dispute between two creditors that each hold a perfected security interest, priority generally is awarded to the creditor that filed or perfected first. § 9-322(a)(1). Bank filed on February 4, and its security interest in the computer system became perfected on July 1. Dealer filed its financing statement, and its security interest in the computer system became perfected, on July 25. So under the general priority rule of section 9-322(a)(1), Bank wins. But section 9-322(a) begins with the caveat, "Except as otherwise provided in this section. . . ." And subsection (f)(1) states that subsection (a) is subject to other provisions of Part 3 of Article 9. One of those other provisions is section 9-324(a), which awards priority to the holder of a purchase-money security interest in non-inventory that is perfected no later than the 20th day after the debtor receives possession of the collateral. Dealer can claim priority under this provision. Its security interest is a purchase-money security interest under sections 9-103(a) and (b)(1) (Dealer has engaged in seller financing). The computer system in the hands of Clinic is equipment, rather than inventory. And Dealer perfected its security interest on July 25, within 20 days after Clinic took possession of the computer system on July 8. Therefore, Dealer's security interest in the computer system enjoys priority, and **Answer (D) is the correct answer**. **Answer (A) is incorrect** but would be correct if Dealer could not successfully invoke section 9-324(a). **Answer (B) is incorrect.** Clinic's violation of its contract may create a default and give Bank a cause of action against Clinic, but it has no effect on the priority rules of Article 9. And **Answer (C) is incorrect** because the twenty-day period in section 9-324(a) starts running when Clinic takes possession of the computer system on July 8, not when Dealer's security interest attaches on July 1.

94. **Answer (D) is the correct answer.** Under section 9-324(a), a PMSI in non-inventory enjoys priority over a conflicting security interest if the PMSI is perfected "when the debtor receives *possession* of the collateral or within 20 days thereafter" (emphasis added). The 20-day period starts running not when the debtor acquires rights in the collateral, but when the debtor receives possession of the collateral. Therefore, **Answers (A) and (B) are incorrect**. And PMSI status is dictated by section 9-103, not when (or if) the PMSI is timely (or ever) perfected (so **Answer (C) is incorrect**). Dealer's failure to timely file its financing statement prevents it

from invoking section 9-324(b), leaving Lender with priority under section 9-322(a). But Dealer's security interest continues to remain a PMSI. Therefore, **Answer (D) is the correct answer**.

95.   Through its after-acquired property clause that encumbers equipment, Midtown Bank has a security interest in the photocopier that is perfected by filing. Dealer also has a security interest in the photocopier perfected by filing. Under the general rule of section 9-322(a)(1), Midtown Bank enjoys priority because its filing date (March 7) is earlier than Dealer's filing and perfection date (August 25). But as noted in sections 9-322(a) and (f), the general rule is subject to other priority rules, one of which is section 9-324(a). Under that rule, Dealer's security interest enjoys priority because its security interest is perfected, its interest is a purchase-money security interest under sections 9-103(a) and (b) (dealer financing), the photocopier is not inventory in Farmington's hands, and Dealer perfected its security interest by filing a financing statement on August 25 (which is not later than the 20th day following August 8 — the date on which Farmington took possession of the item).

(Appreciate that the 20-day period begins to run from the date of possession, not the date of attachment — presumably because the former is more easily determinable.)

96.   **Answer (B) is the correct answer.** Both Dealer and Lender can claim a purchase-money security interest in the piano under sections 9-103(a) and (b)(1). Dealer has a PMSI for the 20% down payment (seller financing), and Lender has a PMSI for the remaining 80% of the purchase price (third-party financing). In the hands of Smalltown College, the piano is equipment. And both Dealer (March 24) and Lender (March 15) perfected their security interests in the piano by filing financing statements no later than the 20th day after Smalltown College took possession of the piano (March 7). Therefore, both Dealer and Lender enjoy priority over BigBank under section 9-324(a). As between Dealer and Lender, Dealer's security interest enjoys priority under section 9-324(g)(1), which favors the seller over a third-party financer. See § 9-324, cmt. 13. So Dealer's down payment is repaid first ($2,000), with the remaining $4,000 paid to Lender (to be applied against its $8,000 loan), and BigBank receives nothing. This result is found in **Answer (B), making it the correct answer** and **Answers (A), (C), and (D) incorrect answers**.

97.   **Answer (D) is the correct answer.** Much of the previous analysis remains applicable. Both ABC Finance and Lender are entitled to PMSI super-priority over BigBank under section 9-324(a) as both filed financing statements within the 20-day period following the delivery date of March 7. Section 9-324(g) resolves the priority between ABC Finance and Lender. Neither creditor was the seller, so subsection (g)(1) does not apply. Instead, subsection (g)(2) applies and directs the reader to the general priority rule of section 9-322(a). Under section 9-322(a)(1), Lender enjoys priority because it filed its financing statement on March 15, three days before ABC Finance filed its financing statement on March 18. So Lender gets repaid first and takes the entire $6,000, leaving nothing for ABC Finance and BigBank. This result is found in **Answer (D), making it the correct answer** and **Answers (A), (B), and (C) incorrect answers**.

98. **Answer (A) is the correct answer.** BigBank has an enforceable security interest in the Items through its after-acquired property clause. That interest is perfected under the facts (presumably by filing, as it is not likely that BigBank would take possession of the equipment). Because BigBank filed its financing statement before Dealer did, Dealer will not enjoy priority in any of the Items or proceeds therefrom unless Dealer's security interest is a purchase-money security interest. Prior to the enactment of revised Article 9, some courts held that the inclusion of after-acquired property clauses and future advance clauses destroyed, or transformed, a PMSI into a non-PMSI because cross-collateralization upset the traditional one-to-one relationship between a unit of collateral and its unpaid purchase price. Some courts disagreed, concluding that a security interest could be both a PMSI and a non-PMSI. As revised, Article 9 adopts this latter approach, often referred to as the "dual status rule." See § 9-103(f) and cmt. 7.

Under the dual status rule, Item #1 secures Dealer's debt of $80,000. Because the contract requires application of payments to oldest debts first (enforceable under section 9-103(e)(1)), the $80,000 represents $40,000 unpaid on Item #2 and $40,000 unpaid on Item #3. (The aggregate purchase price of all three items is $150,000. At the time of default, Debtor owes $80,000 to Dealer, indicating that Debtor has repaid $70,000. Under the contract terms, that $70,000 repaid the entire purchase price of Item #1 [$50,000] and part of the purchase price of Item #2 [$20,000].) To the extent that an item secures repayment of its own purchase price, the security interest is a PMSI. But because the purchase price of Item #1 has been paid in full, the security interest in Item #1 is not a PMSI. So Dealer cannot claim any super-priority in Item #1 under section 9-324(a). Instead, Dealer receives $0 and BigBank receives the entire $36,000 under section 9-322(a)(1) because BigBank filed its financing statement before Dealer did. This result is found in **Answer (A), making it the correct answer** and **Answers (B), (C), and (D) incorrect answers**.

99. **Answer (C) is the correct answer.** Under the dual status rule, Item #2 secures Dealer's debt of $80,000. As noted in the previous answer, the $80,000 represents $40,000 unpaid on Item #2 and $40,000 unpaid on Item #3. To the extent that an item secures repayment of its own purchase price, the security interest is a PMSI. So Dealer can claim a PMSI in Item #2 up to $40,000. And Dealer's PMSI enjoys priority over BigBank's security interest under section 9-324(a). So Dealer enjoys priority for $40,000. Dealer cannot claim a PMSI in the extra $5,000. BigBank receives that $5,000 under section 9-322(a)(1) because it filed its financing statement before Dealer did. This result is found in **Answer (C), making it the correct answer** and **Answers (A), (B), and (D) incorrect answers**.

100. **Again, Answer (C) is the correct answer.** Under the dual status rule, Item #3 secures Dealer's debt of $80,000. As noted in the previous answer, the $80,000 represents $40,000 unpaid on Item #2 and $40,000 unpaid on Item #3. To the extent that an item secures repayment of its own purchase price, the security interest is a PMSI. So Dealer can claim a PMSI in Item #3 up to $40,000. And Dealer's PMSI enjoys priority over BigBank's security interest under section 9-324(a). So Dealer enjoys priority for $40,000. Dealer cannot claim a PMSI in the extra

$2,500. BigBank receives that $2,500 under section 9-322(a)(1) because it filed its financing statement before Dealer did. This result is found in **Answer (C), making it the correct answer** and **Answers (A), (B), and (D) incorrect answers**.

101.   CompuStore is entitled to the entire $30,000. CompuStore offered dealer financing for 75% of the purchase price and held a purchase-money security interest in the computer system to secure repayment of that $45,000. Blumfield Bank offered third-party financing for the 25% down payment and also held a purchase-money security interest in the computer system to secure repayment of that $15,000. (See §§ 9-103(a), (b).) Both creditors are perfected by filed financing statements, so each can claim the super-priority awarded to purchase-money creditors by section 9-324(a). In such a situation, section 9-324(g)(1) applies and awards priority to CompuStore, the seller (which holds "a security interest securing an obligation incurred as all or part of the price of the collateral"), rather than Blumfield Bank, the third-party financer (which holds "a security interest securing an obligation incurred for value given to enable the debtor to acquire rights in or the use of collateral"). (See § 9-324, cmt. 13 for policy reasons.) As the party with priority, CompuStore gets the entire $30,000 because NOS has repaid only $10,000 of its $45,000 debt to CompuStore.

102.   Blumfield Bank is entitled to $10,000 and Friendly Finance is entitled to $20,000. Both creditors engaged in third-party financing and hold purchase-money security interests in the computer system. (See §§ 9-103(a), (b).) Both creditors are perfected by filed financing statements, so each can claim the super-priority awarded to purchase-money creditors under section 9-324(a). In this situation, where neither purchase-money creditor was the seller, section 9-324(g)(2) applies and awards priority under the general rule of section 9-322(a). Under that rule, Blumfield Bank enjoys priority because it filed its financing statement long before Friendly Finance filed its financing statement or perfected its security interest. As the party with priority, Blumfield Bank receives the first $10,000 (the amount of its unpaid debt), and Friendly Finance gets the remaining $20,000 (leaving it with a $10,000 deficiency claim).

103.   **Answer (C) is the correct answer.** This fact pattern is based upon Example 1 in cmt. 4 to section 9-336. It involves commingling of goods, which is governed by section 9-336 (be careful that you do not confuse commingling of non-goods such as deposit accounts. The rules for such intangibles are found in section 9-315(b)).

Section 9-336 specifically permits the continuation of a security interest in a product or mass (think of a pile of grain) that is made up of commingled goods. Its very existence **makes Answer (A) the incorrect answer**. Also, section 9-336 specifically is a separate rule for security interests in commingled goods and does not mention purchase-money priority, so **Answer (B) is also wrong**.

The choice between Answers (C) and (D) turns on what ratio section 9-336 chooses. That answer is given by section 9-336(f)(2), which states that with respect to properly perfected pre-commingled security interests, "the security interests rank equally in proportion to the value of the collateral at the time it became commingled goods." That means the 3:5 ratio (or $300 to $500) found in Answer (C) is the appropriate choice. It reflects the relative values of the collateral, the proper choice, rather than the ratio in Answer (D), which is keyed to debt, not the value of the collateral. Thus, **Answer (D) is incorrect**.

104. **Answer (D) is the correct answer.** This is a priority problem, so we start with the baseline rule for priority between two consensual secured parties: the first person to file or perfect has priority. § 9-322(a)(1). This baseline rule has nothing to do with being paid, or with the manner in which repossession is undertaken. Thus **Answers (A) and (B) are incorrect**. Answer (C) looks like it is attempting to meet one exception to the "first to file or perfect" rule: purchase-money priority. That takes us to section 9-324.

Under section 9-324, secured parties with purchase-money security interests can obtain priority over secured parties who have already filed their financing statements. Does AirCon have a purchase-money security interest? Yes; it is retaining title until paid, which sections 1-201(b)(35) and 2-401(1) convert into a security interest, and because the security interest secures the purchase price of the property encumbered, it is a purchase-money security interest. § 9-103(a).

The way in which this leapfrog in priority is obtained depends on the type of collateral at issue. Here, the air conditioners are clearly Flakey's inventory. As such, to gain priority, AirCon will have to comply with section 9-324(b). This subsection deliberately makes it more difficult to take a purchase-money security interest with priority in inventory than it does to take a purchase-money security interest in other goods, such as equipment (which would be governed by section 9-324(a)). The increase in formality and difficulty is due primarily to the nature of inventory (it is bought to be sold), and the position of the general lender who finances a debtor's inventory purchases.

Section 9-324(b) has four requirements for a purchase-money security interest in inventory to take priority over a security interest in inventory perfected by a previously-filed financing statement: (1) the purchase-money security interest is perfected when the debtor receives possession of the inventory; (2) the purchase-money secured party sends an authenticated notification to the holder of the conflicting security interest; (3) the holder of the conflicting security interest receives the notification within five years before the debtor receives possession of the inventory; and (4) the notification states that the person sending the notification has or expects to acquire a purchase-money security interest in inventory of the debtor and describes the inventory.

The question under these facts is whether the voicemail was an "authenticated notification," and thus met the requirements of item (2) above (which requirement is found in section 9-324(b)(2)). "Authenticate" is defined in section 9-102(a)(7), where it is defined to mean "(A) to sign; or (B) to execute or otherwise adopt a symbol, or encrypt or similarly process a record in whole or in part, with the present intent of the authenticating person to identify the person and adopt or accept a record." Voicemail really does not fit any of these descriptions, and thus AirCon did not satisfy the requirements of section 9-324(b), thereby **making Answer (C) the incorrect answer, and Answer (D) the correct answer,** through a simple application of the general "first to file or perfect" rule of section 9-322.

105.   **Answer (C) is the correct answer.** Initially, we can **eliminate Answer (D);** under these circumstances, with multiple defaults, Jake (the debtor) will not obtain the cart. But what of the other claimants? We can eliminate the IRS, and hence **eliminate Answer (A)**, because the IRS lien is subsequent to both Albert's and Henry's lien, and the IRS does not attempt to disturb the priority of existing liens. See generally 26 U.S.C. §§ 6321-6323.

      As between Henry and Albert, Albert filed first; and, under the first to file or perfect rule of section 9-322(a), Albert enjoys a presumption that he will prevail. The fact that Albert's debtor (Beth) sold the cart to Jake does not affect Albert's perfected position. The interest will continue notwithstanding sale or exchange under section 9-315(a)(1), and the change in the debtor (who, pursuant to section 9-102(a)(28), is defined as the entity who owns the collateral) does not make the financing statement ineffective under section 9-507(a)).

      But is Henry's interest a purchase-money interest? Yes, the security interest was given to secure credit Henry extended to enable Jake to purchase the cart. § 9-103(b). Does it qualify for purchase-money priority? Yes, because it is equipment, the only requirement for such priority is that the security interest be perfected before or within twenty days of delivery, § 9-324(a). That is the case here. Thus, Henry will have priority, notwithstanding his later filing of a financing statement, **making Answer (C) the correct answer** and **Answer (B) an incorrect answer**.

er. **Answer (A) is incorrect**. Friendly Furniture
ndra and can claim a PMSI in the furniture under
ndra's hands, the furniture was a consumer good.
PMSI in consumer goods, its security interest is
ection 9-309(1). **Answer (C) also is incorrect.**
rest survives the sale under section 9-315(a)(1)
ized. And the security interest remains perfected;
to refile a financing statement against Jill, the new
)7(a). But even though Friendly Furniture's interest
ale, Jill's ownership interest enjoys priority under
oke the protection afforded by that section (often
le" provision) because the furniture was a consumer
remains a consumer good in Jill's hands; Jill had no
re's security interest; Jill gave value for the furniture;
never filed a financing statement. Because Jill has
f Friendly Furniture's security interest, **Answer (B) is**
Answer (D) also is incorrect. The Internet sale may
use of action against Sandra, but the contract violation
ty rules of Article 9, or the rights given by Article 9 to
o the Friendly Furniture contract.

ect answer. Section 9-320(b) favors a buyer over the
if certain conditions are met. One condition is that the
umer goods in the hands of the buyer. § 9-320(b)(3). And
the sale occurs before the purchase-money creditor files
9-320(b)(4). Both conditions are present in Answer (A),
correct answer. **Answer (B) is incorrect**. A lien creditor
st arises after the purchase-money creditor's interest is
automatic   will lose a priority dispute, whether or not the purchase-
money creditor has filed a financing statement. § 9-317(a)(2)(A). **Answer (C) also**
is incorrect because a party that purchases consumer goods for resale as its own
inventory cannot invoke the protection afforded to buyers by sections 9-320(a) or
(b), whether or not the purchase-money creditor has filed a financing statement.
The buyer is not protected by section 9-320(a) because the goods are not inventory
in the hands of the seller, so the buyer is not a buyer in the ordinary course of
the seller's business. And the buyer is not protected by section 9-320(b) because
the buyer is purchasing the goods for use as inventory, not consumer goods. Finally,
Answer (D) is incorrect because a purchase-money creditor's failure to file a
financing statement will not affect its automatic perfection, or the nature of its
secured claim, if the debtor files a bankruptcy petition.

108.   No, Article 9 does not permit GCB to recover the piano from Ima. GCB can invoke section 9-201(a) (under which its security interest is effective against Ima except as otherwise provided elsewhere in the UCC) and section 9-315(a) (under which its security interest continues after an unauthorized disposition — such as this one, since Ima did not use cash or a credit card as a form of payment — except as otherwise provided in Article 9). But under section 9-320(a), Ima acquired the piano free of GCB's security interest created by her seller, Warren County Music Company, because Ima is a "buyer in ordinary course of business" as defined in section 1-201(b)(9). She falls within the definition because she has bought goods (the piano) in good faith (section 1-201(b)(20) — no facts suggest otherwise) and without knowledge "that the sale violates the rights of another person in the goods" (as contrasted with her knowledge merely of GCB's security interest). Furthermore, the piano is inventory in the hands of her seller so Warren County Music Company is in the business of selling goods of this kind. And, because Ima's execution of a promissory note was an industry practice for such an expensive purchase, the sale comported with "the usual or customary practices in the kind of business" in which Warren County Music Company was engaged.

109.   Yes, Article 9 permits GBC to recover the photocopier from Ingrid. GCB can invoke section 9-201(a), under which its security interest is effective against Ingrid except as otherwise provided elsewhere in the UCC. And GCB can invoke section 9-315(a), under which its security interest continues after an unauthorized disposition (such as this one, since Ingrid bought a piece of equipment, rather than a unit of inventory) except as otherwise provided in Article 9. Ingrid cannot invoke the protection afforded to buyers under section 9-320(a) because Ingrid is not a "buyer in ordinary course of business" as defined in section 1-201(b)(9) since Warren County Music Company is not in the business of selling photocopiers. Also, Ingrid cannot invoke the protection afforded to buyers under section 9-320(b) because the photocopier is not a consumer goods in the hands of her seller, Warren County Music Company, who had filed a financing statement against the photocopier. And because GCB's financing statement against Warren County Music Company remains effective to perfect GCB's security interest after the sale under section 9-507(a), Ingrid cannot invoke the protection afforded to buyers by section 9-317(b).

110.   **Answer (C) is the correct answer.** When collateral is covered by a certificate of title statute, that statute dictates the means of perfection. It is as if compliance with the certificate of title statute is the equivalent of filing a financing statement. § 9-311(b). Thus, SlowBank was perfected in the Suburban when Harriet sold it to Fairway, and under sections 9-315(a) and 9-102(a), its interest continued in the goods. This is so regardless of whether Harriet paid SlowBank or not, and would especially be the case if Fairway paid less than the debt secured (of course, if Harriet paid the debt in full, she would be entitled to removal of the notation on the certificate of title). Thus, **Answer (D) is incorrect**.

QuickBank was also perfected in the Suburban when Fairway acquired it. The exception to the certificate of title statutes is found in section 9-311(d), which makes perfection by filing a financing statement appropriate when the collateral subject to the certificate of title is held as inventory by the debtor. As between QuickBank and SlowBank, SlowBank would prevail at this point (while the car was in the possession of Fairway). Thus, **Answer (B) is incorrect**.

Bart is a "buyer in ordinary course of business" from Fairway under section 1-201(b)(9), and thus will take free under section 9-320(a) of any security interest created by his seller, Fairway. Unfortunately for Bart, that is only QuickBank; Fairway had nothing to do with the creation of the security interest by Harriet in favor of SlowBank. So **Answer (A) is an incorrect answer**. With no rule or statute to cut off or eliminate SlowBank's interest, it will prevail in a replevin action, and thus **Answer (C) is the correct answer**. (In the real world, Fairway would have breached the implied warranty of title found in section 2-312 and would be personally liable to Bart for any losses. But such a warranty is only as sound as Fairway is, and if Fairway is in default to QuickBank, its unsecured promises may not be worth much.)

111. **Answer (B) is the correct answer**. Under the general rule of section 9-201(a), a buyer acquires collateral subject to any existing security interest. But subsection (a) begins with the caveat: "Except as otherwise provided in the Uniform Commercial Code. . . ." The quoted language indicates that some provisions permit a buyer to acquire collateral free of a security interest created by the seller. One of those provisions is section 9-315(a). But Greg cannot invoke that provision because Kirby Piano did not authorize its customer, Heather, to sell the piano free and clear of the security interest. So **Answer (A) is incorrect**. Another provision is section 9-320(a), which protects buyers in the ordinary course of business. But to be a "buyer in ordinary course of business" as defined at section 1-201(b)(9), one must buy the goods from a person "in the business of selling goods of that kind." Perhaps rephrased, the goods must be inventory in the hands of the buyer's seller. The piano was equipment in the hands of Heather, so Greg is not a buyer in the ordinary course. So **Answer (C) is incorrect**. Yet another pro-buyer provision is section 9-320(b). But it applies only when the collateral is a consumer good in the hands of both buyer and seller. Heather held the piano as equipment, so section 9-320(b) is inapplicable and **Answer (D) is incorrect**. Nevertheless, Greg can invoke section 9-317(b) as a buyer that gave value and took delivery of the piano without any knowledge of Kirby's security interest, which, at the time of delivery, was unperfected. True, Kirby's security interest was perfected by the Illinois filing. But that Illinois filing lapsed in August, four months after Heather relocated her studio in April to California. § 9-316(a)(2). And the effect of that lapse is that the security interest "is deemed never to have been perfected as against a purchaser of the collateral for value," such as Greg. § 9-316(b). Therefore, section 9-317(b) permits Greg to acquire the piano free of Kirby's security interest, **making Answer (B) the correct answer**.

Observe that Kirby would have avoided this unfortunate result if it had filed a financing statement in California before Greg acquired the piano. Article 9 encourages Kirby, and other secured parties, to confirm the location of the debtor at least once every four months.

112. **Answer (D) is the correct answer**. Section 9-201(a) states the general rule that a security agreement is effective not only between the parties (Lender and Dealer), but also against purchasers of the collateral (Edith). And under section 9-315(a),

Lender's security interest in the refrigerator survives the unauthorized sale. Both sections 9-201(a) and 9-315(a) are subject to other provisions of Article 9, one of which is section 9-320(a). That section permits a "buyer in ordinary course of business" to acquire collateral free of a security interest created by the buyer's seller (Dealer), "even if the security interest is perfected and the buyer knows of its existence." Under the last part of the quoted language, Edith's mere knowledge of Lender's security interest does disqualify her from the protection afforded by section 9-320(a). Also, under the definition of "buyer in ordinary course of business" (section 1-201(b)(9)), Edith can be a buyer in the ordinary course of business even if the sale violates the security agreement as long as Edith does not have knowledge of the violation. As noted in section 9-320, cmt. 3: "Reading the definition together with the rule of law results in the buyer's taking free if the buyer merely knows that a security interest covers the goods but taking subject if the buyer knows, in addition, that the sale violates a term in an agreement with the secured party." Therefore, **Answer (C) is an incorrect answer.** The fact that the sale violates the security agreement, by itself, does not prevent Edith from being a buyer in the ordinary course of business. She did not have knowledge that the sale violated the terms of the agreement. Furthermore, the sale "comports with the usual or customary industry practices in the kind of business in which the seller is engaged. . . ." § 1-201(b)(9). Therefore, **Answer (A) is an incorrect answer**. Under section 1-201(b)(9), a buyer in the ordinary course of business must be buying goods from a party that is "in the business of selling goods of that kind." Perhaps rephrased, the focus is on the ordinary course of the seller's business and its use of the collateral, not the buyer's use. And Dealer is in the business of selling refrigerators. The fact that Edith intended to use the refrigerator as a consumer good, rather than inventory, is irrelevant and **makes Answer (B) an incorrect answer**. Edith meets the requirements of section 1-201(b)(9), making her a buyer in the ordinary course of business and **Answer (D) the correct answer**. As a result, Edith acquires the refrigerator free and clear of Lender's security interest.

113. Under section 9-317(a)(2), the general rule used to resolve priority disputes between lien creditors and secured parties, Mason's lien enjoys priority because Dealer had not yet filed its financing statement (and therefore was unperfected) when Mason's lien arose on September 10. But this general rule is expressly subject to section 9-317(e), which awards priority to a security interest that (i) attaches before the lien arises, (ii) enjoys purchase-money status, and (iii) is perfected by a financing statement filed no later than the 20th day after the debtor receives delivery of the collateral. The problem states that Dealer retained an enforceable security interest on September 1, so the interest attached before Mason's lien arose on September 10. And Dealer has engaged in typical seller financing, retaining a security interest to secure repayment of the unpaid purchase price of an item sold on credit, so its security interest enjoys purchase-money status under sections 9-103(a) and (b). Therefore, if Dealer files its financing statement no later than September 25 — the 20th day after Debtor received delivery of the Equipment on September 5 — its security interest will enjoy priority. So the judge should rule in favor of Dealer if Dealer filed its financing statement on September 18 or September 23, but the judge should rule in favor of Mason if Dealer filed its financing statement on September 28.

The purpose of section 9-317(e) is to protect purchase-money creditors against the risk that an unsecured creditor will obtain a lien on collateral during the gap period between attachment and perfection. This gap period arises because many purchase-money creditors do not file a financing statement until after the goods have been delivered to the debtor-buyer.

114. **Answer (A) is the correct answer.** The filing officer's misfiling does not affect the effectiveness of Bank's financing statement. The risk of misfiling is borne by those who search, rather than those who file. § 9-517. So Bank's security interest did become perfected, and **Answer (D) is incorrect.** The applicable priority rule between a secured party and a lien creditor is found in section 9-317(a)(2). Under that section, the secured party enjoys priority if its security interest is perfected when the lien creditor's interest arises (or, alternatively, the security interest is not perfected solely because the secured party has yet to give value). Tim became a lien creditor on March 5, but Bank did not perfect its interest until later, when it filed its financing statement on March 9. Because Bank's security interest was not perfected when Tim became a lien creditor, Tim's interest enjoys priority, **making Answer (A) correct and Answer (B) incorrect. Answer (C) is incorrect** because Bank's security interest is not a PMSI (Debtor already owned the collateral). Therefore, the grace period afforded by section 9-317(e) to purchase-money creditors in a dispute with a lien creditor is not applicable.

115. Under section 9-323(b), the sheriff should pay $80,000 to Bank and $20,000 to Jeremy. That statute makes Bank's security interest subordinate to Jeremy's

155

property interest "to the extent that the security interest secures an advance made more than 45 days after [Jeremy] becomes a lien creditor." Rephrased, Bank's security interest enjoys priority with respect to all advances funded on or before the 45th day after Jeremy became a lien creditor (this 45-day period is absolute and is not shortened if the secured creditor acquires knowledge of the competing lien during the period). Jeremy became a lien creditor on September 15, so advances funded by Bank before October 31 — $30,000 on September 1, $20,000 on October 1, and $30,000 on October 28 — are entitled to priority. The $20,000 advanced on November 4 is not protected because it was funded more than 45 days after Jeremy became a lien creditor. So Bank is entitled to receive $80,000 (covering its first three advances), and Jeremy is entitled to receive the remaining $20,000.

Observe that Bank cannot take advantage of the post-45-day-protection offered by sections 9-323(b)(1) and (b)(2) because Bank had knowledge of the lien on October 25 (before the 45-day period ended) and did not fund the advances pursuant to a prior commitment entered into without knowledge of the lien.

116. Yes, the assumptions permit the Bank to receive the entire $100,000. Bank's agreement to loan $150,000 to Debtor in one or more advances means that all of the advances were funded "pursuant to commitment" as defined at section 9-102(a)(68). Even though Bank is not obligated to fund an advance if an Event of Default exists, the advances are funded "pursuant to commitment." This is so because the definition of "pursuant to commitment" is met even if "a subsequent event of default or other event not within the secured party's control has relieved or may relieve the secured party from its obligation." Because Bank funded the four advances pursuant to commitment, all of the advances are protected against Jeremy's competing $60,000 claim under section 9-323(b)(2) because the commitment was entered into on September 1, before Bank discovered Jeremy's competing claim on October 25. As all of Bank's advances enjoy priority, the sheriff should pay the entire $100,000 to Bank.

117. **Answer (B) is the correct answer.** This problem involves what are sometimes referred to as mechanics' or artisans' liens, which are liens provided by statute in favor of those who add value or repair some item of personalty. These statutes often condition perfection or enforcement of these liens upon possession by the repair person of the item to which value has been added. This sends the clear message that the person repairing or adding value must get paid before it relinquishes possession.

Article 9 deals with these liens in section 9-333(b), which gives priority to the holder of the possessory lien. That means that such liens do not follow the first in time rule. To use high-falutin' language, this is an example of non-temporal priority. But to obtain the priority of section 9-333(b), the non-Article 9 lien has to be a possessory lien. A "possessory lien" is defined in section 9-333(a) as a lien "(1) which secures payment or performance of an obligation for services or materials furnished with respect to goods by a person in the ordinary course of the person's business; (2) which is created by statute or rule of law in favor of the person; and (3) whose effectiveness depends on the person's possession of the goods."

This definition requires us to look at the text of the statutory lien to see if it meets all of these requirements, which it seems to do. The statute satisfies (1) by giving to the person making repairs a lien on the goods repaired "for his reasonable charges for the balance due for such work done and materials furnished." One might quibble here that the statute quoted does not require the repairer to perform the repairs in the ordinary course of the repairer's business as required by section 9-333(a)(1), but the fact that it was done in the ordinary course suffices. (The facts would be changed if you, a law student, fixed a friend's bicycle; under the statute you would have a possessory lien; under section 9-333(b), it would not have priority.) The lien is created by statute, and it thus satisfies paragraph (2) of section 9-333(a). Finally, the state statute makes the lien clearly "dependent upon possession," so paragraph (3) is met.

As a result of this analysis, the state statute means that as between Jim and CR, CR wins. This **eliminates Answers (A) and (D)**, which have Jim prevailing. As between CR and FirstBank, CR wins since, as shown above, the lien given to CR by statute qualifies for the priority under section 9-333. So **Answer (B) is the correct answer** and **Answer (C) is an incorrect answer**.

Note also that this result does not vary depending on whether FirstBank is perfected or not. So the characterization of the collateral as a consumer good (so that perfection would be automatic and not require a financing statement, § 9-309(1)) or as equipment (which would require a financing statement to perfect) is irrelevant.

118. **Answer (B) is the correct answer.** First, focus on what is at issue: the violin. Thus, the security agreement and financing statements covering all other assets are irrelevant; there is no notion under Article 9 that improper attachment in one area (such as an attempt to use "all assets" in the security agreement, a practice that section 9-108 does not permit) infects other independent efforts at attachment. Another way to say this is to note that section 9-203(b)(3) is written in the disjunctive; compliance with any sub-paragraph will be sufficient to complete attachment.

This analysis indicates that **Answer (A) is incorrect**, since it focuses on non-violin collateral. It also indicates that **Answer (C) is incorrect**, since nothing in Article 9 validates a notion of "bad faith" non-attachment.

That leaves Answers (B) and (D). **Answer (D) is wrong** in that local filing is not authorized for anything but fixtures, "as-extracted collateral," and timber to be cut. § 9-501.

But is Answer (B) right? There is no authenticated security agreement. But that does not matter here. An alternate manner of attachment and perfection is the pledge. Under section 9-203(b)(3)(B), attachment occurs if there is value (here present from the past loan), the debtor has rights in the collateral (he owns the violin), and "the collateral is not a certificated security and is in the possession of the secured party under Section 9-313 pursuant to the debtor's security agreement." Since a security agreement is defined in section 9-102(a)(73) as "an agreement that creates or provides for a security interest," and since through section 9-102(c) we incorporate Article 1's definition of "agreement" ("the bargain of the parties in fact as found in their language or by implication from other circumstances"), we can see that so long as the secured party has possession (as is the case here), the agreement to provide security need not be found in a writing or a record. We thus have attachment.

But what about the priority contest? Under section 9-317(a), a judgment creditor such as Crispen is junior only to a perfected security interest; even if Jim's interested attached by way of pledge, it will lose to Crispen if it is unperfected. Was Jim perfected? Jim had possession of the violin. Because the violin is a "good," that possession sufficed for perfection under section 9-313(a) ("a secured party may perfect a security interest in . . . goods, . . . by taking possession of the collateral"). Thus, Jim held a perfected security interest in the violin, and **Answer (B) is the correct answer**.

119. **Answer (B) is the correct answer.** "Commercial financing security" refers to "(i) paper of a kind ordinarily arising in commercial transactions, (ii) accounts receivable, (iii) mortgages on real property, and (iv) inventory." 26 U.S.C. § 6323(c)(2)(C). Accounts and inventory are expressly mentioned, **making Answers (A) and (C) incorrect answers**. Chattel paper ordinarily arises in commercial transactions, **making Answer (D) incorrect**. Equipment is not mentioned in the definition, **making Answer (B) the correct answer**.

120. **Answer (C) is the correct answer.** Under the Federal Tax Lien Statutes (26 U.S.C. §§ 6321-6323), advances funded after the IRS files its tax lien notice may enjoy priority if they were funded (i) within the 45-day period following the filing date of the tax lien notice and (ii) without knowledge of the tax lien notice. 26 U.S.C. § 6323(c)(2)(A), (d). The IRS filed its tax lien notice on August 1, so the 45-day period ended on September 15. But Bank discovered the tax lien filing a few days earlier on September 5. So only advances funded prior to discovery are protected. Those advances aggregate $600,000, **making Answer (C) the correct answer** and **Answers (A), (B), and (D) incorrect answers**.

Appreciate that, unlike section 9-323(b), the 45-day period under the Federal Tax Lien Statutes is not absolute. The period can be terminated by the secured party's knowledge of the competing tax lien, and the period cannot be extended if the debtor and the secured party have entered into a binding commitment without knowledge of the competing tax lien.

121. **Answer (A) is the correct answer.** As used by Fashions Group, the dresses and shoes are inventory, a type of commercial financing security. 26 U.S.C. § 6323(c)(2)(C)(iv). So **Answer (B) is incorrect.** Bank's discovery of the tax lien notice does terminate the 45-day period of protection for advances funded after the tax lien notice is filed. 26 U.S.C. § 6323(c)(2)(A). But Bank's discovery of the tax lien notice does not terminate the 45-day period of protection for collateral acquired by the debtor after the tax lien notice is filed. 26 U.S.C. § 6323(c)(2)(B). So **Answer (C) is incorrect**. (The difference is justified because Bank's knowledge can affect its own funding decision but not necessarily the debtor's purchasing activity.) Because the collateral is commercial financing security and was timely acquired on September 9 (within 45 days following the filing of the tax lien notice on August 1), Bank's security interest enjoys priority, **making Answer (A) the correct answer. Answer (D) is incorrect**, as the relevant 45-day period of protection commences on the date of the tax lien filing, not the date of the assessment.

122. **Answer (D) is the correct answer.** The machines are equipment, which is not included within the definition of "commercial financing security." 26 U.S.C.

§ 6323(c)(2)(C). But the definition of "commercial financing security" becomes relevant only with respect to collateral acquired by the debtor after the IRS files its tax lien notice. Fashions Group acquired these machines on July 20, before the IRS filed its tax lien notice on August 1. So the fact that the collateral is not "commercial financing security" has no effect on priority, **making Answer (A) an incorrect answer. Answer (B) is incorrect** because the tax lien filing, not assessment, dictates priority. And **Answer (C) also is incorrect.** If anything, Bank's lack of knowledge at the time of purchase would favor Bank, not the IRS.

123. **Answer (C) is the correct answer.** Lender has the rights provided by Part 6 of Article 9 after Debtor defaults. § 9-601(a). Those rights arise by statute, not by contract, so the fact that the loan papers may not mention the rights is irrelevant. Lender's ability to repossess the collateral after default is a statutory right under section 9-609(a)(1), so **Answer (A) is incorrect.** Debtor's liability for any post-foreclosure deficiency arises by statute under section 9-615(d)(2), so **Answer (B) is incorrect.** Lender's ability to contact Debtor's customers and request them to remit payment directly to Lender also arises by statute under section 9-607(a)(1), **making Answer (D) an incorrect answer**. Lender's application of foreclosure proceeds is dictated by section 9-615(a). Subsection (a)(1) permits Lender to apply some of the proceeds to pay its reasonable legal fees and expenses only "to the extent provided for by agreement and not prohibited by law. . . ." So if the loan documents are silent on this matter, Lender's counsel should be concerned, **making Answer (C) the correct answer**.

124. **Answer (C) is the correct answer.** As a general rule, a secured party is obligated to send a foreclosure notice to the debtor. § 9-611(b), (c)(1). But section 9-611(d) excuses notice "if the collateral is perishable or threatens to decline speedily in value or is of a type customarily sold on a recognized market." So **Answers (A) and (B) are incorrect answers**. Notice is excused in the first instance on the theory that the debtor will suffer more harm (an increased deficiency) during the time it takes to deliver notice. Notice is excused in the second instance because the recognized market offers an objective benchmark against which the actual proceeds can be compared for commercial reasonableness. That same reason supports excusing notice if the collateral is the subject of widely distributed standard price quotations, but surprisingly section 9-611(d) contains no such exception (**making Answer (C) the correct answer**). (Appreciate, however, that some collateral may be both of a type customarily sold on a recognized market *and* subject to widely distributed standard price quotations, in which case notice is excused for the latter, but not the former, reason.) And **Answer (D) is incorrect** because section 9-624(a) permits a debtor to waive its right to a disposition notice by authenticating a waiver after default.

125. **Answer (C) is the correct answer.** Under section 9-612, AmeriBank can invoke the safe harbor on timeliness by sending notice no later than ten days before the scheduled sale. The sale is scheduled for August 14, so AmeriBank must send its notice no later than August 4. **This result is found in Answer (C), the correct answer**, and not in **Answers (A), (B), and (D), all of which are incorrect answers**.

126. **Answer (B) is the correct answer.** In addition to the information found in section 9-613(1), a disposition notice in a consumer-goods transaction also must include

"(B) a description of any liability for a deficiency of the person to which the notification is sent; (C) a telephone number from which the amount that must be paid to the secured party to redeem the collateral under Section 9-623 is available; and (D) a telephone number or mailing address from which additional information concerning the disposition and the obligation secured is available." § 9-614(1). The only answer with information required by the quoted passage is Answer (B). **Answer (A) is incorrect**. Although Article 9 permits the debtor to attend a public disposition and purchase the collateral, the notice need not mention that the debtor may do so. The notice need not describe the nature of the default, so **Answer (C) is incorrect**. And **Answer (D) also is incorrect**. Article 9 does not provide the debtor with any statutory right to a strict foreclosure (a process by which the secured creditor retains the collateral and forgives all or part of the secured debt).

127. **Answer (C) is the correct answer. Answer (A) is incorrect** because the collateral is sold on a recognized market, so notice is excused under section 9-611(d). **Answer (B) is incorrect** because section 9-611(b) only requires Bank to "send" notice; the statute does not require receipt. **Answer (D) is incorrect** because the information is not required by section 9-613(1). **Answer (C) is correct** because the notice is missing a required piece of information: the time of sale. § 9-613(1)(E).

128. The $2 million is allocated according to the distribution scheme in section 9-615. First, under section 9-615(a)(1), BankTwo can recover its repossession and disposition-related expenses if they are "reasonable" (these expenses include attorney fees and legal expenses "to the extent provided for by agreement and not prohibited by law"). Second, under section 9-615(a)(2), BankTwo receives $400,000 — the amount of its secured debt. Third, under section 9-615(a)(3), BankThree receives $300,000 as a holder of a security interest subordinate (under section 9-322(a)) to the security interest of BankTwo — but only if BankTwo received from BankTwo an "authenticated demand for proceeds before distribution of the proceeds is completed." And fourth, under section 9-615(d)(1), the remaining amount (the "surplus") should be returned to Debtor. (Notice that BankOne, the senior creditor, does not share in the proceeds distribution under section 9-615(a), for a reason explained in the next answer.)

129. The answer is found in section 9-617(a). Under (a)(1), the foreclosure sale transfers all of Debtor's property interest in the Asset to the successful buyer. Under (a)(2), the foreclosure sale terminates BankTwo's security interest. And under (a)(3), the foreclosure sale terminates the subordinate security interest held by BankThree, whether or not BankThree shared in the proceeds distribution under section 9-615(a)(3). But the foreclosure sale does not discharge the senior security interest held by BankOne (which is the statutory protection that BankOne receives in lieu of sharing in the proceeds under section 9-615(a)). Instead, BankOne's security interest survives the sale.

130. As noted in the answer to the previous question, BankOne's security interest survives the foreclosure sale. Therefore, Buyer acquired the Asset subject to a $500,000 encumbrance. Buyer has thus paid too much for the Asset because its current fair market value, if unencumbered, is only $2 million. Buyer has suffered an immediate

loss (at least on paper) of $500,000, because the value of the Asset, as encumbered, is only $1.5 million (this loss is calculated as follows: $2 million fair market value if unencumbered — [$2 million purchase price + $500,000 security interest]). If the unencumbered Asset's fair market value had been more than $2.5 million, Buyer would have received a bargain. For example, Buyer can show a profit (at least on paper) of $400,000 if the fair market value of the unencumbered Asset had been $2.9 million (this gain is calculated as follows: $2.9 million fair market value if unencumbered — [$2 million purchase price + $500,000 security interest]).

131. **Answer (B) is the correct answer.** A debtor's right of redemption is codified at section 9-623(a). Except in a consumer-goods transaction (inapplicable to this problem, which involves inventory and equipment), a debtor may waive its redemption right, **making Answer (A) an incorrect answer**. As a general rule, sections 9-611(b) and (c) obligate a secured party to send a disposition notice to the debtor. A debtor can waive its right to receive the notice under section 9-625(a), but only after a default, so **Answer (C) is incorrect**. Under section 9-610(b), all aspects of a collateral disposition must be commercially reasonable. Section 9-602(7) bars waiver or modification of that obligation, so **Answer (D) is incorrect**. A debtor is entitled to surplus proceeds under section 9-615(d)(1). Section 9-602(5) bars waiver or modification of this right, **making Answer (B) the correct answer**.

132. **Answer (B) is the correct answer.** Partial strict foreclosure is prohibited only in a consumer transaction. § 9-620(g). But the business nature of Bank's loan to Lisa prevents this transaction from being a consumer transaction. § 9-102(a)(26). So partial strict foreclosure is an option, and **Answer (A) is incorrect**. Sometimes the secured party can be forced to dispose of collateral if a certain percentage of the debt has been repaid. (The policy for this rule is that if a high percentage of the debt has been repaid, then presumably the debtor has equity in the collateral that will render a surplus upon disposition.) But this rule applies only if the collateral is consumer goods. § 9-620(e). Lisa has secured the loan with investment property, however, so the rule does not apply and **Answer (C) is incorrect**. Bank is obligated to send its proposal to any secured creditor who has perfected a competing security interest by timely filing a financing statement. § 9-621(a). Priority is irrelevant, so **Answer (D) is incorrect**. Bank may accept collateral in full or partial satisfaction of Lisa's debt only if Lisa consents to Bank's proposal. § 9-620(a)(1). Lisa's extended silence can be deemed consent under section 9-620(c), **making Answer (B) the correct answer**. (Observe that silence cannot be deemed consent to a proposal of *partial* strict foreclosure. § 9-620(c)(1).)

133. **Answer (D) is the correct answer.** Section 9-610(b) imposes on Dealer the duty to conduct any disposition in a "commercially reasonable" manner. Section 9-602(7) prohibits Dealer from waiving or varying that duty, **making Answers (A) and (B) incorrect answers**. Notwithstanding the statutory prohibition against waiver or variance of the duty of commercial reasonableness, section 9-603(a) permits Dealer and its customers to "determine by agreement the standards measuring the fulfillment of . . . the duties of a secured party under a rule stated in Section 9-602 if the standards are not *manifestly* unreasonable" (emphasis added). Therefore, **Answer (D), rather than Answer (C), is the correct answer**.

Whether a standard is unreasonable, manifestly unreasonable, or unconscionable must be determined by specific facts. Therefore, it is possible that courts may not reach uniform results in their conclusions, and their conclusions could be shaped by a variety of factors, including the nature of the transaction and the sophistication and negotiating strength of the parties. Even so, Dealer is encouraged to utilize section 9-602 in an attempt to define the contours of "commercial reasonableness," if for no other reason than to reduce the likelihood of litigation on (or to guide a court in its review of) Dealer's compliance with section 9-610(b).

134. **Answer (C) is the correct answer.** Former Article 9 did not clearly articulate what would happen to a deficiency claim arising from a disposition that was not commercially reasonable. So courts developed three responses over time. One response, the "absolute bar rule," favored the debtor by completely barring recovery of any deficiency, regardless of the severity of the breach or the resulting harm. Another response permitted the debtor to counterclaim for, and recover, any damages that it could prove resulted from the creditor's noncompliance. And a third response was a presumption that compliance would have generated proceeds equal to the debt (and thus no deficiency). The presumption was rebuttable, so the secured party could offer evidence that compliance would have generated proceeds less than the unpaid debt, still leaving a deficiency that the creditor should recover. Revised Article 9 adopts this so-called "rebuttable presumption rule." See § 9-626(a) and cmt. 3. Under this test, the court should enter a deficiency judgment of $2,600, calculated by subtracting the proceeds generated from a commercially reasonable disposition ($5,000) from the unpaid debt ($7,600). Because the "absolute bar rule" is inapplicable and Dealer offered proof rebutting the statutory presumption, **Answer (A) is incorrect**. The "rebuttable presumption rule" requires a determination of the amount of proceeds generated by a commercially reasonable disposition, not necessarily the fair market value (remember, nonjudicial foreclosures are distress sales that attract bargain hunters). So **Answer (B)**, calculated by subtracting the fair market value ($5,800) from the unpaid debt ($7,600), **is incorrect**. And **Answer (D) is incorrect** because Dealer's own evidence revealed that a commercially reasonable disposition might have generated proceeds in excess of $4,300.

135. **Answer (B) is the correct answer.** As noted in the previous answer, Revised Article 9 adopts the "rebuttable presumption rule" when a noncomplying secured party seeks to recover a deficiency judgment. But this rule does not apply in consumer transactions. See § 9-626(a) ("In an action arising from a transaction, other than a consumer transaction. . . ."). Instead, Revised Article 9 "leave[s] to the court the determination of the proper rules in consumer transactions." § 9-626(c). Under the altered facts, the transaction is a "consumer transaction" under section 9-102(a)(26) because Baxter incurred the debt, and acquired the photocopier, primarily for personal, family, or household reasons. Therefore, the court is free to calculate the deficiency under any rule it chooses to follow. The court will probably follow one of the three rules discussed in the previous answer. The court could follow the "absolute bar rule," leaving no deficiency and **making Answer (A) a possible option (and**, because the question asks you to identify the least likely amount that the court will award, **therefore probably an incorrect answer)**. The court also

might follow the "rebuttable presumption rule," **leaving Answer (C) as a possible option (and therefore probably an incorrect answer)**. Or the court might simply honor Dealer's request for $3,300 in the absence of a counterclaim by Baxter for damages. So **Answer (D) is a possible option (and therefore probably an incorrect answer)**. But most courts disregard deficiencies that utilize the fair market value of the collateral, for at least two reasons. One reason is that nonjudicial foreclosure dispositions are forced dispositions and not likely to generate a price anywhere close to the fair market value (a price negotiated between willing parties). Another reason is the statutory admonition found in section 9-627(a): just because a higher amount could have been generated from a disposition at a different time or different method does not prevent the secured party from proving that the disposition was commercially reasonable. Therefore, **Answer (B)**, a deficiency calculated by using the fair market value, **is the least likely amount that the court will award, and, accordingly, the best of the four answers**.

136. **Answer (A) is the best answer.** A secured party may repossess collateral without judicial process, "if it proceeds without breach of the peace." § 9-609(b)(2). This duty cannot be waived or varied by the parties. § 9-602(6). Nor can the parties attempt to define the contours of acceptable behavior through standards (even if the standards are not manifestly unreasonable). § 9-603(b). Therefore, the self-serving provision in the standard form of security agreement will not shield Otto's Auto's from liability for any breach of the peace, **making Answer (B) an incorrect answer.** The overwhelming number of courts have held that the duty to avoid breaching the peace cannot be delegated; therefore, a secured party will incur liability for any breach of the peace by an independent contractor. *See, e.g., Clark v. Associates Commercial Corp.*, 877 F.Supp. 1439 (D. Kan. 1994); *MBank El Paso, N.A. v. Sanchez*, 836 S.W.2d 151 (Tex. 1992); *see also* § 9-609, cmt. 3 ("In considering whether a secured party has engaged in a breach of the peace . . . courts should hold the secured party responsible for the actions of others taken on the secured party's behalf, including independent contractors engaged by the secured party to take possession of collateral."). Therefore, the fact that Towtruck Tim, an independent contractor, repossessed the vehicle should not protect Otto's Autos from liability for any breach, so **Answer (D) is not the best answer**. The speed and silence with which Towtruck Tim repossessed the vehicle no doubt reduced the likelihood of a confrontation with Keith or a nearby neighbor. But the absence of a confrontation does not necessarily prevent a breach of the peace. Most courts have held that a creditor breaches the peace if it removes collateral from a restricted area. *See, e.g., Henderson v. Security National Bank*, 140 Cal. Rptr. 388 (Ct. App. 1977) (removal of car after breaking lock on garage door); *Bloomquist v. First National Bank*, 378 N.W.2d 81 (Minn. Ct. App. 1985) (removal of collateral from business premises after entering cracked, but taped, window and opening garage door secured by deadbolt lock). Given the well-deserved sanctity afforded by courts to a person's home, the locked or unlocked status of the garage should be irrelevant if the garage door is closed. Indeed, the very act of opening the closed door may be a breach of the peace (if not a violation of the local criminal code). Therefore, **Answer (C) is not the best answer**. Instead, **Answer (A) is the best answer**. If a court does find that the repossession triggered a breach of the

peace, Otto's Autos may be liable. And courts have not hesitated in awarding punitive damages in appropriate cases. *See, e.g., Chrysler Credit Corp. v. Turner*, 553 So.2d 64 (Ala. 1989) ($15,000); *Williamson v. Fowler Toyota, Inc.*, 956 P.2d 858 (Okla. 1988) ($15,000). Opening a garage door, even though unlocked, may merit such an award to discourage similar conduct.

137. **Answer (D) is the correct answer. Answer (A) is not correct** because a reservation of title is treated by law as a reservation of a security interest. §§ 1-201(b)(35); 2-401(1). Thus, when Dave signed the contract of sale, he also signed a "security agreement."

Answer (B) might be correct. The baseline rule is that filing is necessary to perfect all security interests. § 9-310(a). But perfection is not necessary to enforce a security agreement against the debtor; only attachment is. So, if there are no other creditors present, an unperfected secured party can enforce its security agreement **(making Answer (B) an incorrect answer)**. As an aside, Fast Freddie probably is perfected even though Fast Freddie never filed a financing statement. Fast Freddie can rely on automatic perfection (upon attachment) if Fast Freddie has a purchase-money security interest in a consumer good. § 9-309(1). Given that Fast Freddie is reserving title is the same as granting a security interest, and given that the security interest is given to secure payment of the computer's purchase price, the security interest in this case is a purchase-money security interest. § 9-103(a), (b)(1). Is the computer consumer goods? And, if so, at what time does the inquiry take place? Section 9-309 is clear that the relevant time is upon attachment. Attachment, in turn, occurs when the debtor has authenticated a security agreement which describes the collateral, value has been given, and the debtor has rights in the collateral. § 9-203(a), (b). This occurs when both parties become bound upon signing the contract (Dave has a "special property" in the computer as soon as it is "identified" to the contract — § 2-501 — and thus has "rights" in the collateral at that time). We are told that until the computer was physically delivered, Dave's intent was to use it in the education of his daughter — something clearly for personal, family, or household use. It is thus a "consumer good" under section 9-102(a)(23) at the time of attachment, and thus no financing statement need be filed. Fast Freddie is perfected upon attachment. § 9-309(1). But as noted above, perfection is not a prerequisite to enforcement against a debtor who has not filed for bankruptcy.

Answer (C) is incorrect. It summarizes the test of section 9-320 for a buyer in the ordinary course of business, which Dave certainly is. Under section 9-320, however, a buyer takes free not of her seller's interest, but of any security interest the seller created in favor of a third party. Thus, Dave will take free of the security interest of any bank that finances Fast Freddie's inventory, but not of any security interest in favor of Fast Freddie. This leaves **Answer (D) as the correct answer**. Dave has no defense to Fast Freddie's attached (and probably perfected) security interest.

138. **Answer (A) is the correct answer.** Default is not a term that is defined by Article 9. It leaves to the parties the task of defining default. See § 9-601, cmt. 3. That

has been done here, but the parties agreed that any default would be dependent upon written notice. That was not given here, so there was no valid default. Without default, GougeBank could not validly repossess under section 9-609. As a consequence, the taking of the tickets was conversion, making (A) the correct answer.

Although Answer (B) is literally true — GougeBank "could" accelerate, it did not do what was required to do so. **Answer (B) is thus not the correct answer. Answer (C) is not correct** because GougeBank did have a perfected security interest in the tickets — they were received in exchange for collateral, and thus are proceeds under section 9-102(a)(64), and less than twenty days have passed, so perfection is assumed under section 9-315(c). **Answer (D) is not correct** again because regardless of whether it was required to make demand, no default had occurred due to the lack of a writing.

(As an aside, most well-drafted security agreements that favor secured parties do not require written notice in order for a default to exist, or else they require that the notice be given within five to ten days after the default exists.)

139. **Answer (B) is the correct answer.** In this scenario, Flake's customer takes subject to a perfected security interest unless it fits under one of the exceptions. § 9-315(a)(1). One exception is for buyers in the ordinary course of business, found in section 9-320(a). Does the buyer qualify here? Probably not. The definition of a "buyer in ordinary course of business" requires that the purchase be "in the ordinary course." § 1-201(b)(9). Swapping plane tickets for a snowmobile, especially on a "whim," does not qualify as "ordinary course." So GougeBank will likely be able to pursue the buyer.

Answer (A) is incorrect because a secured party may (in the absence of marshaling) pursue any and all collateral. See § 9-601(c). It only gets one "satisfaction," however, which means that it must stop collection efforts against the collateral when the debt secured by the collateral is repaid.

Answer (C) is incorrect because a secured party does not have to refile a financing statement if the name of its debtor changes due to a sale. § 9-507(a). This means that those wanting to check financing statements have to know who sold the collateral to a debtor, but the Code considered this, and thought it the lesser evil (since wash sales and other devices could be used to deprive a secured party of its perfected status if there was a duty to refile).

Answer (D) is incorrect because the buyer in the ordinary course exception in section 9-320(a) applies even if a buyer knows of a filed financing statement.

140. **Answer (D) is the correct answer.** Under 11 U.S.C. § 362(d), a court shall grant relief from the stay if (i) BigBank's security interest is not adequately protected or (ii) Karen has no equity in the vehicle and the vehicle is not necessary to an effective reorganization. Under 11 U.S.C. § 362(g), BigBank (as the party requesting relief) has the burden of proof on Karen's equity in the vehicle, and Karen (the party opposing the relief) has the burden of proof on all other issues, including the issue of adequate protection. This allocation of proof is correctly stated in **Answer (D), making it the correct answer** and **Answers (A), (B), and (C) incorrect answers**.

141. **Answer (A) is the correct answer.** Because the trustee cannot set aside the security interests of either creditor, this problem is merely an Article 9 priority dispute. MedCo, a seller-financer, is claiming a purchase-money security interest in the kidney dialysis machine under sections 9-103(a) and (b)(1). Because MedCo filed its financing statement on August 25, within twenty days after delivering the machine to Clinic on August 9, MedCo's security interest in the machine enjoys priority under section 9-324(a). Bank's security interest in Clinic's remaining equipment enjoys priority under section 9-322(a)(1) because Bank filed its financing statement on July 7, before MedCo filed its financing statement on August 25. Clinic owes $80,000 to MedCo, and the kidney dialysis machine has a value of $90,000. So MedCo has an $80,000 secured claim. Clinic owes $120,000 to Bank, and Bank's claim is secured in an amount equal to the remaining collateral: $60,000. The balance of Bank's claim, $60,000, is unsecured. So Bank has a $60,000 secured claim and a $60,000 unsecured claim, and MedCo has an $80,000 secured claim. This result is found in **Answer (A), making it the correct answer** and **Answers (B), (C), and (D) the incorrect answers**.

142. **Answer (C) is the correct answer.** Normally the act of filing a post-petition financing statement violates the automatic stay. 11 U.S.C. § 362(a)(4), (5). But post-petition perfection is permitted by 11 U.S.C. § 362(b)(3) if "the trustee's rights and powers are subject to such perfection under section 546(b) of this title. . . ." Under 11 U.S.C. § 546(b)(1), a trustee's rights and powers are subject to any Article 9 provision that permits perfection to be effective against a lien creditor that acquired its lien prior to perfection. The applicable Article 9 provision is section 9-317(e), which permits a purchase-money creditor to enjoy priority over the competing (and prior) claim of a lien creditor if the purchase-money creditor's interest is perfected no later than the 20th day after the debtor receives possession of the collateral. As Dealer (a seller-financer) can claim a purchase-money security interest in the refrigerator under sections 9-103(a) and (b)(1), and because Dealer timely filed its financing statement, Dealer can invoke the protection afforded by section 9-317(e). Therefore, Dealer did not violate the automatic stay by filing its financing statement after Restaurant filed its bankruptcy petition.

Answer (A) is incorrect because the refrigerator is equipment, and a purchase-money security interest is automatically perfected only in consumer goods. § 9-309(1). **Answer (B) is incorrect** because only individuals can exempt property from the estate. 11 U.S.C. § 522(b) (indicating that "an individual debtor" may exempt property). And **Answer (D) is incorrect** because Chapter 7 is a liquidation chapter, not a reorganization chapter.

143. **Answer (C) is the correct answer.** An after-acquired property clause is ineffective to encumber post-petition collateral unless the post-petition collateral represents pre-petition proceeds. 11 U.S.C. §§ 552(a), (b)(1). (The purpose of this provision is to free up assets needed by the bankrupt debtor to secure post-petition financing in favor of a creditor that will insist on a first-position security interest in unencumbered collateral.) Under this provision, Bank has a security interest in inventory worth $400,000 to $450,000 calculated as follows: $300,000 (yes; collateral existed on the petition date) + $100,000 (yes; proceeds of pre-petition collateral) + $50,000 (perhaps; the post-petition accounts might have been generated by the sale of pre-petition inventory) + $50,000 (no; this amount does not represent pre-petition collateral or its proceeds). And Bank has a security interest in accounts worth $350,000 to $400,000 calculated as follows: $250,000 (yes; collateral existed on the petition date) + $100,000 (yes; proceeds of pre-petition collateral) + $50,000 (perhaps; the post-petition inventory may have been acquired with cash proceeds of pre-petition accounts) + $50,000 (no; this amount does not represent pre-petition collateral or its proceeds). So Bank has a security interest in accounts and inventory that aggregate $750,000 to $850,000, **making Answer (C) the correct answer** and **Answers (A), (B), and (D) incorrect answers**.

144. **Answer (A) is the correct answer.** The strong-arm clause, a moniker given to 11 U.S.C. § 544(a)(1), gives the trustee the status of a hypothetical lien creditor as of the petition date, together with the rights and powers associated with that status, including the right to "avoid any transfer of property of the debtor" that could be avoided by such a lien creditor as of the petition date. Working in tandem with section 9-317(a)(2), the strong-arm clause permits the trustee to avoid any security interest that is unperfected on the petition date, **making Answer (A) the correct answer. Answers (B) and (C) — both incorrect** — quote language from the actual and constructive fraud tests of the fraudulent transfer provision, 11 U.S.C. § 548(a). And **Answer (D), also incorrect**, is a reference to 11 U.S.C. § 522(f), which permits a consumer debtor to avoid certain judicial liens on, and nonpossessory, nonpurchase-money security interests in, property that otherwise would be exempt in the absence of the encumbrance.

145. **Answer (B) is the correct answer.** Under 11 U.S.C. § 544(a)(1), also known as the "strong arm clause," the trustee can "avoid any transfer of property of the debtor" (e.g., a security interest) that could be avoided by a hypothetical lien creditor on the date of the petition. And under section 9-317(a)(2), a security interest is subordinate to the property rights of a lien creditor (e.g., the bankruptcy trustee) if, when the lien arises, the security interest is not perfected (or, in less frequent situations, when perfection has not occurred solely because the secured party has not given value when the lien arises). Taken together, these two statutes permit

the trustee to destroy any security interest that is unperfected on the petition date. Therefore, the reader must determine whether Secured Party's security interest is perfected on September 13. Debtor is a Delaware corporation, making it a "registered organization" under section 9-102(a)(70). Therefore, to the extent that Secured Party is relying on a financing statement for perfection, it must file the financing statement in Delaware. See §§ 9-301(1); 9-307(e). Secured Party is perfected in Answer (A) because it filed its financing statement in Delaware. That is the proper place to file, not because the collateral was in Delaware, but because Delaware is the law under which Debtor was created. The collateral location is irrelevant, so no subsequent filing in Illinois is required. Secured Party remained perfected on the petition date in the Illinois collateral by the Delaware filing, so the trustee cannot avoid the security interest under 11 U.S.C. § 544(a)(1), **making Answer (A) an incorrect answer**. Under section 9-305(c)(1), Secured Party should have filed its financing statement in Delaware to perfect a security interest in investment property. Instead, Secured Party filed in the state where the stock certificate was located (Georgia), a mistake that left Secured Party unperfected on the petition date. Therefore, the trustee can avoid Secured Party's unperfected security interest under 11 U.S.C. § 544(a)(1), **making Answer (B) the correct answer**.

For reasons already mentioned, Secured Party is perfected in Debtor's Texas-based inventory by the Delaware filing. Normally a post-petition filing is ineffective because it violates the automatic stay under 11 U.S.C. § 362(a)(4). But subsection (a) is expressly subject to subsection (b). And 11 U.S.C. § 362(b)(3) permits a post-petition filing "to the extent that the trustee's rights and powers are subject to such perfection under section 546(b) of this title. . . ." Under that section, the trustee's avoiding powers "are subject to any generally applicable law that — (A) permits perfection of an interest in property to be effective against an entity that acquires rights in such property before the date of perfection. . . ." The "generally applicable law" is section 9-317(e), which permits a secured party to perfect its purchase-money security interest after the lien creditor obtains a competing property interest and yet enjoy priority over that competing property interest. Secured Party timely perfected its purchase-money security interest and can invoke the protection afforded by section 9-317(e). Therefore, the post-petition filing did not violate the automatic stay and is effective to prevent the trustee from avoiding the security interest under 11 U.S.C. § 544(a)(1). So **Answer (C) is an incorrect answer**. And Secured Party's security interest in the bank account became perfected by "control" under section 9-104(a)(1) at the moment of attachment and remained perfected on the petition date. Thus, the trustee cannot avoid the security interest under 11 U.S.C. § 544(a)(1), and **Answer (D) is an incorrect answer**.

146. **Answer (B) is the correct answer.** This question focuses on fraudulent transfers and their effect on the transfer of property (so if you are not covering fraudulent transfers in your course, ignore this question). Under the law of fraudulent transfers, a transfer may be set aside notwithstanding compliance with various formalities. It can be set aside in two situations: the first is if the debtor made the transfer with the intent to hinder, delay, or defraud his creditors; the second is if the transfer

is for less than a reasonably equivalent value and the transferor, after the transfer, is left in a poor financial state such as insolvency.

Given the power of fraudulent transfer law to override other formalities, **Answer (A) is incorrect**. Similarly, since fraudulent transfers look at the intent or the financial state of the debtor/transferor, the financial state of the recipient is irrelevant. That **excludes Answer (C) as a correct answer**.

Since this was a gift transaction, with no expectation that Sally would recover or reclaim the car, it does not appear to be a transaction that creates a security interest, and thus filing a financing statement would do no good, and this **eliminates Answer (D) as an answer**.

This leaves Answer (B). Under section 2(b) of the Uniform Fraudulent Transfer Act, if a creditor can show that the transferor/debtor was not paying his or her debts as they become due, then a presumption of insolvency is created. Insolvency, in turn, is otherwise defined as having more liabilities than assets. But it is up to the debtor/transferor to show that he or she was not insolvent; if the debtor does not make that showing, then he or she will be assumed to be insolvent.

But in addition to a bad financial state such as insolvency, the creditor must show that there was a lack of reasonably equivalent value for the transaction. Here, in a gift transaction, not only is there a lack of reasonably equivalent value, but there is no value given. With both insolvency and a lack of reasonably equivalent value, the transaction may be set aside for the benefit of Sally's creditors. Thus **Answer (B) is correct**.

147.   **Answer (C) is the correct answer.** This fact pattern presents the classic leveraged buyout, which is typically held to be a fraudulent transfer. But before we can get to that conclusion, the question is structured so that we have to assess the transaction under both preference and fraudulent transfer law.

Note first that, from the perspective of Article 9, Fred's security interest is valid and properly perfected. The security agreement describes a broad range of collateral, using Article 9 terms as is permitted by section 9-108. The financing statement uses an "all assets" description as is permitted by section 9-504. And the financing statement is filed in Delaware, where GI is located for purposes of Article 9 under section 9-307. But this question points out that more than Article 9 has to be consulted when the debtor has filed a bankruptcy petition.

Is there a preference or a fraudulent transfer? First, preference law requires a "transfer," and fraudulent transfer law will set aside certain transfers. Transfers are defined very broadly in the Bankruptcy Code. They include "every mode, direct or indirect, absolute or conditional, voluntary or involuntary, of disposing of or parting with property or with an interest in property, including retention of title as a security interest. . . ." 11 U.S.C. § 101(54). Here, the transfer is the transfer of a security interest from GI to Fred; this transaction gave property rights to Fred.

But preferences require that the transfer be "to or for the benefit of a creditor," 11 U.S.C. § 547(b)(1), and "for or on account of an antecedent debt owed by the debtor before such transfer was made," 11 U.S.C. § 547(b)(2). Here, there is no indication that the creation of the security interest was for anything but the debt created simultaneously with the sale of the GI stock. Thus, the transfer cannot be a preference, thereby **disqualifying Answers (B) and (D)**.

Is it a fraudulent transfer? In addition to transactions made with the actual intent to hinder, delay, or defraud (which does not seem to be present here), fraudulent transfers include transfers that are made for less than a reasonably equivalent value, *and* which either rendered the debtor insolvent (or nearly so) or were made at a time at which the debtor was insolvent (or nearly so). 11 U.S.C. § 548(a)(2).

Was the transfer for a "reasonably equivalent value"? Probably not. GI, as a separate entity with separate creditors, did not receive anything in return for the grant of a security interest in its assets. It is as if it guaranteed Alice's debt and received nothing in return. (Note: most gift transactions, or transactions without consideration such as the payment of dividends, will be made for less than a reasonably equivalent value.)

Was GI insolvent or nearly so when it granted the security interest? The test for constructively fraudulent transfers under 11 U.S.C. § 548(a)(2) requires *both* a lack of reasonably equivalent value and a shaky or insolvent financial state. Specifically, 11 U.S.C. § 548(a)(2)(B) requires one of the three adverse financial states; namely that the debtor: "(i) was insolvent on the date that such transfer was made or such obligation was incurred, or became insolvent as a result of such transfer or obligation; (ii) was engaged in business or a transaction, or was about to engage in business or a transaction, for which any property remaining with the debtor was an unreasonably small capital; or (iii) intended to incur, or believed that the debtor would incur, debts that would be beyond the debtor's ability to pay as such debts matured." Insolvency, under the Bankruptcy Code, is a balance sheet test. It requires a "financial condition such that the sum of such entity's debts is greater than all of such entity's property, at a fair valuation. . . ." 11 U.S.C. § 101(32).

While there is not enough information here to find without question that GI was insolvent (no financial information at all is given), the speedy decline of GI and its inability to attract any new capital given Fred's security interest probably means that GI was insolvent (no one would lend on its assets in a junior position) or that it had "unreasonable small capital" (since it could not raise any based on its other assets). Given the likelihood of a colorable fraudulent transfer action, **Answer (A) is incorrect, leaving Answer (C) as the correct answer.**

148. **Answer (C) is the correct answer.** First Bank is perfected in all collateral. The facts give the value of that collateral as $6,000,000. What is the secured claim in bankruptcy? That is determined by 11 U.S.C. § 506(a) and 11 U.S.C. § 506(b). Under 11 U.S.C. § 506(a), "[a]n allowed claim of a creditor secured by a lien on property in which the estate has an interest, . . . is a secured claim to the extent of the value of such creditor's interest in the estate's interest in such property." This states that the secured claim has a maximum value of $6,000,000, the value of the collateral. Thus, **Answer (A) is incorrect.**

We also know that bankruptcy will not give First Bank more than its state law claim. That means that we figure out what the debt is under state law, and that also is a maximum value. Here, we know that there is at least $5,000,000 in principal outstanding. Thus, the claim is at least $5,000,000. Is it more? Under state law, that is, under Article 9, First Bank was careful to note that attorneys' fees were also debts that would be secured by the collateral. If First Bank had not indicated that its attorneys' fees were part of the obligation secured, they would just be unsecured claims (that is, not secured by the collateral).

Knowing that interest continues to accrue under state law, we now know that **Answer (B) is incorrect**, since the $5,000,000 answer does not account for any accrued interest and attorneys' fees. Whether these additional amounts — the accrued interest and attorneys' fees — will be added to the secured claim in bankruptcy is a function of 11 U.S.C. § 506(b). That section states that "[t]o the extent that an allowed secured claim is secured by property the value of which . . . is greater than the amount of such claim, there shall be allowed to the holder of such claim, interest on such claim, and any reasonable fees, costs, or charges provided for under the agreement under which such claim arose."

So in cases such as First Bank's, in which the agreement provides for attorneys' fees and costs, post-petition interest and reasonable attorneys' fees and costs will accrue post-petition and be added to the secured claim. First Bank will not get more than its actual claim, **making Answer (D) an incorrect answer**. That **leaves Answer (C) as the correct answer**.

149. **Answer (A) is the correct answer.** Here, the changed fact is the reduced value of the collateral. For all the reasons listed in the preceding answer, the secured claim in bankruptcy cannot exceed the value of the collateral. Thus, it is irrelevant, for purposes of calculating the secured claim, what the amount secured by the debt would be under state law. Under 11 U.S.C. § 506(a), then, the secured claim is limited to the value of the collateral, or $4,000,000. The only answer consistent with this answer is Answer (A), **making Answers (B), (C), and (D) incorrect**.

150. **Answer (C) is the correct answer.** Under 11 U.S.C. § 547(e), a transfer cannot occur until the debtor acquires rights in the encumbered property. Debtor acquired rights in the Item on the sale date, June 8, under UCC § 2-501. As Bank had previously filed a financing statement, its security interest in the item became perfected on June 8. That is the date of transfer. **Answers (A) and (B) are incorrect** because Debtor did not yet have any rights in the Item. And **Answer (D) is incorrect** because Debtor need not have possession in order to have sufficient rights in the Item to use it as collateral.

151. **Answer (A) is the correct answer.** Under 11 U.S.C. § 547(b), the trustee can attack as voidable preferences "any transfer of an interest of the debtor in property." Angela's payment of $500 is a transfer, as is Elliott's conveyance of a security interest in his investment portfolio. But neither Angela nor Elliott are the "debtor." Kirk, the party in bankruptcy, is the debtor. Therefore, because the transfers were made by non-debtor parties, the transfers cannot be attacked by the trustee as voidable preferences. **Answers (B), (C), and (D) are all incorrect** because they suggest that Angela's payment of $500, Elliott's grant of a security interest, or both, can be attacked as voidable preferences.

As easy as this requirement seems to be, students should be very careful when dismissing a preference analysis solely because the transfer did not come from the debtor. For example, the requirement that the transfer be of property of the estate has not stopped courts from recharacterizing a transaction when the effect, but not the letter, of the transaction is to transfer property that would have been property of the estate. This can be seen when someone assumes the debt of another as part of the purchase price for assets (as when a buyer of a business's assets agrees to assume the existing business lease). Payments on that assumed debt from and after the transfer, while made directly from the non-bankrupt buyer, are held to be indirectly made by the bankrupt debtor, since the assumption is part of the consideration the debtor received. This was recently summarized by the Seventh Circuit as follows:

In those cases in which courts have held that a preference was given in the context of an asset sale, there is a fairly direct, traceable link between the consideration given for the debtor's assets and the funds used to pay the creditor. For instance, a debtor may sell its assets to a third party, and, as part of the purchase agreement, the third party may agree to assume the debtor's liabilities. When the third party subsequently pays a creditor of the debtor, courts have allowed the bankruptcy trustee to recover the payment as a preference. *See* [Mordy v. Chemcarb, Inc. (*In re* Food Catering & Housing, Inc.), 971 F.2d 396, 397-98 (9th Cir. 1992)]; Sommers v. Burton (*In re* Conard Corp.), 806 F.2d 610, 611-12 (5th Cir. 1986). In such cases, the third party's assumption of the debtor's debt is consideration for the sale of the debtor's assets.

See In re Food Catering, 971 F.2d at 398. The debtor effectively transferred to the creditor its right to receive a portion of the sale price equal to the amount of the debt. *See In re* Conard Corp., 806 F.2d at 612. The result is the same when, instead of transferring the money directly to the creditor, the third party deposits the money into an escrow account over which the debtor has no control. *See In re* Interior Wood, 986 F.2d at 231. Nor does the result change when the third party, rather than the debtor, specifies which creditor will receive the funds paid into the escrow account. *See* Feltman v. Bd. of County Comm'rs of Metro. Dade County (*In re* S.E.L. Maduro (Florida), Inc.), 205 B.R. 987, 992-93 (Bankr. S.D. Fla.1997).

Warsco v. Preferred Technical Group, 258 F.3d 557, 565 (7th Cir. 2001).

152. **Answer (D) is the correct answer. Answer (A) is incorrect** because the presumption can be rebutted by the secured party. **Answer (B) is incorrect** because 11 U.S.C. § 547(g) places the burden of proving nonavoidability of the transfer on the secured party. **Answer (C) also is incorrect**. For example, debtor borrows money on July 1, and the security interest attaches on July 3 and is perfected on July 9. Because the security interest is perfected within ten days of attachment, the attachment date is the date of the transfer under 11 U.S.C. § 547(e)(2)(B). But the debt date of July 1 remains antecedent (or prior) to the transfer date of July 3. So **Answer (C) is incorrect**. And **Answer (D) is correct** under 11 U.S.C. § 550(c). This provision permits lenders to extract guaranties from insiders (almost all guaranties are executed by insiders) without worrying that its preference period exposure will be extended from 90 days to one year.

153. **Answer (B) is the correct answer.** The "substantially contemporaneous exchange" exception, codified at 11 U.S.C. § 547(c)(1), can preserve any type of transfer, so **Answer (A) is incorrect**. The "enabling loan" exception," found at 11 U.S.C. § 547(c)(3), preserves only security interest transfers, **making Answer (C) incorrect**. The "floating lien" exception of 11 U.S.C. § 547(c)(5) preserves only security interest transfers in specific types of collateral, so **Answer (D) is incorrect**. But the "ordinary course of business" exception, codified at 11 U.S.C. § 547(c)(2), preserves only transfers "in payment of a debt," **making Answer (B) the correct answer**.

154. **Answer (C) is the correct answer.** The "floating lien" exception of 11 U.S.C. § 547(c)(5) permits the secured party to preserve its perfected security interest in inventory and accounts as of the petition date if the deficiency as of the petition date is not less than the deficiency on the later of (i) the date on which the secured creditor first gave value and (ii) the first day of the preference period (generally the 90th day before the petition date). But the security interest on the petition date is voided to the extent that the deficiency on the petition date is less than the deficiency calculated on the earlier date. The statute requires knowledge of the debt amount and the collateral value on two, and only two, dates. One date is the petition date, the other date is the later of the two dates described above. Debt amounts and collateral values on other dates are irrelevant. In this problem, the deficiency on the petition date of October 1 is $200,000 (debt of $2 million and collateral worth $1.8 million). The 90th day preceding October 1 is approximately July 1. But Bank

did not loan money until July 15, so this later date is the date on which the other comparative deficiency is calculated. That deficiency is $300,000 (debt of $2.0 million and collateral worth $1.7 million). Comparing the two deficiencies reveals that Bank has improved its position by $100,000 (the deficiency decreased from $300,000 to $200,000). This amount is subtracted from the collateral value on October 1 ($1.8 million), leaving Bank with a perfected security interest in collateral worth $1.7 million (**making Answer (C) the correct answer** and **Answers (A), (B), and (D) incorrect answers**).

155. **Answer (C) is the correct answer.** Here, we have a non-purchase-money security interest in a consumer good — the security interest in the television was not given as part of its purchase. As such, Friendly had only an unperfected security interest in the television. Being unperfected, however, does not mean unenforceable; indeed, attachment alone is sufficient for the security interest to be enforced. So Friendly could repossess the goods. It had that right under section 9-609, and it accomplished the repossession without a breach of the peace. Therefore, **Answer (D) is incorrect**.

Friendly's sale, however, is not in accordance with Article 9. It does not give proper notice under section 9-611(c), and the process of sale is likely not commercially reasonable under section 9-610(b), given its timing and the ultimate purchaser. But that may not matter, if the teller who purchased the set paid an amount equal to its fair market value. Moreover, such actions would affect Friendly's deficiency, not the sale itself.

Thus, the focus should be on Friendly's receipt of the $2,500. **Answer (B) is not correct** because the sale has already occurred. The strong arm power of 11 U.S.C. § 544(a)(1) that gives the trustee the status of a lien creditor only matters with respect to property that the debtor still has at the time of the bankruptcy filing. That leaves Answer (A) — under which Friendly keeps the money — and Answer (C) — which requires a preference analysis.

Is the receipt of the $2,500 preferential? Here, our determination that Friendly's security interest was unperfected matters. Friendly meets all of the requirements for a preference. It is a transfer (that it was involuntary does not matter) to a creditor (Friendly) on account of an antecedent debt (the $5,000 loan) within 90 days of the filing, and which, if Friendly were allowed to keep it, would allow it to receive a better dividend than other unsecured creditors (if there is a 10% dividend, then Friendly will collect $2,750 on its loan ($2,500 from the sale, and $250 in the form of a 10% dividend on the $2,500 deficiency). Had it not repossessed the goods, it would received only $500 (10% of the $5,000 debt). Since there are no applicable defenses under 11 U.S.C. § 547(c), this means that Friendly will have to turn over the $2,500 it received, **making Answer (C) the correct answer** and **Answer (A) the incorrect answer**.

156. **Answer (D) is the correct answer.** The only transfer in Answer (A) is the loan repayment. But the loan was repaid by Debtor's brother, not the bankrupt party (Debtor). Therefore, the loan repayment does not represent a "transfer of an interest of the debtor in property" under 11 U.S.C. § 547(b), making **Answer (A) an**

incorrect answer. Answer (B) also is incorrect. Dealer is fully secured at all times (the collateral is always worth at least $80,000 — the amount of the original credit). Because Dealer is fully secured, Debtor's loan repayment of $35,000 does not permit Dealer to receive more than it would under a Chapter 7 liquidation if the payment had not been made. If Dealer keeps the $35,000 it will file a proof of claim for $45,000, a fully secured claim. If Debtor never made the $35,000 payment, then Dealer will file a proof of claim for $80,000, also a fully secured claim. In both instances Dealer is repaid in full. Therefore, the trustee cannot satisfy 11 U.S.C. § 547(b)(5), **making Answer (B) incorrect. Answer (C) is incorrect** because the transfer occurred on May 1, a date that falls outside the 90-day preference period preceding the petition date of August 15. 11 U.S.C. § 547(b)(4)(A). **Answer (D) is correct** because all elements of 11 U.S.C. § 547(b) are present. The transfer is Debtor's grant of a security interest to Finance Company (a pre-petition creditor) in early February, within the 90-day period preceding the petition date of April 25. And the transfer permits Finance Company to receive more than it would in a Chapter 7 liquidation without the security interest. If Finance Company keeps the security interest, it will file a proof of claim for $10,000, a fully secured claim. But if Debtor never grants the security interest, Finance Company will file a proof of claim for $10,000 — an unsecured claim. So the transfer does favor Finance Company by converting an unsecured claim to a secured claim (the type of behavior that the voidable preference statute seeks to condemn).

157. **Answer (B) is the correct answer.** This question involves a priority dispute between a secured creditor and a lien creditor. In some respects, the question is too easy; on the date that Crazy Creditor became a lien creditor, July 15, LargeBanc did not have a security interest in any of JHI's assets; it had yet to loan any money (give value) and thus its security interest was not even attached, let alone perfected. It is as though JHI had given some interest in its property to someone else before the closing. Under the general principle of *nemo dat* (you can only give that which you have), LargeBanc thus took subject to Crazy Creditor's lien because LargeBanc's interest attached afterwards. The only answer that takes this into account is (B), which indicates a lack of attachment. The trick here is that the rule in section 9-322 allocating priority on the basis of the first to file or perfect (and thus permits priority to turn on actions occurring before perfection) is *not* applicable to a contest between a lien creditor and an Article 9 secured creditor. Section 9-322 applies only to priority contests when all creditors claim their entitlements under Article 9.

    The section that resolves priority between Article 9 secured creditors and lien creditors such as Crazy is section 9-317(a)(2). That section states that the rights of a holder of an Article 9 security interest are subordinate to the rights of "a person that becomes a lien creditor before the earlier of the time: (A) the security interest or agricultural lien is perfected; or (B) one of the conditions specified in Section 9-203(b)(3) is met and a financing statement covering the collateral is filed." Here, LargeBanc was not perfected, and *none* of the conditions specified in section 9-203(b)(3) (in most cases, the authentication of a security agreement that adequately describes the collateral) were in place on July 15. That makes **Answer (A) true but incomplete, and hence incorrect**. **Answer (D) is a red herring**; nothing in section 9-317 implicates any four-month rule. Last, Answer (C) may be true, but a secured party cannot bring a preference action; the Bankruptcy Code affords that right to the bankruptcy trustee and makes the initiation of such actions discretionary with the trustee. Thus, **Answer (C) is incorrect**.

158. **Answer (A) is the correct answer.** This question requires knowledge of how to calculate secured claims in bankruptcy. The summary of these rules, found in 11 U.S.C. § 506, is fairly simple to state: a secured creditor has a secured claim in bankruptcy to the extent of the *lesser* of: (i) the amount it is owed on the date of filing; and (ii) the value of its collateral. This general rule is subject to the following exception: interest accrued after the filing date, together with reasonable costs and attorneys' fees, can be added to the secured claim *only* if provided for by the agreement or the law creating the claim, and then only to the extent of the value of the collateral.

    Here, LargeBanc's security agreement specifically creates an obligation of JHI to pay attorneys' fees and costs. And LargeBanc was oversecured; that is, its collateral value of $110,000 exceeds its debt of $100,000. Thus, **Answer (B) is incorrect** since it would not allow post-petition interest or costs.

Answers (C) and (D) require an analysis of whether granting a security interest is a preference. Initially, **Answer (D) can be rejected** because, even if the grant of a security interest were preferential, LargeBanc would still have an unsecured claim for the amount left. Preference law is not punitive. 11 U.S.C. § 502(h).

Was the grant of a security interest preferential? (Note that since there were no payments on the loan, the only "transfer" within the 90-day look-back period is the granting of the security interest itself.) Most likely, it was not. This can be supported on one of two theories. First, 11 U.S.C. § 547(b) requires as an element of a preference that the transfer be made "for or on account of an antecedent debt owed by the debtor before such transfer was made." When was the transfer made? Under 11 U.S.C. § 547(e)(2)(A), a transfer is made "at the time such transfer takes effect between the transferor and the transferee, if such transfer is perfected at, or within 10 days after, such time." When did the transfer "take effect" under 11 U.S.C. § 547(e)(2)(A)? At the time of attachment, since that is when the security interest is enforceable against the debtor. When did that attachment occur? On July 31 -that is when: JHI, the debtor, signed a security agreement describing the collateral; when JHI had rights in the collateral; and when value (in the form of the loan agreement's commitment) was given. That was also the date of perfection, since filing of the July 1 financing statement legitimately covered the collateral described in the security agreement signed on July 31. Thus, there is no antecedent debt. The debt to which the transfer (the security interest) related arose at the same time -not before -as the transfer (or grant) of a security interest. Thus, one of the elements of a preference -the existence of an antecedent debt -is missing.

The second theory is that the "transfer" was substantially contemporaneous with the grant of the security interest, and thus LargeBanc has a complete defense under 11 U.S.C. § 547(c)(1). The only difference here is procedural. The trustee or estate representative has the burden of proving all the elements of a preference stated in 11 U.S.C. § 547(b). The preference defendant has the burden of proving a defense under 11 U.S.C. § 547(c). 11 U.S.C. § 547(g).

With the lack of a preferential transfer (or a complete defense), **Answer (C) is incorrect**, leaving **Answer (A) as the correct answer.**

159. BigBank, the party to whom the security interest is granted, is the "secured party" under section 9-102(a)(72)(A) ("a person in whose favor a security interest is created or provided for under a security agreement"). Jill, whose assets are serving as collateral, is the "debtor" under section 9-102(a)(28)(A) ("a person having an interest, other than a security interest or other lien, in the collateral"). Ace, the party to whom the loan is made, will most likely execute the promissory note and be an "obligor" under section 9-102(a)(59) ("a person that, with respect to an obligation secured by a security interest in . . . the collateral (i) owes payment or other performance of the obligation"). In addition to being the "debtor," and depending on the contractual terms of the transaction, Jill also could be an "obligor" (under the same quoted language) and perhaps (again, depending on the contractual terms of the transaction) a "secondary obligor" under section 9-102(a)(71).

For purposes of attachment, the security agreement must provide a description of the collateral being offered by Jill. Additionally, Jill, the debtor, must authenticate the security agreement. See § 9-203(b)(3)(A).

160. BigBank's security interest attached to the 100 shares of Zinnergy capital stock when all three requirements of section 9-203(b) were met. The security agreement (presumably describing the collateral and authenticated by Jill, the debtor) was executed on September 1, satisfying section 9-203(b)(3)(A). BigBank also gave value on September 1, satisfying section 9-203(b)(1). (Although BigBank did not fund the initial advance until September 15, its commitment in the loan agreement dated September 1 is "value" under section 1-204(1).) And Jill acquired rights in the Zinnergy shares on the purchase date of September 5, satisfying section 9-203(b)(2). As BigBank had previously given value, and as the security agreement had already been executed, BigBank's security interest attached to the Zinnergy shares when Jill acquired rights in the shares on September 5.

161. Under section 9-308(a), BigBank's security interest in the Markelli shares became perfected when the security interest attached under section 9-203(b) and BigBank had taken any necessary step required by statute. The security interest attached to the Markelli shares when Jill acquired the shares on September 20 (the security agreement had been authenticated and BigBank had given value almost three weeks earlier). Under section 9-312(a), a security interest in investment property may be perfected by filing. As BigBank had previously filed its financing statement on September 8, before the security interest attached, perfection occurred at the moment of attachment on September 20 (section 9-308(a), last sentence).

162. The answer depends on whether the credit card receivables and the installment sales contracts are "accounts," the only type of collateral listed in the security agreement. Credit card receivables are "accounts" (section 9-102(a)(2)(vii)), so Providence Bank has a security interest in them. Because the installment sales contracts evidence "a right to payment of a monetary obligation . . . (i) for property that has been or is to be sold, leased, . . . or otherwise disposed of," they may indeed be "accounts" and part of the collateral. But the definition of "accounts" expressly excludes "rights to payment evidenced by chattel paper or an instrument." It is possible that the installment sales contracts are chattel paper under section 9-102(a)(11) (e.g., if Ed's Electronics retains a security interest in the item sold until the customer has completed its contractual obligation) or an "instrument" under section 9-102(a)(47) (e.g., if the contract is either a "negotiable instrument" under section 3-104 or a writing "that in the ordinary course of business is transferred by delivery with any necessary indorsement or assignment"). Only if the installment sales contracts are not chattel paper or instruments will they be accounts and part of the collateral in which Providence Bank has an enforceable security interest.

The credit card receivables are not "rights to payment evidenced by chattel paper or an instrument" -and therefore excluded from the definition of "account" -because the definition of both "chattel paper" and "instrument" expressly excludes credit card receivables.

163. **Answer (B) is the correct answer.** Start the analysis of this problem with the hint in Answer (C) -that Article 9 does not apply. It certainly seems, on a formalistic analysis, as if it does not. There are no security interests or reservations of title. But look at the transaction -no one sells a $1,500 ring for $500 if a true sale or other actual transfer is anticipated. This hesitation is intensified to a full stop when the option is factored in.

Section 9-109, which defines Article 9's scope, adopts a form over substance approach. Specifically, section 9-109(a)(1) states that article 9 applies to: "(1) a transaction, regardless of its form, that creates a security interest in personal property or fixtures by contract." Do the facts in this problem indicate the creation of a "security interest"? A security interest is defined in section 1-201(b)(35) as "an interest in personal property or fixtures which secures payment or performance of an obligation." Here, it is fairly easy to recharacterize the transaction as a loan from Linda secured by Hank's ring -Hank has "pledged" his ring to Linda, and he can buy it back (or redeem it) by paying an amount that very conveniently looks to be the original purchase price (or loan) plus 10% interest. As such, a court would very likely characterize the transaction between Hank and Linda as one for security, rather than one for outright sale. This has significant consequences. Under this analysis, Hank still "owns" the ring and would have rights under Article 9 upon any default.

While Article 9 may govern the transaction, did Linda's interest attach? Two of the requirements for attachment are easy to see: Hank clearly has rights in the collateral, and Linda has given value in the form of $500. But there is no written security agreement. That, however, is not an impediment. Under section 9-203(b)(3), having a signed security agreement with a collateral description is only one of four ways (albeit the most common way) to satisfy the third prong of attachment. Under subparagraph (C), this requirement is satisfied if "the collateral is not a certificated security and is in the possession of the secured party under Section 9-313 pursuant to the debtor's security agreement."

Here, the collateral is a ring, and Linda has possession. The agreement of "sale" can suffice for a "security agreement," since the definition of security agreement does not require the labeling of the agreement as such, or even acknowledgment that an Article 9 transaction is intended. Under section 9-102(a)(73), a "security agreement" is just "an agreement that creates or provides for a security interest." The term "agreement," is defined in Article 1 to mean "the bargain of the parties in fact as found in their language or by implication from other circumstances . . . ." (Article 1 definitions are explicitly incorporated into Article 9 via section 9-102(c).) Note that this avenue of attachment does not require a *written* agreement, just an agreement to create a security interest, by that name or in substance to that end. So Linda possesses the ring pursuant to agreement, and that agreement in substance is one for security (one way to see this is to scrutinize Hank's options at the end of the year -it is economically certain that Hank will exercise his "option;" who wouldn't pay $550 to obtain an asset worth $1,500?). Thus, there is (at least until Linda gives up the ring) attachment.

There also is perfection so long as Linda keeps possession. Under section 9-313, a secured party may perfect a security interest in goods by possessing them. Since Article 9 applies, **Answer (C) is not the correct answer**.

If Article 9 applies, then the security interest presumptively follows the ring upon its sale to George. § 9-315(a)(1). Only if there is some exception can the transfer be free of the security interest. The buyer in the ordinary course exception hinted at in Answer (D) is wrong; to be a buyer in the ordinary course under section 1-201(b)(9) the buyer has to buy from someone in the business of selling the goods at issue. Hank is not a jeweler, so this requirement is not met, and thus **Answer (D) is not correct**.

That leaves us Answer (B) -which mentions George's knowledge -or Answer (A) -which applies the default rule. To puzzle this out, note that Linda lost her status as a perfected secured party by giving the ring back to Hank. Under section 9-313, the debtor cannot hold assets for the benefit of the secured party (there is also an argument that Linda also lost attachment, since she can no longer rely on section 9-201(b)(3)(C)). In any event, under section 9-317(b), "a buyer, other than a secured party, of . . . goods . . . takes free of a security interest . . . if the buyer gives value and receives delivery of the collateral without knowledge of the security interest . . . and before it is perfected."

Here, George has made the ring part of the consideration of a larger sale of sewing machines. He has thus given value and has received delivery of the ring during a period in which Linda's interest is unperfected. So long as he has no knowledge of Linda's interest, he will take free of the security interest (**making Answer (A) an incorrect answer**). That is the core of **Answer (B), the correct answer.**

164. **Answer (B) is the correct answer.** The name change from PhysiCare to Southwest Physicians is most likely seriously misleading under section 9-506(c) because a search against "Southwest Physicians, Inc." will not reveal the earlier filing against "PhysiCare Inc." As a result, the original financing statement is not effective to perfect a security interest in equipment acquired by Southwest Physicians more than four months after the name change (but it will remain effective to perfect a security interest in collateral acquired before, and within four months after, the name change). See § 9-507(c). The security interest in Item #3 is unperfected because Southwest Physicians acquired Item #3 on September 15, more than four months after the name change on April 1. But the original financing statement continues to be effective (even after the four-month period following the name change) to perfect a security interest in Item #1 (acquired on March 15, before the name change) and Item #2 (acquired on July 15, within four months after the name change on April 1). Because Bank continues to have a perfected security interest in Items #1 and #2, but not Item #3, **Answer (B) is the correct answer. Answer (A) is incorrect** because it is overinclusive (including Item #3), and **Answers (C) and (D) are incorrect** because they are underinclusive (omitting Item #1, Item #2, or both).

This problem illustrates that a secured party should, at least once every four months, assure itself that its debtor has not changed its name. And in order to avoid being unperfected in collateral acquired by a debtor more than four months after a seriously misleading name change, the secured party should file an amended financing statement within that four-month period. § 9-507(c)(2).

165.   The bankruptcy judge may, or may not, grant the motion under 11 U.S.C. § 362(d)(1). If the photocopiers are valued on the high end ($19,000), then Landmark's property interest is adequately protected by the $1,000 equity cushion at the present time. But within a few months, the monthly depreciation (and, as permitted by 11 U.S.C. § 506(b), post-petition interest on the oversecured claim) will eliminate the equity cushion, at which time the judge may lift the stay unless Aspen can offer "adequate protection" under 11 U.S.C. § 361 (e.g., a monthly cash payment equal to the depreciation). If the photocopiers are valued at less than the debt of $18,000, then Landmark's property interest already is declining in value, and the judge should immediately lift the stay unless Aspen can offer "adequate protection" under 11 U.S.C. § 361 (e.g., a monthly cash payment equal to the depreciation, or additional collateral). The bankruptcy judge will not grant Landmark's motion under 11 U.S.C. § 362(d)(2) -regardless of the valuation -because the photocopiers appear to be necessary to Aspen's effective reorganization (assuming, of course, that Aspen can propose a feasible plan of reorganization).

166.   **Answer (D) is the correct answer.** This problem presents questions of the relationship between junior and senior creditors after default. First, did Henry have the right to seek replevin? Yes, notwithstanding any other interests in the property, Henry at least had attachment (a signed security agreement adequately describing the collateral, rights in the collateral, and the presence of value). As such, under section 9-203, his interest was enforceable. Under section 9-609, enforceable security interests (or "attached" security interests) can be enforced, after default, by repossession, which is what Henry did by his replevin action.

Henry then conducts a non-complying foreclosure sale. Henry failed to comply with Article 9 because he did not give the required notice to the debtor, § 9-611(c), and he did not proceed in a commercially reasonable manner for the sale, § 9-610(b). These actions, however, probably only affect the deficiency that Q Corporation, Inc. may owe. The focus of this question, in part, is the effect on Beth's interest.

Beth also appears to have an attached security interest. She also appears to be perfected: she has filed a financing statement in the same appropriate place as Henry, and she has gotten Q Corporation, Inc.'s name correct –that is, she has given the name recognized by section 9-503. Under section 9-503(a)(1), a financing statement is sufficient with respect to a registered organization's name "only if the financing statement provides the name of the debtor indicated on the public record of the debtor's jurisdiction of organization which shows the debtor to have been organized." Beth did this; Henry did not.

Moreover, Henry's listing of only "Q Corp." is "seriously misleading," invalidating the piece of paper he filed. Under section 9-507(c), "[i]f a search of the records of the filing office under the debtor's correct name, using the filing office's standard search logic, if any, would disclose a financing statement that fails sufficiently to provide the name of the debtor in accordance with Section 9-503(a), the name provided does not make the financing statement seriously misleading." Our situation is the converse: Henry's financing statement indexed under "Q Corp." would not be returned in a search under the true name. This means that Henry's filing is seriously misleading, and hence ineffective: the fact that a search under Q Corporation, Inc.

(the correct name under section 9-503) would not turn up a filing showing just "Q Corp." is what makes the filing seriously misleading (sort of like the difference, as Mark Twain would have noted, between "lightning" and "lightning bug").

What is the consequence of this? Beth had a superior property interest: she was perfected, Henry was not. She was thus senior under section 9-322. As a consequence, when Henry refused to turn over possession when Beth requested it, Henry thereafter maintained possession contrary to Beth's rights. This usually results in a conversion action. § 9-609, cmt. 5. This means that Answers (C) and (D) are potentially correct. (Answer (A) can be easily dismissed. Henry's botched foreclosure does not affect Beth's rights against the debtor, so the debtor, Q Corporation, Inc., still owes the original $15,000, **making Answer (A) an incorrect answer.** Answer (B) does not mention conversion, and thus while correct as far as it goes, does not go far enough. Thus, **Answer (B) is not the correct answer.**)

But what about Beth's rights against the purchaser, Sarah? It is a fundamental premise of foreclosure that the sale extinguishes the interest of the person conducting the sale as well as all interests junior to it. § 9-617(a). Senior interests are not affected (which explains why senior creditors do not share in the distribution of foreclosure proceeds under section 9-615(a)). So, effectively, Sarah has become a new debtor since she now owns the collateral. Beth may thus pursue the property in Sarah's hands, but nothing else that Sarah owns. She will get, against Sarah, the value of the property, but must stop when her debt of $15,000 is satisfied. Because Answer (C) omits the option to pursue Sarah, **Answer (C) is not the best answer. Answer (D) is the most complete answer.**

167. **Answer (C) is the correct answer.** This question pulls together basic notions of state law perfection with the issues involved in federal intellectual property. Take them separately. With respect to all collateral other than copyrights, the issue is twofold: whether the financing statement filed in 2000 can operate to perfect any security interests which attach in 2004; and whether the security agreement with the future advance clause picks up and will secure (provide for attachment of) the proposed 2004 loan.

Take the issues somewhat backward. A financing statement, once filed and authorized, can serve to perfect any loan at any time, if the information contained in the financing statement is not seriously misleading. Put another way, you do not have to intend or match the filing of a financing statement with the loan in contemplation at the time the financing statement is filed. If the original financing statement was authorized, it is effective for its five-year life. § 9-509. (Of course, David had the power to request a termination in 2002, § 9-513, but the fact that the debtor has an unexercised power to terminate is not the same as removing authorization for the effectiveness of a filing.) As a consequence, if there is proper attachment, the security interest will be perfected with a priority date under section 9-322 of 2000.

Now for attachment. Without a new security agreement, there has to be some connection between the proposed 2004 loan and the 2000 security agreement. That connection is the future advance clause in the original security agreement. The clause as given here is very broadly drafted. If the intent was to pick up what it says -"all debts now *and hereafter* owing to Edgar" -a court will give that clause effect and find attachment. See § 9-204, cmt. 5 ("Indeed, the parties are free to agree that a security interest secures any obligation whatsoever. Determining the obligations secured by collateral is solely a matter of construing the parties' agreement under applicable law. This Article rejects the holdings of cases decided under former Article 9 that applied other tests, such as whether a future advance or other subsequently incurred obligation was of the same or a similar type or class as earlier advances and obligations secured by the collateral."). As a consequence, there was attachment and perfection. Thus, **Answer (A) is incorrect.**

The remaining options require analysis of the status of Edgar's interest in copyrights. Note first that the original collateral description does not include copyrights. But that may not be fatal: if a copyright falls into the definition of "general intangibles" -a category that is included -then copyrights will get picked up. And they do -copyrights are personal property that are not other defined collateral types, and thus fit within the definition of "general intangibles" in section 9-102(a)(42). The trouble is that copyrights registered with the federal Copyright Office have been fairly uniformly held to require perfection by filing with that office; a state filing is not effective to perfect. *See, e.g., National Peregrine, Inc. v. Capitol Federal Savings & Loan Association (In re Peregrine Entertainment, Ltd.),* 116 B.R. 194 (C.D. Cal. 1990). That means that **Answer (B) cannot be correct** because, without a filing in the Copyright Office, Edgar is, at best, unperfected. But does Edgar have any interest at all? The question boils down to whether the preemption of federal law is total -nothing done in the name of Article 9 and state law is effective -or partial. Current thinking is that it is partial -no one argues that the federal copyright law governs the parties' actions upon, for example, default. But does it also preempt attachment? Article 9 does not think so in the absence of express preemption. §§ 9-109(c); 9-311. And what scant authority we have indicates that a security interest can attach to an unregistered copyright; it would be odd if that interest were severed upon registration. *See Aerocon Eng'g, Inc. v. Silicon Valley Bank (In re World Aux. Power Co.),* 303 F.3d 1120 (9th Cir. 2002). Thus, **the better answer is Answer (C),** which indicates that Edgar would have a junior interest.

168. Under the general rule of section 9-322(a)(1), conflicting perfected security interests rank according to priority in time of filing or perfection, whichever is earlier. Bank One filed on March 2, and Bank Two filed on March 28, so Bank One was the first creditor to file. Bank One's security interest became perfected on April 13, when Bank One gave value to Debtor and Debtor authenticated the security agreement (the financing statement had been previously filed, and Debtor had acquired rights in the item of equipment on April 1). Bank Two's security interest became perfected on March 28 when it filed its financing statement (the security interest had attached on April 1, when Debtor acquired the item of equipment, because Bank Two had already given value on March 21, the same date as the authenticated security agreement). So Bank Two's security interest became perfected before Bank One's security interest became perfected. But because Bank One filed on March 2, before Bank Two perfected its interest on March 28, Bank One enjoys priority. This seems only fair, as Bank Two was (or should have been) on notice of a possible competing

security interest by the financing statement that Bank One filed before Bank Two made its loan.

169. **Answer (C) is the correct answer.** We know that Poltroon starts out with a valid security interest in inventory and equipment, perfected (as is permissible under section 9-504(2)) by the filing of a financing statement that simply says "all assets." The question is whether this interest is somehow lost due to the despicable transactions described. Before starting this inquiry, we can **toss out Answer (B)**. The facts say that all that Connie bought was inventory, and thus the cashier's check, if anything, is proceeds of that inventory. Poltroon's security agreement and financing statement cover inventory, so there is no gap.

We can also **eliminate Answer (D)**. There is no "four-months rule" for change of ownership. The four-months rules that exist in Article 9 are: section 9-316 (giving secured parties four months to reperfect when the jurisdiction governing perfection changes, as when a debtor moves to a new state); section 9-507(b) (giving secured parties four months to change their financing statements to reflect a "pure" change in the debtor's name (without a concurrent change in ownership or title), such as when John Jones changes his name to Jimmy Johnson); and section 9-508(b) (giving secured parties four months to file a financing statement against a "new debtor," as when X Corp. merges with the debtor whose name is dissimilar from X Corp.'s, and under non-Article 9 law X Corp. becomes liable on the security agreement with the secured party).

That leaves Answers (A) and (C). Answer (A) indicates that the sale divests Poltroon of its security interest. As a general matter, that assertion is wrong. Under section 9-315(a)(1), a security interest continues notwithstanding sale or other disposition. The cutoff of section 9-320(a) will not help, because it only protects buyers in the ordinary course of business. Under the definition of such buyers, section 1-201(b)(9), the buyer must buy "in the ordinary course" and must buy in "good faith." Neither of these requirements are present here (this is not the way most transactions occur, and thus the transaction is not in the ordinary course, and the transaction apparently was plotted and planned in an effort to defeat the secured party's interests, so it is not in good faith), thereby denying Connie of buyer in the ordinary course status. That leaves **Answer (A) as an incorrect answer** and **Answer (C) as the correct answer**.

170. **Answer (C) is the correct answer.** This question requires knowledge with respect to purchase-money interests in consumer goods, continuation of perfection upon unauthorized sale, and proceeds from a bank account.

Start first with the pinkie ring. The security interest is given as part of the purchase of the ring, and the loan proceeds are used to buy the ring. Thus, the security interest is purchase-money under section 9-103(b). Next, was the ring acquired for personal, family, or household purposes? Yes, as it was acquired for daily wear. Thus, under section 9-309(1), the security interest was perfected without the necessity of filing a financing statement.

This matters due to the sale of the ring. The general rule on sales of collateral is that the security interest continues after the sale. § 9-315(a)(1). Thus, you need to go through the exceptions to the general rule. One exception, section 9-317(b), terminates a security interest only if it is unperfected at the time of the sale. (Note here that perfection continues even if the collateral is sold to someone (who then becomes a debtor) whose name is different than the original debtor -section 9-507 does not require the secured party to refile under the name of the new debtor.) The larger exceptions are in section 9-320: the buyer in the ordinary course exception, and the "garage sale" exception. Under section 9-320(a), a buyer in the ordinary course of business takes free of a security interest. Under section 1-201(b)(9), a person is a buyer in the ordinary course of business if it buys in good faith from someone in the business of selling goods of the type sold. Here, Larry does not sell rings as his business, so the diamond merchant is not a buyer in the ordinary course of business. Under section 9-320(b), however, someone who sells goods used as consumer goods to another person who will use them as consumer goods can sell free of even a perfected security interest, so long as there is no financing statement filed (as might happen at a "garage sale," hence the shorthand expression). Here, however, although the ring for Larry is consumer goods, the ring is not consumer goods in the diamond merchant's hands. Thus, the diamond merchant took subject to Vapid's security interest (and incidentally, Larry thus violated the warranty of good title on the sale under section 2-312).

Thus, those answers which do not include the ring are not correct. That **excludes Answer (D).** What about the account at Dumstruck? Here we need to look at proceeds. The check received upon the sale of the ring was proceeds under section 9-102(a)(64). Funds deposited into the bank account at Dumstuck upon collection on that check were thus also proceeds (or proceeds of proceeds). From this point, however, we have to engage in tracing -we are told that the lowest intermediate balance rule ("LIBR") applies as a method "of tracing, including application of equitable principles, that is permitted under law other than this article with respect to commingled property of the type involved." § 9-315(b)(2). This means that the assumption is that the first funds expended from the account will *not* be proceeds; it is as though the existing balance was oil and the proceeds deposited were water; the water will sink to the bottom and the oil will float to the top. Any withdrawals of liquid will thus be first from the "oil," or non-proceeds. Moreover, since we can "identify" the cash proceeds by the LIBR, the secured party's interest is continuously perfected for more than 20 days, at least as to all such funds identified. § 9-315(d)(2).

From this, we can deduce two things. First, we are told that after the deposit, the account had a zero balance. Thus, all proceeds were spent. That means that any subsequent deposits had to be from non-proceeds, and thus under the LIBR there are no identifiable cash proceeds in the account, and Vapid will not have a superior interest in that account. **Answer (A) is therefore incorrect**.

Answers (B) and (C) differ in whether Vapid has a perfected security interest in the watch. Since there was only $10,000 in Larry's account at Dumstruck before deposit of the ring proceeds, the expenditure of $20,000 to acquire the watch immediately after the deposit had to be at least half proceeds. But that is enough. So the watch was proceeds. Is it perfected for more than 20 days? Here's the rub. None of the exceptions in section 9-315(d) seem to fit; the "same office" rule in paragraph (1) might work, but it requires a filed financing statement to apply, and Vapid did not file one. The watch is not cash proceeds, so paragraph (2) does not apply. And Vapid did not perfect by any other means (such as by filing a financing statement against the watch), so paragraph (3) does not apply. Thus, Vapid is unperfected as to the watch, so **Answer (B) is incorrect.** That leaves Answer (C); Vapid has a superior interest in the ring only.

171. Alamo Finance holds a perfected security interest in the Item because its collateral includes after-acquired equipment and Alamo Finance filed a financing statement. BigBank has an enforceable security interest in the Item under section 9-315(a)(2) because the Item represents proceeds of the deposit account that are identifiable therefrom (via the canceled check); and the security interest in the Item is perfected by the financing statement filed by BigBank on September 1. Under the general priority rules of sections 9-322(a)(1) and (b)(1), BigBank's security interest enjoys priority because BigBank perfected its security interest in the deposit account on April 20, long before Alamo Finance filed its financing statement on June 15 and perfected its security interest in the Item on September 1. But as noted in the preamble to sections 9-322(a) and 9-322(f), the general rules are subject to other priority rules, one of which is section 9-322(d). And under that rule, if BigBank's security interest in the deposit account is perfected (as in this situation) by a method other than filing (*i.e.*, control), then conflicting perfected security interests in any proceeds of the deposit account (such as the Item) rank according to priority in time of filing. Therefore, Alamo Finance's security interest enjoys priority because Alamo Finance filed its financing statement on June 15, before BigBank filed its financing statement on September 1.

172. **Answer (D) is the correct answer. Answers (A) and (B) are incorrect** because a financing statement need not mention any after-acquired property clause (or future advance clause). § 9-502, cmt. 2 (third paragraph). **Answer (C) is incorrect** because SMC acquired the Steinmark pianos in August, within four months after its name change on June 1. Therefore, even if the name change is "seriously misleading" under section 9-506, TNB's original financing statement remains effective to perfect its security interest in the pianos under section 9-507(c)(1). Furthermore, the name change has no effect on the enforceability (or attachment) of TNB's security interest; it affects only the perfection of that interest. TNB has an enforceable security interest in the pianos because the collateral includes inventory (and the pianos are inventory -goods held for sale or lease -in the hands of SMC) and the security agreement included an after-acquired property clause. And that security interest is perfected by TNB's financing statement. Because SMC acquired the pianos within four months after the name change, the name change has no bearing on perfection. So **Answer (D) is the correct answer**.

173. **Answer (B) is the correct answer.** TNB has a perfected security interest in all of the pianos for reasons given in the previous answer. Steinmark also has a perfected security interest in all of the pianos. But because TNB filed its financing statement long before Steinmark did, TNB enjoys priority under section 9-322(a)(1)

unless Steinmark can successfully claim the superpriority afforded by section 9-324(b) to purchase-money security interests in inventory. Steinmark has engaged in seller financing, so it can claim a purchase-money security interest in the pianos under sections 9-103(a) and (b)(1). And the pianos, held for sale or lease by SMC, are inventory. Nevertheless, Steinmark enjoys superpriority only if the four numbered conditions of section 9-324(b) are satisfied. The facts indicate that Steinmark met the three notice-related conditions of (b)(2) (notice sent to TNB), (3) (notice received by TNB on August 12 before pianos are delivered on August 15 and 22), and (4) (substance of notice adequate). Subsection (b)(1) requires Steinmark to perfect its security interest before the pianos are delivered to SMC. Steinmark perfected its interest by filing a financing statement on August 19. It delivered the grand pianos thereafter on August 22, so Steinmark enjoys superpriority in the grands under section 9-324(b). **This eliminates Answers (C) and (D).** But Steinmark delivered the upright pianos earlier on August 15, before the filing date of its financing statement, so Steinmark cannot claim any superpriority in the uprights. Instead, TNB enjoys priority in the uprights under section 9-322(a)(1) because its filing on April 2 predates Steinmark's filing on August 19. **This eliminates Answer (A).** As TNB enjoys priority in the uprights and Steinmark enjoys priority in the grands, **Answer (B) is the correct answer.**

174. **Answer (B) is the correct answer. Answer (A) is incorrect** because Quark has engaged in seller financing and is retaining a security interest in the computer system to secure repayment of the purchase price. Therefore, Quark has a purchase-money security interest in the system under sections 9-103(a) and (b)(1). Quark cannot invoke the superpriority of section 9-324(a) because it filed its financing statement on November 29, more than 20 days after delivering the computer system on November 7. But the lack of superpriority has no effect on the purchase-money status of the security interest. Therefore, **Answer (C) is incorrect. Answer (D) is incorrect** because neither section 9-322(a)(1) nor section 9-324(a) require Quark to give any notice to TNB. (Section 9-324(b), which does require a purchase-money creditor to give notice, is not applicable because the computer system is not inventory in the hands of SMC.) As between TNB and Quark, Quark's security interest enjoys priority. True, Quark cannot invoke the superpriority of section 9-324(a) for reasons given. But Quark still enjoys priority under the general rule of section 9-322(a). TNB has an enforceable security interest in the computer system because its security agreement referenced equipment and included an after-acquired property clause. But SMC acquired the computer system in November, more than four months after SMC's name change on June 1. The name change is seriously misleading under the facts (and probably also under section 9-506), and TNB's failure to timely file an amendment means that its security interest in the computer system is unperfected under section 9-507(c)(2). Therefore, Quark enjoys priority under section 9-322(a)(2) because its perfected security interest in the computer system trumps TNB's unperfected security interest.

175. **Answer (A) is the correct answer.** NBI clearly has a perfected security interest in the car before the sale. It has a valid security agreement which adequately described the collateral, FCI has ownership rights in the collateral, and NBI has given

value in the form of a loan. It perfected by filing in the proper place. Note that even if the cars were covered by a certificate of title statute, the financing statement would still be sufficient. Under section 9-311(d), a security interest in cars held as inventory is perfected by filing a financing statement, even if the cars are subject to a certificate of title statute.

Answers (C) and (D) require some rule that cuts off a security interest to a good faith purchaser for value. Although that is the standard for acquiring a superior ownership interest from one who has voidable title under section 2-403(1), that section is not incorporated into Article 9, and no rule utilizes that status. **Answers (C) and (D) are thus incorrect answers.**

Under section 9-315(a)(1), the security interest continues notwithstanding sale unless some other provision of article 9, or section 2-403(2), so provides. Section 2-403(2) permits a buyer in the ordinary course of business to take free of an owner's interest if property is sold by one to whom property had been entrusted, and if the person entrusted is in the business of selling goods of that type. That does not help here, except to the extent a buyer in the ordinary course took from Harriet. Is NBI a buyer in the ordinary course of business? For that matter, is Harriet a buyer in the ordinary course of business that can take free of NBI's interest? This requires an examination of a buyer in the ordinary course of business.

Section 1-201(b)(9) defines "buyer in ordinary course of business," as follows:

"Buyer in ordinary course of business" means a person that buys goods in good faith, without knowledge that the sale violates the rights of another person in the goods, and in the ordinary course from a person, other than a pawnbroker, in the business of selling goods of that kind. . . . A person buys goods in the ordinary course if the sale to the person comports with the usual or customary practices in the kind of business in which the seller is engaged or with the seller's own usual or customary practices. . . . A buyer in ordinary course of business may buy for cash, by exchange of other property, or on secured or unsecured credit, and may acquire goods or documents of title under a pre-existing contract for sale. *Only a buyer that takes possession of the goods or has a right to recover the goods from the seller under Article 2 may be a buyer in ordinary course of business. A person that acquires goods in a transfer in bulk or as security for or in total or partial satisfaction of a money debt is not a buyer in ordinary course of business.*

(Emphasis added.)

The key to this question is the highlighted sentence. We know that Harriet did not take possession of the goods, but she otherwise met all the requirements: she bought in good faith and without knowledge that her purchase violated anyone's property rights; she also bought from someone in the business of selling goods of the kind bought (cars) and in the ordinary course of business (no odd terms).

That takes us to her lack of possession. In the alternative, the definition says that Harriet may be a buyer in the ordinary course if she "has a right to recover the goods from the seller under Article 2." Under Article 2, a "right to recover goods" is a right of specific performance governed by section 2-716. In this regard, the last sentence of section 2-716(3) was amended at the same time as current Article 9 was introduced, and now reads: "In the case of goods bought for personal, family, or household purposes, the buyer's right of replevin vests upon acquisition of a special property, even if the seller had not then repudiated or failed to deliver." So Harriet's specific performance right, her buyer in the ordinary course status, and her ability to prevail over NBI rest on the acquisition of a "special property" interest. As a consequence, it does not matter that Harriet did not take immediate possession, and thus **Answer (B) is incorrect.**

The acquisition of a "special property" interest is governed by section 2-501, which states that the special property interest arises upon identification of the goods to the contract. Identification occurs when the parties agree, or in the absence of agreement, "when the contract is made if it is for the sale of goods already existing and identified." § 2-501(a)(1). Thus, Harriet acquired a special property interest in the car no later than the signing of the contract. She was thus a buyer in the ordinary course and took free of NBI's interest.

Did Harriet's entrustment wind up revesting the superior interest in the car to NBI? No. NBI cannot be a buyer in the ordinary course of business and take free under section 2-403(2), because, under the last sentence in the definition, "A person that acquires goods . . . as security for . . . a money debt is not a buyer in ordinary course of business." Since NBI's purchase would be as security, it cannot thus be a buyer in the ordinary course of business.

That leaves Harriet as a buyer in the ordinary course of business who takes free of NBI's interest under section 9-320(a), **making Answer (A) the correct answer.**

176.   **Answer (C) is the correct answer.** This question raises the issues of when a secured party may exercise its rights, and the consequences of trying to prematurely exercise those rights. Throughout Article 9, the exercise of rights of repossession and foreclosure are contingent upon the existence of a default. § 9-609. **Answer (A) is thus wrong** because, while it is true that FCI owed NBI $1,000,000, that fact is irrelevant unless FCI was in default, it does not matter that a debt is still owing. Similarly, **Answer (B) is also incorrect** because the issue of whether the peace was breached was a condition to the conduct of the repossession, as opposed to something that validated the repossession in the first place.

Default, however, is not defined in Article 9. It has to come from the parties. Here, the parties have defined default, but the lender, in apparent good faith, has sought to exercise remedies when it has no contractual right to do so. Such an exercise is typically a conversion of the debtor's property under state law -the unlawful exercise of dominion or control of the property of another without adequate consent. And conversion remains a viable option. "Remedies available under other law, including conversion, remain available under this Article in appropriate cases. See Sections 1-103, 1-106." § 9-621, cmt. 12.

When NBI sought to repossess prior to FCI's default, it acted contrary to the property interests not only of FCI, but also Harriet. It thus committed conversion with respect to all cars (including the car described in Harriet's contract), **making Answer (C) the correct answer** and **Answer (D) an underinclusive and incorrect answer**.

177. **Answer (B) is the correct answer.** The degree of protection afforded to Bank's future advances is found in section 9-323(b). Under that section, Bank's future advances (*i.e.*, advances funded after a party becomes a lien creditor) are protected if Bank funds the advance (i) within the 45-day period after the party becomes a lien creditor, (ii) without knowledge of the lien, or (iii) pursuant to a commitment entered into without knowledge of the lien. Bank's advance funded on June 1, before PramCo became a lien creditor on June 15, is entitled to repayment. Bank's advances that were funded on June 30, July 10, and July 20 also are entitled to repayment because those advances were funded within the 45-day period following the date (June 15) when PramCo became a lien creditor. (Notice that the 45-day period is absolute. It is not shortened by the secured party's knowledge of the lien -as Bank so learned on July 15.) Bank's advance funded on August 5 is not entitled to repayment. Bank funded the advance outside the 45-day period, with knowledge of the lien, and not pursuant to any commitment. So Bank is entitled to $100,000, with the balance of $20,000 payable to PramCo. This result is found in **Answer (B), making it the correct answer** and **Answers (A), (C), and (D) incorrect answers**.

178. **Answer (A) is the correct answer.** Under section 9-323(b) all of Bank's advances are protected because Bank funded them "pursuant to a commitment" entered into without knowledge of the lien. This result is found in **Answer (A), making it the correct answer** and **Answers (B), (C), and (D) incorrect answers**. The phrase "pursuant to commitment" is defined at section 9-102(a)(68) and is met even if Bank is excused from funding an advance if Borrower is in default. Also note that Bank's knowledge is examined when it commits to making the loans, not when it funds the advances.

179. The court should enter a declaratory judgment awarding priority to First Bank. Because First Bank failed to timely file its continuation statement, the effectiveness of its original financing statement lapsed. One result of the lapse is that First Bank is retroactively unperfected against "a purchaser of the collateral for value" (section 9-315(c)). However, Tort Victim is not a "purchaser" under section 1-201 because it did not acquire its property interest in Debtor's inventory by a voluntary transaction, but rather by judicial process. Therefore, First Bank's security interest (although now unperfected) continues to enjoy priority over Tort Victim's judgment lien under section 9-317(a)(2) because First Bank's security interest was perfected when Tort Victim's judgment lien attached to Debtor's inventory. See § 9-515, cmt. 3.

180. **Answer (B) is the correct answer.** Because Sally uses the boat for weekend recreational use, the boat is a "consumer good" as defined in section 9-102(a)(23). When collateral is a consumer good, First Bank must send its notice only to the debtor and any secondary obligor. § 9-611(c). Sally, who owns the boat that is serving as collateral, is the debtor under section 9-102(a)(28)(A). Mary, the guarantor on First Bank's loan, is a secondary obligor under section 9-102(a)(71)(A). So **Answer (B) is the correct answer. Answer (A) is underinclusive and incorrect.** First Bank can send its notice to other parties, such as Dealer and Second Bank. But Article 9 does not require First Bank to do so, **making Answers (C) and (D) incorrect**.

181. **Answer (A) is the correct answer.** Under section 9-615(a)(3), First Bank must remit proceeds to <u>subordinate</u> creditors who have provided an authenticated demand for proceeds. Dealer, who gave written demand, is not a subordinate creditor (**eliminating Answers (B), (C), and (D)**). True, it never filed a financing statement. But Dealer -who has engaged in seller financing -can claim a purchase-money security interest (section 9-103(a) and (b)(1)) in a consumer good, so its security interest is automatically perfected on attachment (section 9-309(1)), giving it priority under section 9-322(a) over the competing claims of other subsequent secured creditors like First Bank and Second Bank. Therefore, Dealer is not a subordinate creditor and cannot claim any of the proceeds. Second Bank is a subordinate creditor. However, Second Bank is not entitled to any proceeds because First Bank never received from Second Bank an authenticated demand for proceeds (**making Answers (C) and (D) incorrect answers**). Therefore, all remaining proceeds revert to the debtor, Sally, as "surplus" under section 9-615(d). This result is stated in **Answer (A), the correct answer.**

182. **Answer (C) is the correct answer.** This is a consumer-goods transaction under section 9-102(a)(24) because the boat is a consumer good and all of the loans are personal. Therefore, First Bank must send a notice that complies with section 9-614. The notice must include the information described in subsection (1)(A)-(D). Subsection (1)(A) cross-references section 9-613(1), which requires a collateral description. So **Answer (A) is incorrect.** Subsection (1)(B) requires a description of any liability for which the recipient remains liable, so **Answer (B) is incorrect.** Subsection (1)(C) requires a telephone number that can be dialed to determine the redemption price. So **Answer (D) is incorrect.** But the notice need not include a description of the default, **making Answer (C) the correct answer.**

183. **Answer (A) is the correct answer.** The boat is a consumer good, and Sally's debt is personal (rather than commercial), so the transaction is a consumer transaction under section 9-102(a)(26). Section 9-620(g) prohibits partial strict foreclosure in a consumer transaction, so **Answer (A) is correct.** Therefore, First Bank must propose a full strict foreclosure. In a full strict foreclosure, First Bank need not send its proposal to Mary, a secondary obligor (presumably because a secondary obligor will never object to a full strict foreclosure, which effectively cancels the obligor's contingent liability). § 9-621(b). **So Answer (B) is incorrect.** Under section 9-620(c)(2)(C), Sally's prolonged silence can indeed create constructive consent, so **Answer (C) is incorrect.** And **Answer (D) is incorrect** because First Bank must order a UCC search report to ensure that it complies with section 9-621(a)(2), which requires First Bank to send its proposal to other parties that have timely filed a financing statement against the boat.

184. **Answer (B) is the correct answer.** The first thing to check is the status of Sears' security interest. Its sales slip appears to contain all the requisites for attachment under section 9-203: it is a record which Ed authenticates by signing, and it describes the collateral; it represents value given in the credit it extends; and it evidences that Ed has rights in the collateral (Sears actually does this with its own in-house credit card). So there is attachment. Is there perfection? There is no financing statement filed, so the baseline method of perfection is absent. § 9-310(a).

Are there any exceptions available? Note first that the security interest is purchase-money; that is, the security interest in the television secured the obligation incurred to buy that same television. § 9-103(a), (b)(1). If the television is "consumer goods," as defined in section 9-102(a)(23), then perfection occurs upon attachment; that is, it is automatic. § 9-309(1). We are told that Ed takes the television home and watches his favorite shows, which looks to be the type of "personal, family or household" purposes that would make the collateral a consumer good. Thus, Sears was perfected when Ed walked out of the store.

This analysis thus shows that **Answer (C) is incorrect**. Sears did not have to file a financing statement. It also shows that **Answer (A) is incorrect**. The other answers seem to focus on changes brought about by the sale to Jane, Ed's neighbor. The baseline rule here is stated in section 9-210 generally and in section 9-315(a)(1) specifically: "a security interest or agricultural lien continues in collateral notwithstanding sale, lease, license, exchange, or other disposition thereof . . . ." Answer (A) is not responsive to this in that it states some of the requirements for a person to take free of an *unperfected* security interest under section 9-317(b). But Sears was perfected, and thus section 9-317(b) is irrelevant and **Answer (A) is thus incorrect.**

Answer (D) seems to indicate that Sears might have some duty to file a financing statement since the debtor now is Jane (recall that the debtor is the one who owns the collateral). But under general *nemo dat* principles, and under section 9-315(a)(1), the security interest continues. Answer (D), however, is consistent with Sears always winning in this situation. If we look to other rules terminating or subordinating a security interest, and find one, the statement is overbroad. One such section that shows this overbreadth is section 9-320(b), the so-called "garage sale" exception. That section, in pertinent part, states that "a buyer of goods from a person who used or bought the goods for use primarily for personal, family, or household purposes takes free of a security interest, even if perfected, if the buyer buys: (1) without knowledge of the security interest; (2) for value; (3) primarily for the buyer's personal, family, or household purposes; and (4) before the filing of a financing statement covering the goods." Paragraphs (1), (2), and (4) are met: Jane did not know of Sears' interest, paid cash for the goods, and Sears never filed a financing statement. Paragraph (3), however, provides the answer: Jane's use is not for personal, family, or household purposes; she uses it in her profession as a teacher. That makes the television "equipment" under section 9-102(a)(33). Thus, this means that **Answer (D) is not the best answer. Answer (B) provides the more complete and accurate answer.**

185. Yes, Wally should be very concerned. The trustee will contend that Wally's security interest is unperfected because the financing statement is seriously misleading (and therefore ineffective) under section 9-506 because the financing statement referred to the debtor by a trade name ("The Plumber's Helper"), rather than the legal name ("Robby") (see §§ 9-503(a) and (c)). The trustee will then invoke its powers under the "strong arm clause" of 11 U.S.C. § 544(a)(1). Under that provision, the trustee is given the status of a hypothetical lien creditor as of the date of the bankruptcy petition. And because Wally's security interest was never perfected, the trustee can

invoke section 9-317(a)(2) and argue that its hypothetical lien enjoys priority over Wally's unperfected security interest. As a result, Wally's unperfected security interest is avoided and his claim in the bankruptcy is unsecured (presumably resulting in a bankruptcy dividend significantly less than if he had held a fully secured claim).

186.   **Answer (A) is the correct answer.** As a general rule, the automatic stay (11 U.S.C. § 362(a)) prevents a secured party from taking any action against the debtor, the estate, or the collateral. For example, 11 U.S.C. § 362(a)(1) halts the commencement of any lawsuit against the debtor that could have been commenced pre-petition, **making Answer (D) an incorrect answer. Answers (B) and (C) are incorrect** under 11 U.S.C. § 362(a)(3), (4), (5), and/or (6), which, among other things, prohibit a secured party from taking collateral from the estate, exercising control over estate property, enforcing any security interest in estate property, enforcing any lien against the debtor's property, and recovering a pre-petition claim against the debtor. Answer (A) would appear to be incorrect because 11 U.S.C. § 362(a)(4) and (5) block a secured party from taking any action to perfect a security interest in property of the debtor or the estate (query, however, whether attempting to maintain or continue perfection is the same as attempting to perfect). But 11 U.S.C. § 362(a) is expressly subject to subsection (b). And subsection (b)(3) permits a secured party to take action "to maintain or continue the perfection" of a security interest "to the extent that the trustee's rights and powers are subject to such perfection under" 11 U.S.C. § 546(b). 11 U.S.C. § 546(b)(1)(B) subjects the trustee's rights and powers to any applicable law (e.g., Article 9) that "provides for the maintenance or continuation of perfection of an interest in property to be effective against an entity that acquires rights in such property before the date on which action is taken to effect such maintenance or continuation." Under section 9-515(c), a security interest perfected by a financing statement becomes unperfected when the financing statement ceases to be effective (generally after five years from the date of filing). Upon the lapse, the security interest is deemed "never to have been perfected as against a purchaser of the collateral for value." But the trustee, a "lien creditor" under section 9-102(a)(52)(C), is not a "purchaser of the collateral for value" since section 1-201 defines "purchaser" as one who acquires a property interest in a voluntary transaction. Therefore, even though a secured party may become unperfected when its financing statement lapses, the security interest continues to enjoy the same pre-lapse priority over any lien; the post-petition filing of a continuation statement does not affect the priority between the secured creditor and the trustee. The trustee's lien remains subject to the security interest perfected on the petition date, whether perfected or unperfected thereafter. Thus, the post-petition filing of the continuation statement is effective against an earlier lien, triggering application of 11 U.S.C. §§ 546(b) and 362(b)(3). Because the post-petition filing of the continuation does not violate the automatic stay, **Answer (A) is the correct answer**.

187.   **Answer (C) is the correct answer.** The "strong arm clause," codified at 11 U.S.C. § 541(a)(1), permits the trustee to avoid a security interest that is not perfected on the petition date. **Answer (A) is incorrect** because the security interest, a purchase-money security interest in a consumer good, is automatically perfected

on attachment. § 9-309(1). **Answer (B) is incorrect** because Lender's security interest was perfected by the financing statement filed on December 20. (But Lender's act of filing so close to the petition date may permit the trustee to avoid the security interest as a voidable preference under 11 U.S.C. § 547.) **Answer (D) also is incorrect**. Although Merchant's security interest was not perfected on the petition date, the trustee's strong-arm powers are subject to Merchant's priority rights under section 9-317(e). See 11 U.S.C. § 546(b)(1)(A). **Answer (C) is the correct answer** because Nelson's father cannot rely on automatic perfection of his security interest. A purchase-money security interest in consumer goods is automatically perfected on attachment. § 9-309(1). But the collateral is investment property, not consumer goods. Furthermore, investment property is excluded from the definition of "goods" under section 9-102(a)(44) so Nelson's father cannot claim that his security interest is a purchase-money security interest. § 9-103(b).

And the post-petition filing does not violate the automatic stay. Post-petition perfection is permitted by 11 U.S.C. § 362(b)(3) if "the trustee's rights and powers are subject to such perfection under section 546(b) of this title . . . ." Under 11 U.S.C. § 546(b)(1), a trustee's rights and powers are subject to any Article 9 provision that permits perfection to be effective against a lien creditor that acquired its lien prior to perfection. The applicable Article 9 provision is section 9-317(e), which permits a purchase-money creditor to enjoy priority over the competing (and prior) claim of a lien creditor if the purchase-money creditor's interest is perfected no later than the 20th day after the debtor receives possession of the collateral. As Dealer (a seller-financer) can claim a purchase-money security interest in the photocopier under sections 9-103(a) and (b)(1), and because Dealer timely filed its financing statement on July 25 (a date not later than twenty days after the delivery date of July 8), Dealer can invoke the protection afforded by section 9-317(e). Therefore, Dealer did not violate the automatic stay by filing its financing statement after Merchant filed its bankruptcy petition.

188.   **Answer (D) is the correct answer.** Under 11 U.S.C. § 547(e)(2), the transfer date of the security interest is the date of attachment (August 3), rather than the date of perfection (August 4) because the security interest was perfected within ten days of attachment. Nevertheless, the transfer on August 3 was for an antecedent debt because the loan was made on August 1. Therefore, the trustee can indeed prove that the transfer was for antecedent debt, making **Answer (A) an incorrect answer**. With the transfer, Bank will have a secured claim in the bankruptcy; without the transfer, Bank's claim is unsecured. Therefore, the trustee can prove that Bank is in a better position with the transfer than it would be without the transfer in a Chapter 7 liquidation, **making Answer (B) an incorrect answer**. (Generally, the trustee cannot prove the existence of 11 U.S.C. § 547(b)(5) when the transfer is a loan repayment to an oversecured creditor. In this problem, however, the trustee is attacking a collateral transfer, not a payment transfer.) The first parts of Answers (C) and (D) are correct, as the trustee can prove all elements of a voidable preference under 11 U.S.C. § 547(b). But the second part of Answer (C) is incorrect because the "ordinary course of business" exception protects only payment transfers (note the language in 11 U.S.C. § 547(c)(2): "to the extent that such transfer was -(A) in payment of a debt . . . ."), **making Answer (C) incorrect**. In this problem, the

trustee is attacking a security interest, not a loan repayment. The second part of Answer (D) is correct because when the "new value" was given (*i.e.*, when the loan was made) on August 1, Bank and Debtor intended the loan to be unsecured, rather than secured. Perhaps rephrased, when the loan was made, the parties did not intend any security interest transfer. Therefore, even if the security interest on August 3 could be deemed a "substantially contemporaneous" exchange for new value given on August 1 (satisfying 11 U.S.C. § 547(c)(2)(B)), the facts prohibit Bank from proving the intent required by 11 U.S.C. § 547(c)(2)(A) when the loan was made. Thus, Bank cannot successfully invoke the contemporaneous exchange exception and protect the security interest from attack. As a result, **Answer (D) is the correct answer.**

189.   **Answer (C) is the correct answer.** There are two items of collateral (or their proceeds) involved here: the ink and paper, and the printing press. The security agreement simply says "all equipment." Was the ink and paper "equipment," and thus is the check for the purchase of the ink and paper proceeds? No. First, we start with the interpretive provision in section 9-108(b). That section says that a description is sufficient if it "identifies the collateral by: . . . (3) . . . , a type of collateral defined in [the Uniform Commercial Code]." Equipment is such a term. It is defined in section 9-102(a)(33) as "goods other than inventory, farm products, or consumer goods." It is thus the "residual" category for tangible collateral. Are the paper and ink included in any of the other categories? If so, they cannot be equipment. And they are in another category. Section 9-102(a)(48)(D) defines inventory to include "goods, other than farm products, which: . . . (D) consist of raw materials, work in process, or materials used or consumed in a business." Since the ink and paper would be "used or consumed" in Darren's business, they would be inventory, and First Bank would have no interest in them.

This **eliminates Answers (A) and (B)** because they both indicate an interest in the ink and paper. In choosing between Answers (C) and (D), we have to determine whether the used printing press was "equipment." It is not inventory (because it is not held for sale or lease). See § 9-102, cmt. 4.a. ("Implicit in the definition is the criterion that the sales or leases are or will be in the ordinary course of business. For example, machinery used in manufacturing is equipment, not inventory, even though it is the policy of the debtor to sell machinery when it becomes obsolete or worn."). Because no farming operations or consumer use is present, it is not farm products or consumer goods. It must thus be equipment, and thus there is attachment given the terms of the security agreement.

Is the security interest perfected by an "all assets" description in the financing statement? First, note that Article 9 permits supergeneric descriptions such as "all assets" or "all personal property" only in financing statements; such descriptions are insufficient for a description in a security agreement. §§ 9-108(c) (inappropriate in security agreement); 9-504(2) (appropriate for financing statement). Next, note that the financing statement was filed in Nevada, where Darren, a resident of Nevada, is located for purposes of section 9-307(b)(1) at his "principal residence," which the facts give us as Nevada. Finally, note that Darren authorized the filing, so there is no problem under section 9-509(a)(1). But ultimately, he only authorized it for equipment. Can the overbroad financing statement work with respect to those areas agreed to be within its ambit? Yes. Section 9-509, cmt. 4, ex. 1, makes this clear: "Debtor authenticates a security agreement creating a security interest in Debtor's inventory in favor of Secured Party. Secured Party files a financing statement covering inventory and accounts. The financing statement is authorized insofar as it covers inventory and unauthorized insofar as it covers accounts."

With the filing thus authorized, **Answer (D) is incorrect** since it excludes the used printing press, and **Answer (C) is the correct answer**.

190. **Answer (A) is the correct answer.** This question involves the scope of the grant of the security interest: does "all equipment" mean just those pieces of equipment Darren possessed on the date of attachment, or does it extend to other pieces of equipment as well? While there is no hard and fast rule here, there is enough information in the problem to answer this question. First, start with guidance from the comments. Section 9-108, cmt. 3, states: "Much litigation has arisen over whether a description in a security agreement is sufficient to include after-acquired collateral if the agreement does not explicitly so provide. This question is one of contract interpretation and is not susceptible to a statutory rule (other than a rule to the effect that it is a question of contract interpretation). Accordingly, this section contains no reference to descriptions of after-acquired collateral."

That might seem to stymie this inquiry, but for the fact that the problem indicates that the security agreement anticipated the acquisition of the printing press on July 1, and that this printing press was purchased with loan proceeds. This should be sufficient indication that the proper interpretation of the contract would include this new printing press as collateral to which First Bank's lien would attach. Because the prior problem established that First Bank had a security interest in the existing printing presses, that **makes Answer (A) the proper answer**, and **leaves Answers (B), (C), and (D) underinclusive and incorrect**.

191. **Answer (B) is the correct answer.** The change in facts indicates a change of residence for Darren. He is now a resident of California. Section 9-307(b)(1) states: "A debtor who is an individual is located at the individual's principal residence." Under section 9-301(1), "while a debtor is located in a jurisdiction, the local law of that jurisdiction governs perfection, the effect of perfection or nonperfection, and the priority of a security interest in collateral." With Darren's residence in California, the filing in Nevada is meaningless. The law of Nevada (that is, Nevada's version of sections 9-301 and 9-307) will point to Darren's "location," which under the law of Nevada (that is, Nevada's version of section 9-307) is in California. California law will point to the same place. Thus, only a filing in California according to California law will be sufficient to perfect an interest in any collateral owned by Darren. All of First Bank's security interests are thus unperfected (**eliminating Answers (A), (C), and (D)**), and the trustee would have a superior interest in them pursuant to its status as a judicial lien creditor under 11 U.S.C. § 544(a)(1).

192. **Answer (C) is the correct answer.** This question looks to whether First Bank can take action (it can, because there is a default), and if the collateral which it wants

to pursue is subject to its perfected security interest (the perfection being necessary, otherwise the trustee would have a superior interest under the "strong arm" provision in 11 U.S.C. § 544(a)(1)).

As indicated previously (see the answer to the initial question of this five-question set), the ink and paper were not part of First Bank's collateral. Thus, any answer which selects the $5,000 check, which is proceeds of that ink and paper, is incorrect. This reasoning **eliminates Answers (A) and (B).**

The difference between Answers (C) and (D) is the inclusion of the $100,000 downpayment check (the account due from SPI is proceeds, and there is no need for reperfection because accounts are perfected in the same office as equipment, and because there was no intervening cash proceeds, § 9-315(d)(2)).

The check is also proceeds under section 9-102(a)(64) as something received on the exchange or sale of collateral. It will be perfected for more than twenty days if provided for in section 9-315(d). Section 9-315(d)(2) provides for continuous perfection if the proceeds are identifiable cash proceeds. A check is "cash proceeds" under section 9-102(a)(9), and because it can be traced directly to the sale, then it is identifiable. Thus, **Answer (C)**, which includes the check, **is the correct answer, rather than Answer (D).**

193.   **Answer (D) is the correct answer.** First Bank's sloppiness means that it will be junior to MFI under the first to file or perfect rule of section 9-322(a). This **makes Answer (A) an incorrect answer**, because the presumption given the earlier filing will be that MFI is senior to First Bank. The remaining answers require us to look at First Bank's interest in the check and the new printing press.

Although First Bank has a perfected security interest in the check (as we have seen in prior questions), it is junior to MFI, since priority extends not only to original collateral, but as to proceeds as well. As stated in section 9-322(b)(1): "the time of filing or perfection as to a security interest in collateral is also the time of filing or perfection as to a security interest in proceeds." **So Answer (C) is incorrect.**

What about the printing press purchased on July 1? Here, we need to determine whether this is a purchase-money security interest, because if it is, First Bank has a shot at priority (at least to the extent of its purchase-money debt) under section 9-324. Under the original facts, the acquisition of the new printing press was anticipated by the security agreement, and the loan funds were used to acquire the press. It thus appears to be a purchase-money security interest under section 9-103(b). Because it is equipment, the priority rule is found in section 9-324(a), which states that "a perfected purchase-money security interest in goods other than inventory or livestock has priority over a conflicting security interest in the same goods, . . . if the purchase-money security interest is perfected when the debtor receives possession of the collateral or within 20 days thereafter." Was First Bank perfected when Darren received possession? Yes. Perfection occurred when the last item of attachment occurred; that is, when Darren had rights in the collateral, which had certainly occurred upon delivery. Value had been given in the form of the loan, and there was a written security agreement describing the collateral. The financing statement was filed before delivery. Thus, First Bank would qualify for purchase-money priority under section 9-324(a), **making Answer (D), rather than Answer (B), the correct answer**.

194. **Answer (C) is the correct answer**. This question involves a priority dispute in an "accession." Section 9-102(a)(1) defines an "accession" as "goods that are physically united with other goods in such a manner that the identity of the original goods is not lost." The sound board and the piano each retained their identity after the sound board was installed in the piano. Therefore, from Sound Great's perspective, the piano is an "accession;" from Salem Bank's perspective, the sound board is the "accession." See § 9-335, cmt. 3. But the collateral does not involve a certificate of title, so priority in the insurance proceeds is dictated by rules found outside section 9-335. See § 9-335(c).

Determining which priority rule resolves the dispute between Sounds Great and Salem Bank requires knowing whether their security interests are perfected and qualify for purchase-money status. Both creditors hold a purchase-money security interest under section 9-103; Sounds Great offered seller financing for the piano (but not the sound board), and Salem Bank offered third-party financing for the sound board. True, Salem Bank cannot claim superpriority of its security interest in the sound board under section 9-324(a) because it filed its financing statement on August 30, more than twenty days after Stine Company delivered and installed the sound board on August 8. But Salem Bank's inability to claim superpriority does not adversely affect the purchase-money status of its security interest in the sound board. Therefore, **Answer (D) is incorrect**.

Because Salem Bank filed its financing statement too late to qualify for the superpriority afforded by section 9-324(a) to purchase-money creditors, it appears that Sounds Great is entitled to priority in all of the insurance proceeds under the first-to-file-or-perfect rule of section 9-322(a)(1). But that rule does not apply because Sounds Great does not have a perfected security interest in the piano. Sounds Great filed its continuation statement on April 1, outside the six-month window (April 15-October 15) mandated by section 9-515(d). Therefore, even though the premature filing is recorded in the public records, the filing is ineffective to continue perfection. § 9-510(c). So the initial financing statement filed by Sounds Great in 2001 lapsed in 2006, its security interest in the piano became unperfected, and its security interest is deemed never to have been perfected against Salem Bank. §§ 9-515(c); 1-201(b) (defining "purchaser" in a manner that includes a secured party). This means that Sounds Great cannot enjoy priority in any part of the insurance proceeds solely because it filed and perfected its security interest in the piano before Salem Bank filed and perfected its security interest in the sound board, so **Answers (A) and (B) are incorrect**.

Salem Bank holds a perfected purchase-money security interest in the sound board, and Sounds Great has an unperfected security interest in the piano (including the sound board). Therefore, Salem Bank enjoys priority in the sound board because a perfected security interest trumps an unperfected security interest. § 9-322(a)(2). Since Salem Bank has priority in the sound board, it also has priority in that part of the insurance proceeds that can be allocated to the sound board. So, **Answer (C) is the correct answer**.

195. **Answer (B) is the correct answer.** This question explores the extent to which parties have freedom to contract for what a default might be, and once that is decided, what freedom they have to contract for specific remedies or results upon such a default. As stated in section 9-601(a), "[a]fter default, a secured party has the rights provided in this part and, except as otherwise provided in Section 9-602, those provided by agreement of the parties." As explained in the comments, this "leaves to the agreement of the parties the circumstances giving rise to a default." See § 9-601, cmt. 2. As there are no limits in the statute as to what private parties can agree, **Answer (C) is incorrect**; it is simply the case that due process does not apply in this context (as an aside, while such clauses are probably valid, and often used, they beg for a waiver or estoppel analysis if, contrary to the facts in this problem, the secured party waits before taking any action. As stated in section 9-601, cmt. 2: "This Article does not determine whether a secured party's post-default conduct can constitute a waiver of default in the face of an agreement stating that such conduct shall not constitute a waiver. Rather, it continues to leave to the parties' agreement, as supplemented by law other than this Article, the determination whether a default has occurred or has been waived.").

This analysis also calls into question Answer (D), because it would be correct only if a court utilize some equitable analysis to ensure that parties receive what they bargain for. But that claim can only stand if RLC is not otherwise precluded from taking the actions it took. And it likely is. It is a basic tenet of Article 9 that non-judicial actions such as those used by RLC are taken without a "breach of the peace," a concept that is undefined within the words of Article 9. See § 9-609(b) ("A secured party may proceed under subsection (a) [relating to repossession]: . . . (2) without judicial process, *if it proceeds without breach of the peace*.") (emphasis added).

We do know, however, that section 9-602 states, in relevant part, that "[e]xcept as otherwise provided in Section 9-624, to the extent that they give rights to a debtor or obligor and impose duties on a secured party, the debtor or obligor may not waive or vary the rules stated in the following listed sections: . . . (6) Section 9-609 to the extent that it imposes upon a secured party that takes possession of collateral without judicial process the duty to do so without breach of the peace." Thus, RLC's effort in the security agreement to obtain an agreement that involves a breach of the peace is not enforceable. That **eliminates Answers (A) and (D)**, because each of them would validate a clause that section 9-602 would not enforce.

196. **Answer (A) is the correct answer**. This question continues the examination of post-default behavior. As we saw in the previous answer, **Answer (C) is incorrect** because concepts of due process do not apply to the agreement of private parties with respect to the definition of default. Similarly, **Answer (D) is also incorrect** because the concept of matching benefits does not apply here. The clause stands or falls depending on whether Article 9 validates the activity generally.

Thus, the choices narrow to Answer (A) or Answer (B). The difference in this question is that instead of acting peremptorily and in breach of the peace, RLC negotiates its repossession. VILCC's consent means that there is no breach of the peace, since VILCC's consent removes that element. But what of the other agreements extracted from VILCC? Section 9-602, which invalidated the clause as it applied in the last question, is also applicable here. Note, however, that the introductory clause to Section 9-602 qualifies the prohibitions of that section "[e]xcept as otherwise provided in Section 9-624 . . . ."

Section 9-624, in turn, validates certain agreements made post-default, and only if made post-default. That section validates three types of waivers if made in writing; in particular, it states:

(a)   A debtor or secondary obligor may waive the right to notification of disposition of collateral under Section 9-611 only by an agreement to that effect entered into and authenticated after default.

(b)   A debtor may waive the right to require disposition of collateral under Section 9-620(e) only by an agreement to that effect entered into and authenticated after default.

(c)   Except in a consumer-goods transaction, a debtor or secondary obligor may waive the right to redeem collateral under Section 9-623 only by an agreement to that effect entered into and authenticated after default."

The first and third types of agreement are present in this question. VILCC waived the right to be notified of the sale of the collateral, as provided for in section 9-624(a). It also waived its right to redeem the collateral as provided for in section 9-624(c). Both of these agreements were made after default (as defined by the security agreement) and both were memorialized in an authenticated record (the signed agreement). Since the trustee only takes what the debtor had as of the filing date, these waivers will bind the trustee and VILCC's estate in bankruptcy. The trustee thus has no ground to dispute the taking, **making Answer (A) correct, and Answer (B) incorrect.**

INDEX

INDEX